The Answers to Your Everyday Money Questions

Personal Finance *for* Real People

Common money questions covered in an easy-to-understand way,

to help you understand the elements of your personal finances and money issues.

Sandra Winters

Money Service Centers of Hawaii, Inc.

4-901G Kuhio Hwy. Kapaa, HI 96746

Second Edition

Paperback ISBN: 9781091710979

For information on licensing content or purchasing customized print editions please visit https://personalfinanceforrealpeople.com or call 808.822.5115.

Personal Finance for Real People

Table of Contents

Personal Finance *for* Real People

Introduction

The Need for Answers to Real-Life Money Questions

Welcome! In *Personal Finance for Real People*, you'll find articles that cover typical personal finance topics in an easy-to-understand way, and provide you with the additional resources you need.

This book is meant to be a resource to, well, real people—people like you or me, with very common money problems. Problems that you didn't have answers to—until now! How do you create a budget? Should you loan money to family? How do you work your way out of debt? Don't worry—we'll cover many more subjects.

We suggest reading through the *Introduction* chapters first. That way you'll have a beginning understanding of the elements of your personal finance.

There is a large population in our country, whose people choose to live (or have to live) away from the world of banks, financial analysts, and investment consultants. Those who DO live in the world of banks have plenty of people to help them, and more than plenty of resources of which they can avail themselves.

But what about the non-banked? People who are maybe just like you, or me. Where do we go to get advice and answers to the financial issues we face? How can we handle our paychecks and bills, and what about savings? Sometimes the answers to money questions are fairly easy and common sense; but sometimes they require a lot of research. That's time and possibly facilities you may not have available to you.

But still, you need to find out what to do if you owe back taxes, how to budget and ways to meet that budget, what are other ways to make extra income, how can government programs help you when you need it, how to get started saving, the ins and outs of credit and loans, and how you can get out of debt—*realistically*.

This is why we started this program. Each section focuses on one of the larger issues and how it can help you manage your life. Each section will go into specific details on the most common issues and problems people face. We know you are smart enough to figure these issues out once you have the resources, and a place to go for advice.

The 11 Elements of Financial Health

No matter where any of us are in life, or what our income is, we each deserve to have financial health and the benefits that come from it. But what exactly does the term "financial health" mean?

Personal financial health—just like a company's financial health—has certain markers. Meeting those markers enables one to keep functioning, growing, and achieving success. Simply put, financial health means you can sleep easier at night, and look forward to tomorrow.

What are the ingredients in the recipe for financial health, the markers or elements that we just spoke of?

Here are the 11 key elements of financial health:

- You are able to borrow.
- Your overall credit scores are good.
- You make payments on time.
- Your debt fits into your budget.
- You have emergency savings.
- You are saving for your other goals, short and long-term.
- You have a budget for income and expenses.
- Your taxes are filed and up-to-date.
- You are receiving all the benefits and entitlements for which you are eligible.
- You have a Will, a Power of Attorney, and an Advance Health Care Directive.
- You know where you can go for financial information and help.

Not all of us can check off each of these elements as done and in good condition.

If you can, congratulations! You are in good financial shape, no matter what your income is. If you are not able to count all these elements as true for you, start working on them gradually, and eventually you'll get your financial house in order. Don't let the length of the list overwhelm you. Start with one element you think you can work on, and tackle it. Even doing just one at a time will make a big difference to your financial health. And then you'll have the confidence you need to tackle the next on the list.

Remember, this is not an exercise in self-punishment! It's about finding out how to get what you want out of life. With a little work, a year from now you could be happier and better off.

Give Yourself a Financial Checkup

Mid-year is a good time for contemplation. Perhaps you've been on vacation, and had a chance to think. Or maybe your office or work is slower this time of year. Either way, it's a good point to take a breather and evaluate where you are financially, where you are with your goals, and where you want to go for the rest of the year.

Back-to-School
School is starting, and it's time to get the kids ready. By now, back-to-school sales will have started, so be sure to bargain-hunt. Stock up now for the rest of the school year, and note those amounts in your budget so you can plan for school supplies next year.

College Planning
Speaking of school, if you have high school-age children, this fall is the time to start planning for college costs and shopping for scholarships. Have a family discussion, and decide what you can and can't afford. Scholarships and grants will need to make up the difference. Make sure that the college selection only includes those you can afford or to which your student can get scholarships.

Get Ready for the Holidays
Fall means...the holidays will be arriving soon! Hopefully you've already set aside money for holiday gifts and celebrations, but if you haven't, now is the time to start planning. Set your holiday gift budget: how many people you are giving presents to, and how much you want to spend on each. Set your holiday entertaining budget: Are you hosting any holiday meals or events? Calculate your budget for each, and stay within it!

Establishing a charitable giving budget is good to do also, and don't forget about planning for any holiday travel.

Review Your Monthly Budget
End of summer is also an ideal time to run a checkup on your monthly budget. Check over your expenses of the last six months. What was unexpectedly high? How can you offset that higher expense? Are there items or expenses that you can cut? For example: Don't pay for expanded cable if you aren't fully using it, eat out fewer times a month, don't get newspaper delivery if you end up with a pile of unread papers—same for magazines.

Remember, a budget isn't something that keeps you from enjoying life. A realistic budget will help you meet your goals and make sure you can and do enjoy life!

Start Saving!
The website http://www.AmericaSaves.org has many suggestions on ways to save an extra $100 in one month.

Tax Planning

Plan for next year's tax bill—it seems a bit early, but there are things you can do now to make it go much easier come next April. If you are self-employed, make sure you are keeping up with your estimated tax payments. Keep your records organized: Put copies of all deductible expenses in your tax folder—don't wait till January to find everything. If you have a 401-K, try to max out your contributions. And if you have questions, from last year or for next, now is a good (as in slow) time to meet with a tax accountant.

Understand Your Healthcare Options

What does the Affordable Care Act—Obamacare—mean? Signup starts each year in the fall, and it's good to start thinking about it ahead of time. Your state may already has very strict employer mandated insurance for those working over 20 hours per week. But for those who work less than that, who are unemployed, who are self-employed, or have pre-existing conditions, Obamacare is certainly worth exploring.

Revisit and Review Your Goals

Remember your goals from the beginning of the year? Now is the time to see how you tracked to the goals you set. If you missed some of them, figure out why and how you can get them on track again. If you still have some to meet, understand what you need to do now to get there. And if you met some of your goals, congratulations!

There's more advice on a mid-year financial review on the website America Saves.com.

A mid-year checkup gives you a heads-up on issues that need to be addressed, shows you where you are making progress, and still gives you time to make any important changes.

Personal Finance *for* Real People

Manage Your Income

Types of Income

Income falls into several categories—especially for the IRS. You may be asked about your various incomes if you apply for a larger loan, a credit card, and of course on your tax form. Here are the major groups of income:

`Wages & salary:` What you get paid for work you do.

`Tips`

`Pensions`

`Business income:` The net income from your business.

`Rental income:` The proceeds if you rent a property, or a room in your home.

`Capital gains:` For example: If you buy a house for $140,000, and then sell it for $160,000, that $20,000 you made is capital gains and is taxed differently.

`From government programs:` Social Security, disability, federal grants and scholarships, unemployment, government and military pensions, government health care credits.

`Certain tax issues:` Earned Income Tax Credit, and your tax refund.

`From investments:` Interest earned on accounts, dividends from stock investments, annuities, from your 401k after you start drawing from it, selling stock options, stock that is given to you.

`Other miscellaneous sources:` Clergy earnings, gambling income, bartering income, some categories of cancelled debt, alimony.

`Child support:` This is NOT taxable, or tax deductible, though it is income.

Manage Your Life with a Budget

Here's a question: What is the single action you can take to have enough money to meet all your current needs?

Hint: It's not winning the lottery—although that could go a long way to meeting your future needs and wants!

It's something that's initially slightly painful, but not difficult—kind of like a vaccination.

Ready?

It's making a budget. Really. Before you can effectively manage your money, you need to know, realistically, where it goes and where it needs to go.

1. First, figure out where you are currently spending your money.
Start tracking how much you're spending, and on what, each and every day. You can use a computer program like MS Money or Quicken, or you can simply just write down each purchase and expense in a pocket journal. Try to do this for at least two weeks—preferably a month—so you get a full picture of all your expenditures. Be sure to track the cash that goes out of your pocket, too (a prime area of overspending). Next, do the same with your income.

Remember that your expenditures each month should be less than your take-home income. If you operate at a negative each month (spending more than you are making), you will very quickly go into debt, and not be able to accomplish everything you want to do.

2. Second, set up your budget; again, on the computer, or just on a pad of paper.
Make a line item for each of your projected expenses. It's easier if you create budget categories for like-types of expenses: One section for utilities; one for health and medical expenses; one for auto, transportation, car insurance, and fuel; one for food, groceries, and dining out; etc.

Be honest. Don't under-budget an item because it makes you squirm. And, conversely, don't be too hard on yourself by eliminating all "fun" items.

Your goal now is to plan each monthly expense in line with what it has been historically, tweaking here and there to come out below your monthly take-home income. This is your chance to prioritize the money you spend. Living costs come first, of course. But you might decide to spend less on eating out so you can save for a vacation. Or set some of your clothing allowance aside for education.

If you can (and you really should try), set aside a set amount each month in both short- and long-term savings. Short-term savings will help in case of a sudden emergency (surprise doctor visit, car trouble), and long-term savings for retirement.

Now you are in control!

3. Third, monitor your spending.

Now that you have a plan, it's time to put it into action. Track your spending against your budget each month. See if you need to change any of your expense items: Perhaps your insurance rate went down (a good opportunity to put an additional amount in savings, by the way), or you have a new regular expense, or you want to add one or more special savings accounts.

The key is to know where your money is going each day, and why.

How to Budget Your Income

We covered the importance of setting up a budget, and how to calculate it—estimating your monthly expenses and subtracting that from your income (and making sure you don't go in the negative!). But for some of us, trying to figure out just what our monthly income actually is can be a little challenging. Using myself as an example, as a freelance writer and consultant, my income can vary from month to month, depending on what jobs come in and when I receive the payment for each job. So I don't really have a set amount that I know will land in my checking account each month.

Maybe you are paid hourly, and your hours can vary from week to week. Business can pick up, and you are needed for more hours, or slow down and your hours get cut. If you are not paid sick leave, any time you're ill and miss work reduces the hours for which you are going to get paid.

If you are paid each week, trying to estimate your monthly take-home pay can be confusing: Some months have four pay periods and paychecks, and others have five pay periods and paychecks. It seems like a nice surprise when you get that "extra" paycheck in a month, but it can make the other months seem a little lean.

To calculate your income for your budget, you are just going to have to do a little guesswork and estimating. First list all the income you can reasonably expect for the year, going month-by-month. Maybe you have a regular part-time job that you are expecting to keep. If your hours vary each week, take the average weekly hours for a six-month period (your hours over the last six months, divided by the number of weeks—26). Then multiply that times your hourly take-home pay rate, and by 26 to get your six-month income total.

Add to that any additional income you might be expecting: Extra work, a holiday period when you might be getting extra hours, child support or alimony, gifts, etc. Now you should have a total average income for a six-month time period. Divide that by six to get your monthly-expected average income. Use this figure on which to base your monthly budget.

Don't forget to change your budget if your circumstances change! You get a raise, or get laid-off for a while; or move and your rent goes up or down, etc. It may seem like a lot of effort to go to, but having a budget, and knowing how you are either meeting it or missing it puts you in control of your finances and your life.

Create Specific Budgets

We've been talking about budgets, mostly applying to general household budgets. And those are important, of course. They are the budgets you need to do first. But there are other, more specific budgets you can do, that you'll find quite helpful—and even necessary:

`Christmas and holiday budget`:
Spending at the holidays can easily get out of hand, leading to painful credit card bills in January. Establish what you can afford, and assign a dollar amount to each gift. Track it as you buy your holiday gifts. Most importantly, don't go over your budget!

`Special event budget`: The same holiday budget strategy applies also to back-to-school, birthdays, quinceaneras, vacations, and weddings. Make a realistic budget, fill in your actuals as you go along, and stick to your budget.

`Charitable giving budget`: If you're like me, this can easily get out of control—so many need so much help! But here again, you only have so much you can spend, and you have to budget it somehow. Decide, just for a specific time period, what are the top three charities you want to support. However much you can afford to give them, divide it by three. In the next time period—like the next holidays—you can choose another three.

`Small-business budget`: If you decide to start a part-time business, you will definitely need to have a budget. In the Worksheets section we've included a sample business budget you can use to start with—you will want to tailor it for your own business needs.

What's Your Budget Personality?

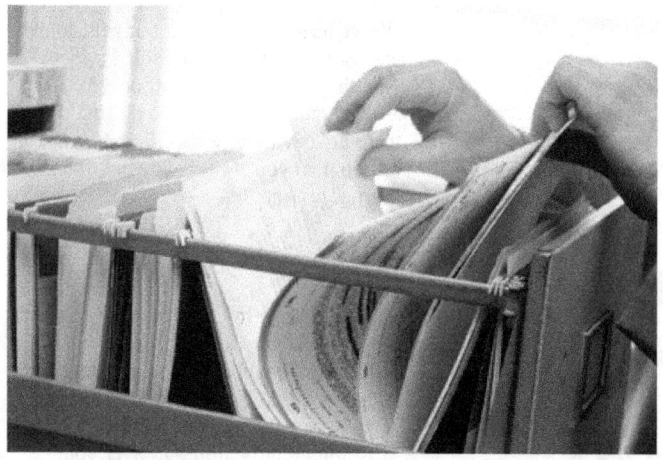

It's no surprise that we all have different talents and abilities, or that we like to do things differently than everyone else. What can be surprising is that your personality affects how you approach (or avoid) budgeting.

Some people are good at math, some are naturally organized, some prefer to go with their instincts, and some operate best within an established framework. Whatever your budget personality, there are ways to make this valuable tool work better for you.

We all know that creating a budget and having a clear, ongoing, picture of your finances is the best way to be financially successful and to meet your financial goals. Work *with* your personality and your talents to most effectively set up and follow your budget.

See if you recognize yourself from these budget personality types:

THE MASTER BUDGETER

You have a budget and financial goals and you follow your plan. You set aside money for each goal: retirement, a new car, a down payment, or paying off debt—and you stick to your budget. You are focused and disciplined.

`Where you could use help:`
Unexpected expenses: In your master goal planning, don't forget to plan for the unexpected and for emergencies. Be sure to set aside money for situations like car repair, unexpected medical expenses, moving, or family events.

`Budgeting to try:`
Take a look at your budget and actual expenses from last year, or your bank statements—there were probably a few surprise expenses there. Think about what small to medium to large unexpected events could happen this year, what happened last year, and factor those into your budget. Also, relax a little. You are in great control of your finances, so use a little to enjoy life.

THE SYSTEMIZER

You have a system for everything, set up just so you don't have to think about each task again. You use paycheck direct deposit, automatic bill pay, automatic deposits to savings, etc. You don't enjoy finance, and don't want to spend extra time on it, but you are handling your responsibilities, even if you don't have an actual budget.

Having all your finances set up to process automatically means you might be letting some areas slide, and might not be spotting problems. If your paycheck is deposited automatically, you might not see a mistake on your check, and the same thing applies to your bills. Without stopping and taking a look at your finances periodically, you may be missing out on opportunities to save money, or to maximize your savings.

Budgeting to try:
Set up a systemized budget and stick to it: Download bank statements and credit card statements that already have expenses in categories. Review your finances, and look for services you may not be using, and for any fees you could avoid. Check your deposits and make sure they've all been credited, and that they are correct. Take a look at your bills and investigate any large variances.

THE LAST MINUTE MANAGER

You do handle all your finances, but you don't use a budget, and you don't really have a clear idea about where exactly you are financially. You manage your busy life via your phone, paying bills online at the last minute, and using to-do lists. Your life is all about the next thing that has to happen today.

Where you could use help:
You need to step back and take a look at the big financial and life picture. Where do you want to be in a year, five years, or ten? Are there any big financial issues you need to be planning for (college, a house or car purchase, paying off debt)? You most likely make impulse purchases, especially those that "save" you time, and you probably don't have much of an emergency fund plan.

Budgeting to try:
Using even a simple budget will help you not just set yourself up for the future, but will help you handle your last-minute tasks not so last-minute. Tracking your expenses will help you see where you can save time and money. There are quite a few budget apps for your phone that are perfectly suited for you.

THE OSTRICH

You have your head in the sand when it comes to money and finances. You'd like to avoid the whole issue, and you do so as much as you can. You pay bills when you get a late notice, you pay extra service fees and late charges, and you miss opportunities. You don't know how to balance your checking account, if you have one, and you have no idea what your financial picture is. If you have cash in your pocket, you feel perfectly fine about spending it.

Where you could use help:
You need help everywhere! It seems overwhelming to even think about taking charge of your money, especially if it seems like you don't have enough to go around, but you can do it. Just take it slow and one step at a time.

Budgeting to try:
Start off by going week by week: keep track of what you spend and what you make each week. You can use a computer spreadsheet, a budget printout, a phone app, or just scribble it all on a piece of paper—the important thing is that you are keeping track. At the end of each week, see how you did: Did you have money left at the end of the week, or were you short? Look at your spending habits and see where you could improve. Gradually move to a slightly more formal and ongoing budget. This will help keep you on track, and let you compare the past and plan for the future. Also, use services that will help you keep on top of paying bills and avoid unnecessary fees:

Automatic bill-pay services, apps that help you track your spending and your bills. Or, try the "envelope budgeting" trick: Use an envelope for each of your regular expenses, and once a week put a budgeted amount of cash in each one.

Keeping your specific financial personality in mind when approaching your budget will help you become more successful in managing your money and in planning for the future.

Budget Tips: Easy Ways to Calculate Your Spending

We've reviewed the importance of establishing a budget for yourself and your family. Without that, you can't even begin to manage your money. Remember that you need to know what money is going out so you can make sure it's less than what's coming in.

If you're like me, the thought of tracking and calculating every single expenditure makes you think that maybe you'll just go to a movie, rather than digging into that task.

But it doesn't really have to be a painful process!

Here are some easy ways to calculate your spending:

- Do you use a credit card for most of your spending? Download your purchase data (or look at your statement) from the previous month and put each line item into a general subject area (dining out, groceries, clothes, fees, etc.).
- The same applies if you use mostly a debit card—download your transactions (or look at your statement) for a month, and assign each one a spending category.
- Some companies provide you with a year-end purchase summary that, while a little painful to look at, really gives you a good picture of where your money went that year.
- If you mostly use cash, keep a small notebook with you for one week, and write down (in round numbers—don't make yourself crazy over two cents!) what you spend and where each day. Multiply this by four to get an average month's expenses.

Look into the future:

- Sit down and think about the next six months.
- Now make a "shopping list" of everything you think you'll have to spend money on. Rent? Check! Dentist visit? School fees? New tires? Check! Check! Check!
- Also include any financial plans you might have: paying off a credit card or loan, setting aside savings, etc.

Next:

- Add up your "shopping list" and divide it by the number of months it's for—in this case, six.
- Add this to the monthly expenses you've tracked in the first section.

- Take a look at the total and see how it compares to your household's monthly income. You probably know what your paycheck usually is, and don't forget to check on your spouse's average monthly income, and any other sources you might have (disability, Social Security, alimony, etc.).

Hopefully, your spending is less than what you are bringing in. If not, you know what to do—see where you can cut spending here and there.

Congratulations! You now have a spending plan, or budget! Even without writing everything down each and every month, you'll know what your financial picture is, and what you can—and can't—afford.

The Cash Advantage

In any tough economy, more and more people move away from using traditional banks. Why? Sometimes it's distrust of Wall Street and banking systems. Often high- or under-employment leaves Americans strapped financially. They are unable to cover high bank fees and penalty charges; staying with a bank just puts them in a worse financial position.

There's another group of people: Those who choose to manage their finances outside of the banking system. They are employed, often at higher salaries, but they are frustrated with banks and their ever-increasing fees.

Millions of Americans fall into these categories; they are termed "the unbanked." They choose to have neither a checking nor savings account, and to use prepaid debit cards, bill-paying services, money orders, small loans, check-cashing services, and...cash.

Cash has so many advantages:

- First, there are no fees, no penalties, no paperwork, and no interest charges for using cash.
- In fact, if you are purchasing something, you can frequently negotiate for a cash discount.
- There's no danger of identity theft when using cash.
- Cash is accepted—and welcomed—almost everywhere.
- Unlike almost everything else you touch, cash is anonymous and private, and leaves no trail.
- Cash is what you want to have quickly at hand in case of an emergency—you should have some in your emergency "go-bag."
- Cash, even just your leftover pocket change, is easy to set aside to save for one or more specific goals.
- Just think—no PINs or passwords to remember!

With cash it's easy to stay on budget—you can't spend what's not in your pocket. It's easy to calculate how much you have available—just count it!

Financial Planning Tools

Now that you're ready to get your financial house in order, how do you start? In what direction do you make that first step?

When I start something new, I always like to start with a list or a worksheet.

A list gives you a tangible reference to what you need or what you need to remember.

A worksheet gives you structure and makes the process much easier. Instead of starting from scratch, you just need to plug in the information that you already have.

You don't even need to be that organized first!

As you start your financial makeover, luckily, there are a lot of resources out there for you: the library, the bookstore, schools, professionals, and the internet. For now, let's focus on the internet. There are quite a few non-profit organizations online that can provide you with basic financial planning tools for free.

What you can find:

- Household budgeting worksheets
- Savings calculators
- Loan calculators
- Interest rate calculators
- Retirement calculators
- Auto purchase evaluators
- Home purchase, mortgage, and rent evaluators
- And much, much more!

What you can do:

- Print out a worksheet, or use a worksheet online
- Go through a lesson plan on a financial topic
- Calculate a purchase
- See how much your debt is really costing you, and see the best way to pay it off
- Evaluate your insurance coverage
- Set up your household budget
- Participate in a webinar, watch a video, listen to a podcast, read an article

However you want to learn, and whichever way is easiest for you, there's a financial planning tool ready and waiting.

No excuses!

Here are some good websites to start with:

- In addition to worksheets and referrals, The Financial Planning Association (http://www.plannersearch.org) also provides links to brochures, articles, webinars, and may other helpful resources.
- FINRA (http://www.finra.org) has links to investment research tools, financial calculators, a glossary of financial terms, and even a couple of financial games for kids.
- At Money Management International (http://www.moneymanagement.org) you can use different calculators to evaluate your car purchase (or sale), expense budgeting and calculating, loan decision making; plus they have many more resources such as financial lesson plans, podcasts, webinars, etc.
- TIAA (http://www.tiaa.org) also has a wide variety of resources, from articles to worksheets to webinars.

Use Technology to Manage Your Income

Although we've been emphasizing using a budget printout, or a cash envelope to help you keep track of your income and expenses, those aren't the only methods available.

New apps make it possible to track your spending, your income, pay your bills, check your accounts, put money into savings, and many more tasks.

Here are some of the more popular money-managing apps:

FOR MONEY MANAGEMENT

Mint: Free, and available for iOS, Android, and Amazon.
Easily pulls all your accounts, cards, and investments into one place so you can track your spending, create a budget, receive bill reminders, and get customized tips for reducing fees and saving money. Syncs with your bank account and/or credit card to track your spending patterns, and lets you know when you're slipping up.

Level Money: Free, and available for iOS and Android
A simple tool to automatically analyze your financial picture, Level Money is a day-to-day expense tracker, helping you understand how much you have left to spend in a given day, week, or month. If you're puzzled about how you ended up with an empty wallet by the end of the day or week, this is perfect for you.

Bills Monitor: 99¢, and available for iOS
Never be late paying your bills! Bills Monitor will track and check your bills, and remind you to pay them.

Daily Budget Original: Free, and available for iOS
Warning: There are numerous in-app purchases you can make for additional services. Make sure it's something you really need and will use before purchasing.

Daily Budget is simple and easy way to calculate and track your daily budget. It will calculate your daily budget based on your income and fixed expenses. If you save today, you'll have a larger daily budget tomorrow. Save for large purchases or other purposes—an amount will automatically be withdrawn from your daily budget.

`Prosper Daily`: Free, and available for iOS
View all your accounts in one place, track your credit score, know exactly what you are spending and what you are spending it on, checks for fraudulent charges, and comes with ID protection.

FOR SAVING

`Acorns`: Free, and available for iOS and Android
`Acorns` makes it possible for anyone to slowly build an investment portfolio. It rounds up everyday credit and debit card purchases to the next dollar, and deposits the difference into a savings account. For example, if you buy a coffee for $2.63 using a linked card, it will charge you $3 and automatically deposit the $.37 into your diversified portfolio. Plus, it only costs $1 a month to manage your savings investment account, and you may withdraw whenever you want without a penalty.

`RetailMeNot`: Free, and available for iOS and Android.
You may already know about http://www.RetailMeNot.com, where you can download coupons and look up discount codes. Now they've taken it a step forward: All you need to do is launch the `RetailMeNot` app while you're shopping and it will gather all the deals and discounts available in that store, then display a barcode for any you want to redeem at checkout.

PODCASTS

Listen to podcasts focused directly on managing your income, saving money, and improving your financial life.

`The Dave Ramsey Show`: Dave Ramsey's show is about real life and how it revolves around money, teaching you how to manage and budget your money, get out of debt, build wealth, and live in financial peace.

`Money Girl's Quick and Dirty Tips for a Richer Life`: Money Girl provides short and friendly personal finance, real estate, and investing tips to help you live a rich life.

`The Savings Angel Show with Josh Elledge`: Each week TV personality and improv comedian Josh Elledge shares how to save money, make more money, and live a more abundant life.

`The Clark Howard Podcast`: The nationally syndicated show covers how to save more, spend less and avoid consumer rip-offs.

`You Need a Budget (YNAB)`: Not just a podcast, but an app, too. The app will help you organize your spending and income, and the podcast shares honest and upfront financial thoughts and discussions to help you take control of your financial life.

`Follow Me Out of Debt with Tom Merlino`: Get out of debt and into prosperity!

`The Clever Girls Know Podcast`: Bola Onada Sokunbi is a Certified Financial Education Instructor and money expert who teaches women to ditch debt, save money, and build real wealth.

Remember, there are all kinds of ways you can manage your income and your spending—now there are no excuses!

Improve Your Life: Set Up a Part-Time Business

We've mentioned before about getting an additional job or taking on some freelance work. The purpose in those cases was to find a way get yourself out of a temporary time of short income or extra debt.

But what if you could find a way to add that income on an ongoing basis? "Easy for you," you say, "but what can I do that people would pay money for, and how would I find them anyway?"

People all around you are starting their own small—sometimes very small—businesses. With so much available—including service-based businesses—on the internet, it's not hard to research what your options could be.

"But I have a job already!" you say. We suggest: Think about starting a second type of business: part-time self-employment.

We've put together a starter-kit of suggestions and resources to get your ideas flowing. You already have a talent or a skill, now you just have to hone in on two things:

- What will give you pleasure to do?
- What will generate the extra income that you need, whether it's large or small?

Do you have something you can sell? Your options are almost limitless online. You can sell through a website company designed just for that (eBay, Etsy), and/or you can start your own website. You can also sell in person: at craft shows, through local stores, at church bazaars, antique shows or flea markets.

eBay:
eBay (http://www.ebay.com) is the granddaddy of all kinds of goods for sale online. Are you interested in a specific kind of antique? Do you have a batch of collectables you'd like to sell? Can you resell regular merchandise in like-new condition—clothes, toys, fabric, or tools?

eBay will charge you a set of fees throughout the selling process. More information on that is on eBay's website: go to Seller Center, and then to Fees and Features. They will also help you get started and walk you through the entire process of selling and shipping just a few items or setting up a virtual eBay store.

Etsy:
Do you have a craft or art you love to do? Set up a virtual shop on Etsy (http://www.etsy.com). It's similar to eBay, but it is for artists, crafters, and makers of all kinds. You can also set up a shop selling the supplies all

those makers need (beads, fabric, ribbons, paper, etc.). A few of the categories include: printed artwork of your own, cards, wedding invitations, wedding signage, handmade clothing and accessories, screen-printed t-shirts, handmade objects crafted out of wood, tech accessories like stands and sleeves, and jewelry. Plus many more!

Etsy will also charge you fees: A fee for listing your product each six months, and a fee for when you sell your product. Just like eBay, they will help you get started and walk you through the whole process. They have a good shipping and postage helper, and there are many, many articles on various Etsy-related topics. Read through their `Seller Handbook` on the Etsy website.

Other online options for craft and artwork include:

- Deviant Art (http://www.deviantart.com)
- Artfire (http://www.artfire.com)
- And more listed in this `Business News Daily` website article: http://www.businessnewsdaily.com/5287-etsy-alternatives-handmade-sites.html

Everyone has a skill for something—the trick is viewing it as a skill that people will pay you to do.

- Are you a skilled mechanic? Start your own small auto repair and auto service in your garage.
- Do you know about computers? So many people panic when something goes wrong with their computer. Think about a Computer Repair shop on the side. Or teaching customers about their software.
- Can you do gardening and enjoy landscaping? There is a booming market for that kind of service.
- Choose something easier, but still in demand:
  - Window washing
  - Housecleaning
  - Dog walking and pet sitting
  - Household and office indoor plant care
  - Pool cleaning
- If you can qualify, child-care services are always needed.
- Provide a delivery service: for offices, medical offices, or just people who don't have the time to take care of it themselves.
- Instruction classes: Do you have an artistic skill? Can you speak with small groups of people? Think about offering an instructional class at a local art center, the library, or the community college.
- Do you have a traditional skill? People, and especially tourists would love to experience that. Put together a simple presentation, and approach tour guides, convention planners, wedding planners, and museums.
- Do you have office skills, and are organized? Become a Virtual Assistant. VAs can do anything from transcribing recording, doing internet research, handling travel bookings, and so, so much more. Start your research with the IVAA—the International Virtual Assistant Association (https://ivaa.org).
- Go to a service such as Amazon Mechanical Turk (https://www.mturk.com/mturk/welcome) where businesses offer short-term tasks, and pay whatever they think that is worth. Depending on your talents, training and skills, you may be able to make a decent amount of money.
- Traditional services like editing, writing, blogging, and copywriting, have mostly gone online now. If you are good in those areas, offer your services through your website, list on appropriate sites, and apply for projects at businesses.

"These all sound great," you say, "but how am I supposed to both research and set up a business?" You need multiple partners.

Website

Yes, you will need a website. Think about social media later on in the process. You can easily set up a template website with companies such as GoDaddy (http://www.godaddy.com) and Squarespace (http://www.squarespace.com).

Setting up a business license

Your local financial services company may be able to help you with your license paperwork. They can help you fill out the paperwork, and point you in the direction to go next.

Funding

Yes, sometimes you don't have the immediate funds to cover a small business start-up, even if it's buying a sewing machine or business cards. You might be able to get a small business loan, or a loan from family, or you just might have to save up for a while. Also think about crowdsourcing: You post on a verified website like Kickstarter (http://www.kickstarter.com) or GoFundMe (http://www.gofundme.com), and people from all over contribute (if they love your ideas) to your fund. The great thing is that they can contribute $10, $100, or $1,000, or any amount in between, depending on their own financial situation and on how much they like your business idea or specific need.

Promotional materials

Probably the only thing you need at first is a business card. Printing services now have templates (nice ones!) you can choose from, and they have frequent sales. Compare pricing, quantity required, and think about what you want your card to say and how it will be used. Good online printers include Moo, Vistaprint, and GotPrint. Of course, there are many more.

Advice

Take advantage of advice from people who have been there. The Small Business Administration (http://www.sba.gov) has a program in which retirees offer advice and guidance to those just starting out.

Community colleges also frequently have business-oriented courses for people just like you. Or, take the opportunity to get knowledgeable about computer programs. Your community college most likely has an entire Career and Technical Education department. Also don't forget your community center—they can offer useful classes, too.

There are many online courses and webinars, especially in the art and craft areas, but more as well. Companies include SkillShare (http://www.skillshare.com), CreativePro (https://creativepro.com), and CreativeLive (http://www.creativelive.com).

Set Your Financial Goals

Whatever time it is, it's a good time to take a few minutes and think about getting your financial goals in order. A little time now will pay off next year! Let's take a look at some worthwhile financial goals you should consider:

Plan your savings

We'd all like to have a hefty amount set aside for an emergency or special purchase, and the key to that is making a plan and sticking to it. Think about what you can afford to set aside each week or month. Even if it's just $5 a week, that will add up.

- Only pay for your purchases in bills. Keep your change in a jar and cash it in at the end of the year.
- Pay yourself $5 or $10 a week or month, in cash, and hide it away in an envelope where you won't see it every day.
- Buy yourself a $20 (or more!) prepaid debit card once a month, and collect them all in an envelope or box until you reach your goal.
- If you give up something—like going to the movies, or a morning coffee—to save money, set that money aside in your savings stash.

Think about what savings goals you might have for next year: Will you have expenses for education, for medical or dental, a new car/car repair? Or maybe you want to save for a vacation. Start planning for it now.

Double-check your personal information

- Look at your most recent paycheck to make sure your name, address, and Social Security number are right—it's much easier to correct now than later.
- Order your free copies of your credit reports, if you have not already done so this year. http://www.AnnualCreditReport.com is one site that offers this service.
- Consider adjusting your withholding. Did you withhold enough from your paycheck this year, or will you have to find more money come tax time? Or did you withhold too much, and will get a big tax refund? Both mean that you should think about tweaking your withholding amount for next year.

Insurance

- If you do have insurance, check how you've met your deductibles this year. If you have met your deductible, now is the time to take care of any other needs—it's like free money!
- Now is a good time to review your insurance for next year, too. Are there any discounts you might be eligible for? Is there any coverage that you need   to add, or that you can eliminate?

IRA and 401-K contributions

- If you are lucky enough to have an IRA or 401-K retirement savings plan, the end of the year is a great time to put a little extra into your fund.

Tax prep

- This is probably the last thing you want to think about, but the next year is right around the corner!
- If your paperwork isn't organized for tax filing yet, it's time to make a start.
- Are there any receipts or documents that you need to get before filing your taxes? Now is definitely better than later to arrange all that.
- And while you're at it, start a folder for next year's tax documents—that way you've made it easy for yourself to keep organized.

Set your financial goals for next year

- Take some time to consider what your financial goals will be.
- Think about the year ahead, what might be coming up, and also any changes or improvements you want to make.

A few financial suggestions:

- Set a monthly income and expense budget.
- Plan and save for large expenses, and also for unexpected expenses.
- Start a plan to pay off your credit cards and other debt.

The last weeks of the year are perfect to think about the past and the future.

What would you change? Did you accomplish what you set out this to do this year?

Don't criticize yourself if you didn't meet your goals; recognize your mistakes and set yourself up with plans to avoid repeating them, and to reach your goals for next year.

What Financial Records Should You Keep?

After you've finished preparing your taxes is a good time to look at what paperwork and records you should keep, and what you should dispose of. You've gone through all your financial paperwork for the previous year—how much of it should you keep? What does the IRS require, and what's really necessary?

You have to keep some records for backup to a possible tax issue, for proof that you did something (made a payment), for legal records (birth certificates), or to refer to it later (warrantees/receipts).

What you should keep:

Tax returns:

- Keep these a minimum of three years from the date you filed your taxes.
- If you operate your own business (and not just retail or professional businesses—contracting and freelancing apply here, too), the IRS has six years to audit you, so keep your records for seven years.
- However, keep in mind that there is no period of limitations for audits when a tax return is fraudulent, or if no tax return was filed at all, so consider if you just want to keep ALL tax returns.

Supporting tax return documents you should keep for the same length of time:

- W-2s, 1099s, interest statements, alimony collected, any other income reports.
- Deduction records: receipts, cancelled checks, charitable contributions, retirement plan contributions, statements.
- Bank statements: Keep for one year, unless they contain information you are using to support your tax return filing.

Vehicle documents:

- Keep the title until you have sold or disposed of the vehicle.
- Keep maintenance records if you plan on selling the vehicle.
- Keep insurance records for as long as you own the vehicle.

Home or property documents:

- Keep the real estate deed for as long as you own the property.
- Also keep all property purchase documents for as long as you own the property.
- Keep records of any permanent home or property improvements, and keep records of any expenses incurred in the purchase or sale of the property. Make sure these don't get "stuck" in previous years' tax returns.

Loan documentation:

- Keep any documentation related to loans, including the original loan document and statements, until you have paid off the loan.
- Once the loan is paid off, keep the documents that prove you paid in full.
- After you have sold the item or property that you got the loan for, shred the records.

Medical and health insurance records:

- Keep your paperwork for as long as you have the policy, or until you renew it.
- Keep documents for any unresolved/unreimbursed or unpaid claims.
- Keep documents for any ongoing treatments.
- If you think your out-of-pocket medical expenses are going to exceed the minimum deduction of your adjusted gross income (after you take out your other tax deductions), then keep all medical, medication, and dental expense records that year for a tax deduction. Check on www.irs.gov for qualifications.

Investments:

- Keep annual investment statements and certificates until you sell the investment.
- If you made a nondeductible contribution to an IRA, keep the records indefinitely to prove that you already paid tax on this money when the time comes to withdraw.
- Keep brokerage statements until you sell the securities. You will need the purchase or sales slips from your brokerage or mutual fund to prove whether you have capital gains or losses at tax time.

If you are self-employed:

- Make sure to keep copies of any bills that support deductions on your tax return—utilities if you claim a home office, telephone bills if you claim it as a business expense.
- Keep your bank statements.
- Keep credit card statements if you need them to support a deduction.
- Keep these records for as long as you keep the corresponding tax return.

Receipts:

- Keep receipts that are used to support a tax deduction.
- Keep receipts that are for large purchases, or large-ticket items, until you sell or dispose of that purchase.

What to keep forever:

- Birth certificates, marriage licenses, divorce decrees, passports, education records, military service records, Social Security cards, other legal resolutions,   adoption records, wills (until updated), life insurance.

What you should discard:

- Utility and telephone bills once your payment has been processed (unless you are self-employed—see above).
- Cancelled checks for cash or non-deductible expenses.
- Receipts for purchases not tax-deductible (although, do keep receipts for credit card purchases until you reconcile your statement).
- Expired warranties, and warranties/documentation for items you no longer own.
- Pay stubs after reconciling with year-end W-2s.
- Credit card statements, once payments and charges have been processed and reconciled (unless you are self-employed—see above).
- Social Security statements—only keep the most recent one.
- ATM receipts, unless you want to keep the check image in a deposit.
- Unnecessary "sales" or information that sometimes comes with a credit card or utility statement.

Remember! Always shred anything you are discarding that contains any personal information at all.

Where to Keep Your Financial Records

Financial records: They are here to stay. We all have financial records, whether they're pay stubs or tax returns, but there still isn't a one-stop solution to track all your finances.

Should you use online storage, or just keep hard copies? Here are a few options to consider:

THREE WAYS TO STORE YOUR DOCUMENTS

- Keeping hard copies: Although it's not so convenient, hard copies are still a viable—and easy—option for storing your financial records. At its simplest level, all you have to do is dump everything in a box! Even if you store most of your records online, hard copies are useful for backup, especially if you get audited. These should be records that you will need to consult only in case of an audit, or if you are doing research. You can't bring these along with you on a long trip away from home.
- Online storage: You can store your information on "the cloud" (server farms located hundreds of miles away from your home), but are you willing to trust that data doesn't get hacked or that the servers don't go down? These records should be non-sensitive information that you will need to access frequently.
- Storing on your computer: A third option would be to store your digital financial records on your own computer. If that's what you prefer, consider getting a portable external hard drive as a backup.

It's all about back-up: The best system is to have current files on your own computer, hard copies in storage, non-sensitive files in the cloud, an external hard drive to back-up your computer files and to store sensitive information, and irreplaceable items and documents in either a fire-safe or safety deposit box.

You'll be backed up in case you lose your hard copies through theft or fire, or if you are hacked. Don't forget to put a password on your hard drive.

Where to keep everything:

- Irreplaceable documents and valuable items should go in your own fire safe, or in a safety deposit box.
- Hard copies should be stored in labeled boxes in a dry, secure place, out of the sun, and away from anything flammable. This could be your house, or a storage unit.
- Your portable, external back-up hard drive can also go in your fire-safe, storage unit, or safety deposit box. A fire-safe is easiest—you can easily retrieve it to back up your computer when you need to.

Easy Math for Personal Finances

I bet that when you were in school you thought to yourself, "I'll NEVER have to use all this math!"

But the truth is, you use math every day.

For example:

- Making sure you get correct change when you make a purchase.
- Figuring out how much carpet to get for the bedroom.
- Calculating your gas mileage, and more.

You also need to use some basic math when handling your personal finances. Here are a few reminders of what you've forgotten since you left school:

Making a Budget: A budget lists all your monthly expenses: The areas in which you spend money each month (utilities, rent or mortgage, insurance, food, etc.); and as well lists your monthly net (take-home) income amounts. Your total expenses should be less than your total net income.

1. (total monthly expenses) < (total monthly net income)
2. (total monthly net income) - (total monthly expenses) = over budget (in debt) or under budget (doing well)

Gross Income: Your original pay amount, without any deductions.

Net Income: Your gross income, with deductions subtracted. If you look on your pay stub, you'll see that your employer (or Social Security, etc.—whoever is paying you) has deducted a few items from your check. These are usually taxes and possibly insurance or other items the company is charging you for: taxes, Social Security, Medicare, etc. If they aren't on your check—perhaps you do contract work or freelance—you will still have to pay these at the end of the year in your taxes, so remember to subtract them from your gross income now.

1. (your gross income) – (deductions from your paycheck: Federal tax, state tax, Social Security, possibly more) = (your net income)

Cash Flow: What's left over after you've paid your bills—how much you earn vs. how much you spend. Are you living within your budget and always have enough to pay bills as they come in, or going into debt?

1. income – expenses = cash flow

Simple Interest: The most basic interest formula—the amount that is earned (or that you owe) on the principal. This is the interest you earn on a savings account or what you may pay on a loan or on a credit card.

1. Monthly interest: (your principal amount) x ([your interest rate] divided by [number of months you are calculating for]) = interest
2. Annual interest: (your principal amount) x (your interest rate expressed as .00) = interest

Compound Interest: The interest you earn (or pay, in the case of a debt) on the principal PLUS any interest that has been earned and added to the principal. Compound interest is most often used in long-term loans, such as a mortgage, and in long-term investments.

1. (your principal amount) x ([1 + your annual interest rate expressed as .00] ÷ (the number of times interest will be calculated and added in]) = (amount accumulated)

Change Your Interest Percentage into Decimals: Usually we think of interest rates as percentages (7% or 2.4%, for example). In the formulas above, you'll see we mentioned expressing your interest rate as a decimal (.00). You have to do this in order to make a mathematical calculation. But it's easy!

1. (your interest rate) ÷ 100 = (your interest rate expressed as .00)
2. The easy way: Take (your interest rate), remove the percentage sign (%), and move the decimal sign (.)—which is at the far right of (your interest rate) even though you don't see it—and place that decimal sign two places to the left.
3.5% = .05

How Much House Can You Afford? If you are getting a home loan, most lenders will want your monthly home loan payment to equal no more than 30% of your available monthly income (after you've paid all other monthly debts like insurance, credit card, student loans).

Step one: Calculate your available monthly income.

1. (net, or take-home, income) – (regular monthly debts) = (available monthly income)

Step two: Calculate the monthly mortgage payment you can afford.

1. (available monthly income) x (.30, or 30%) = (your affordable monthly mortgage payment)

Calculate a Tip: Using the standard tip rate of 18% (please feel free to leave more if your server did a good job!):

1. .18 x (your check total) = (amount of tip)
2. Now just add it to your check total, and you're done!

Calculate a Sale Price: Multiply the discount percentage ("25% off!") times the original price:

1. .25 x (product's original price) = (how much you will save on your purchase)

Remember that the more you know about your finances—what money comes in and what goes out—the more able you are to control it and meet your goals. If you understand exactly how these various calculations are arrived at and where the numbers come from, you take that much more control over your future.

Also, Practical Money Skills (https://www.practicalmoneyskills.com/) is a good website that offers easy calculators for many financial purposes.

Anatomy of a Personal Check

Name, address: In the **upper left-hand corner** is your name and address. Make sure the information shown here is up to date. Do not add your phone number or driver's license number, and definitely not your Social Security number!

Check number: In the **upper right-hand corner** is a check number, which falls in line chronologically with other checks in your checkbook. This number helps you identify each check after it has been written to a person or business.

Date: Below the check number is a space to write down the date the check is written.

Pay to the order of: Below your name and address is where to write in the name of the person or business the check is written to, also called the payee line.

Dollar sign: On the **right-hand side**, this is where to write the dollar amount of the check, that amount that will come out of the checking account. For example, "$62.00."

... Dollars: Below the "Pay to the order of" section is where to write out the dollar amount being paid. For example, "Sixty-two dollars."

Bank address: The check might—or might not—also contain the bank's address.

Memo: At the **bottom left-hand corner** of the check is a space where notes can be made about what the check is being written for.

Signature: In the **bottom right-hand corner** is where to sign the check. Without an account holder's signature, the check is invalid.

Bank routing number and account info: At the **bottom** of the check are various numbers. The first nine digits are the bank's routing number. The 10-digit series in the middle is the personal account number. The last four number grouping is the check number.

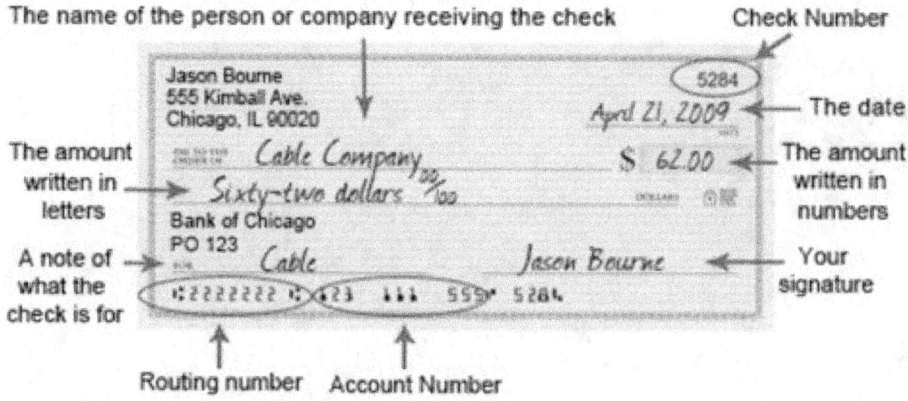

Handy Personal Budget Worksheets

MONTHLY HOUSEHOLD BUDGET

Copy this budget, and use it to not just establish your expected monthly expenses, but also to compare how you did in real life that month. There may be areas you need to adjust—up or down.

FAMILY MONTHLY BUDGET SCHEDULE

	January	February	March	April	May	June	July	August	September	October	November	December	Yearly Total
INCOME DESCRIPTION													
Wages (takehome) - partner 1													
Wages (takehome) - partner 2													
Interest and dividends													
Miscellaneous													
TOTAL INCOME													
Auto expense													
Auto fuel													
Auto insurance													
Auto payment													
Beauty shop and barber													
Cable TV													
Charity													
Child care													
Clothing													
Credit card payments													
Dues and subcriptions													
Electricity company													
Entertainment and recreation													
Gas company													
Gifts													
Groceries and outside meals													
Health insurance													
Home repairs													
Home or renter insurance													
Household													
Income tax (additional)													
Laundry and drycleaning													
Life insurance													
Medical and dental													
Miscellaneous													
Mortgage or rent payment													
Other debt payments													
Prescriptions													
School expenses													
Telephone bill													
Tuition													
Vacations													
Water company													
Work expenses													
Other													
Other													
Other													
Other													
TOTAL EXPENSES													
CASH (SHORT) EXTRA													

ENVELOPE CASH BUDGET

Copy the worksheet (enlarge if necessary); cut out on exterior lines; fold on dotted lines; glue or tape into envelope shape.

CATEGORY

DATE	WHERE	+/- $'	BALANCE

CATEGORY

DATE	WHERE	+/- $'	BALANCE

CATEGORY

DATE	WHERE	+/- $'	BALANCE

Paycheck One

Bill	Username	Password	Amount Due
			$
			$
			$
			$
			$
			$
			$
			$
			$
			$
			$
			$

	Total	$

Paycheck Total	
Bills Total	
Amount Short/Over	

Paycheck Two

Bill	Username	Password	Amount Due
			$
			$
			$
			$
			$
			$
			$
			$
			$
			$
			$
			$

	Total	$

Paycheck Total	
Bills Total	
Amount Short/Over	

WEEKLY CASH FLOW

FOR THE WEEK OF:

Date	Description	In	Out
	Balance at the start of time period		
	Total input		
	Total output		
	Difference		
	Balance carried forward		

BILL PAY RECORD

BUDGET ITEM	January	February	March	April	May	June	July	August	September	October	November	December
Mortgage/Rent												
Internet												
Cable												
Electricity												
Gas												
Water												
Telephone												
Trash Pickup												
Home/Renter Insurance												
Taxes												
Auto payment												
Auto fuel												
Tuition/Child care												
Health Insurance												
Student Loan												
Credit Card												
Credit Card												
Credit Card												
Credit Card												
Loan												
Savings												
Emergency Fund												
Charity												
Other												
Other												

BANK RECONCILIATION FORM

PLEASE EXAMINE YOUR STATEMENT AT ONCE. ANY DISCREPANCY SHOULD BE REPORTED TO THE BANK IMMEDIATELY.

CHECKS OUTSTANDING	
Number	Amount
TOTAL	

1. Record any transactions appearing on this statement but not listed in your checkbook.

2. List any checks still outstanding in the space provided to the right.

3. Enter the balance shown on this statement here.

4. Enter deposits recorded in your checkbook but not shown on this statement.

5. Total Lines 3 and 4 and enter here.

6. Enter total checks outstanding here.

7. Subtract Line 6 from Line 5. This adjusted bank balance should agree with your checkbook balance.

Small Business Worksheets and Forms

PETTY CASH

Petty Cash Reconciliation Sheet

Department: Month:

Description	Quantity	Amount
Total petty cash counted		
Paid vouchers counted		
Total petty cash and paid vouchers		
Total authorized petty cash float		
Difference		

Comments

Prepared by: Date:

BUSINESS BUDGET

INCOME	Actual	Budget	Difference
Sales	$	$	$
Sales Quarter 1	$	$	$
Sales Quarter 2	$	$	$
Sales Quarter 3	$	$	$
Sales Quarter 4	$	$	$
Other	$	$	$
TOTAL SALES	$	$	$
Cost of Goods	$	$	$
Beginning inventory	$	$	$
Goods Purchased or Manufactured	$	$	$
Shipping Charges	$	$	$
Labor (wages and payroll)	$	$	$
Other	$	$	$
Less Ending Inventory (subtract)	$	$	$
COST OF GOODS SOLD	$	$	$
Gross Profit	$	$	$
Non-Operating Income	$	$	$
Interest income	$	$	$
Rental income	$	$	$
Gifts received	$	$	$
Donations	$	$	$
Other	$	$	$
TOTAL NON-OPERATING INCOME	$	$	$
TOTAL INCOME	$	$	$
EXPENSES			
Operating Expenses			
Accounting and legal	$	$	$
Advertising	$	$	$
Depeciation	$	$	$
Dues and subscriptions	$	$	$
Insurance	$	$	$
Interest expense	$	$	$
Maintenance and repairs	$	$	$
Office supplies	$	$	$
Payroll expense	$	$	$
Postage	$	$	$
Rent	$	$	$
Research and Development	$	$	$
Salaries and wages	$	$	$
Taxes and Licenses	$	$	$
Telephone	$	$	$
Travel	$	$	$
Utilities	$	$	$
Web hosting and domains	$	$	$
Other	$	$	$
TOTAL OPERATING EXPENSES	$	$	$
Non-Recurring Expenses			
Furniture, Equipment, Softward	$	$	$
Gifts Given	$	$	$
Other	$	$	$
TOTAL NON-RECURRING EXPENSES	$	$	$
TOTAL EXPENSES	$	$	$
Net Income Before Taxes			
Income Tax Expense			
NET INCOME	$	$	$

[Company Name] Invoice

	Invoice No.	[Invoice Number]
	Invoice Date:	[Date]
[Address Line 1]	Bill To:	[Contact]
[Address Line 2]		[Company]
[Address Line 3]	Address:	[Customer Address Line 1]
[Phone]		[Customer Address Line 2]
[Web Site]	Phone:	[Customer Phone]
[E-mail]	E-mail:	[Customer E-Mail]
[Fax]	Fax:	[Customer Fax]

Description	Units	Cost Per Unit	Amount
Invoice Data 1 description	40	$ 100.00	$ 4,000.00
Invoice Data 2 description	30	75.00	$ 2,250.00
Invoice Data 3 description	40	50.00	$ 2,000.00
Invoice Data 4 description	5	100.00	$ 500.00

Invoice Subtotal	$ 8,750.00
Tax Rate	8.25%
Sales Tax	721.88
Other	
Deposit Received	5,000.00
TOTAL	**$ 4,471.88**

Make all checks payable to [Company Name]
Total due in 15 days. Overdue accounts subject to a service charge of 2% per month.

Thank you for your business!

Personal Finance *for* Real People

Saving & Investing

Get Started Saving

When you have bills to pay, it's hard to think about saving and setting aside a little each month for the future.

But just think of the last time you had a financial emergency: An unexpected car repair, a medical expense, or a large insurance deductible, or expenses that were not covered.

Think about things you would like to—or need to—get: A new car, a home repair, a computer, or even just a movie and dinner night out.

And finally, think about larger expenses you want to be prepared for in the future: College or training, a medical procedure, a vacation, or even retirement.

Sound overwhelming? Not if you take it one simple step at a time.

Set Your Budget
We've talked about establishing your income and expense budget, and we've provided a budget template that you can use. All you have to do is fill it in! Once you do that, you can see where you have opportunities to save.

Finding Money to Save
We'll give you a good start with suggestions on easy ways to save, from bringing your lunch to work instead of eating out, to negotiating better rates on some of your bills (cable, for example). And there's more! Save all or part of your tax refund. Think about other ways you can set aside $5, $10, or $20 at a time. Start with stashing all the coin change you bring home in your pocket or purse. Small amounts really add up!

The Interest Advantage
How to get free money? By putting at least some of your savings where it will earn interest. And especially compound interest—where you earn interest (money added to your savings account) on top of both your original savings amount plus the interest that you've previously earned. Interest on your interest!

An easy way to start: With a NetSpend prepaid debit card. NetSpend offers a 5.00% interest (Annual Percentage Yield)—one of the highest interest rates in the country.

Now Set Your Goals
You can save more by having a goal in mind. Visualizing what you want to save for gives your savings a purpose; otherwise you may be tempted to withdraw from what you've saved. But once you have a goal in place, you know that taking money out of your savings is taking away from that ultimate goal.

Your savings goals can be small or large, and you can even have more than one. Maybe you want to put money into an emergency savings fund AND want to start saving for a car or house purchase. That's fine—just set up both, and make sure you contribute regularly to both.

Keep track of what you are spending (here's where your budget comes in) and what you are saving. Nothing motivates you more than seeing those savings add up!

Savings Strategies

Thinking about saving, and your personal finance plan, early in the year sets you up for success for the entire year. While others are drifting away from their annual goals, you will have set yourself up to end the year in much better financial shape than you started. And really, it won't be hard! No trips to the gym, and no dieting required!!

The non-profit organization America Saves (https://americasaves.org) offers even more great ways to get started saving.

If you haven't started setting aside savings yet, it can be a little overwhelming to think about. But really, it's very simple.

First, set a goal. Or go crazy, and set two or three goals! Do you want to have money for emergencies? Save for college expenses? For a new car? For moving expenses, or even a vacation? Or maybe you just want to get rid of your debt. Name your goal!

Second, make a plan. How are you going to achieve your goal? This is probably the hardest part, harder even than actually setting aside the savings. Just take it step by step, and you'll be through it in no time. Start with looking at your expenses and making a monthly budget. You'll find a handy Budgeting Worksheet included on our site and in this book. Once you know where your money is going each month, you can cut down on unneeded spending and save the difference.

Now put your plan into action. It's easy to say "just save the difference," but what are some easy ways to do that?

Determine an amount to set aside in savings each week. It doesn't matter if it's not a large amount at first. Can you save $50 a month? If $25 or $50 a month is too high, just start saving the loose change you've collected at the end of each day. It adds up quickly, and helps you get into the saving habit. Set it aside in cash, load it onto a debit card, or into a savings account.

Earn money on your savings. With a NetSpend prepaid debit card, you are eligible for a NetSpend Savings Account: No minimum deposit, and NetSpend offers a 5.00% interest (Annual Percentage Yield)—one of the highest interest rates in the country. Load your card with funds from your savings account, or use it to deposit funds. And it's FDIC insured.

Use cash. For an easy way to control spending, consider switching over to a cash-only system. Decide ahead of time—each week for example--how much you want to spend, and set aside that much in cash. You can find more insight on the cash-only lifestyle is on the WiseBread (https://www.wisebread.com/) website.

Use pre-paid debit cards. Sometimes you do need a credit card. What to do if you are trying to avoid adding to your credit card debt, or if you just get too tempted to spend with a credit card in your pocket? Use a pre-paid debit card for those situations in which you can only use a credit card. You can limit the amount of money available to use by only loading that much on the card.

Examine your optional expenses. Take a good look at what you spend money on each month. There are the necessary basics, like groceries, rent or mortgage, insurance, utilities, gas, and car repair. What else do you spend money on, and can you cut those expenses back a little? Limit dining out at restaurants, even fast food ones. Borrow movies and books from the library for free. Look for free museum nights and art shows, and discount programs at attractions and movie theaters. Trade babysitting services with friends.

Take a look at the regular services you pay for each month. Are you using all your cell phone minutes, or could you go to a more inexpensive plan? What about your car or home insurance? By going to a higher deductible, you will save on your premium each month. Think about your cable service, internet service, etc. Negotiate with your provider, and shop around for better deals.

Pack your lunch, and clean out your pantry. One of the keys to saving is developing thrifty long-term habits, such as bringing your own lunch to work instead of eating out. If you're worried you don't have time, cook something on Sunday and put it in individual portable containers. Start this week, and over the course of a couple of months, you can easily save $100. Plan meals around the ingredients you already have in your cupboards. You'll slash your next grocery bill, and you'll help ensure that food doesn't go stale.

Put your tax refund in savings. Get the most from your tax refund by paying down your high-interest debt, or by putting it into your savings account.

Find even more saving strategies on the America Saves website (https://americasaves.org). Take the America Saves Pledge now to set your savings goal and make a plan to save.

America Saves is a campaign managed by the non-profit Consumer Federation of America. It seeks to motivate, encourage, and support low- to moderate-income households to save money, reduce debt, and build wealth.

The Ways to Save

Many people think that having a traditional savings account at a bank is the only way to save. Not true!

Today there are quite a few ways you can set your savings aside. See which you feel more comfortable with, which will encourage you to keep saving, and what the fees and withdrawal requirements and/or penalties are for each.

- Reloadable prepaid debit card: Set aside cash that you save, and then load it on to your prepaid debit card weekly, monthly, or whenever. Make sure you stash that debit card where it won't get lost, and where you won't be tempted to use it! Start a card for each of your savings goals.
- NetSpend prepaid debit card: As mentioned previously, this prepaid debit card offers interest, and its FDIC insured.
- Savings Bonds: Purchase in amounts as low as $25, guaranteed by the Federal government, earns a fixed interest rate.
- CD or Certificate of Deposit: Purchased through traditional banks and credit unions, often available in amounts starting at $500.
- Credit Union savings and bank account
- Traditional bank account
- Cash—no fees involved!

40 Easy Ways to Save

We've put together a list of easy ways you can save.

There are probably more ways that you can think of!

Remember to set your savings goal!

- Save your loose change.
- Wait before you make an impulse purchase. Think about it overnight.
- Get a receipt for everything you purchase. Look them over at the end of the week, and see where you could have saved a few dollars.
- Do a savings match for each non-essential thing you buy. Coffee at Starbucks? Put a matching $3.00 into your savings stash.
- Shop clearance items first.
- Keep track of sales. Get store print circulars, sign up for email notifications, and ask store staff.
- Sign up for customer rewards programs: Safeway's Club Card, or Cartwheel at Target. You'll get points that will turn into discounts or credits, and additional coupons.
- Don't shop without a coupon! Always check online for coupons to the store you're going to be shopping in. RetailMeNot (https://www.retailmenot.com) is a good place to start.
- Shop in bulk, if it makes sense for your family.
- If you don't have a membership to a warehouse club like Costco, see if any of your friends or family members are, and go with them on their next shopping trip.
- Buy a regular coffee instead of a latte.
- Buy one fewer soda per week or day, and set that money aside.
- Stop smoking.
- Bring your lunch to work.
- Eat out one fewer time per week or month.
- Make a list before you go grocery shopping.
- Don't go shopping while you are hungry.
- Buy store brands instead of name brands.
- Eat vegetarian once a week or more.
- Start a vegetable and herb garden.
- Cook extra and freeze for later.

- Shop around for gas—if you have a smart phone, use an app like *Gas Buddy* to see what's cheapest close to you.

- If you can, have your doctor prescribe generic rather than brand-name drugs.
- Know your health insurance. Annual visits and other well-care services are free under the Affordable Care Act.
- Do you have a spare bedroom or extra space in your garage? Rent it out!
- Make sure to know and monitor your data usage and minutes on your phone, and don't go over your limit each month.
- Visit your local library: You can borrow books, e-books, and DVDs for free, participate in many free entertainment programs, use computers, use copying services, and take classes, and read newspapers and magazines. It's also a great place for finding out what's going on in the community.
- You'll find bargains in entertainment at concerts at colleges, high schools, and even churches.
- Don't go to shopping centers for entertainment!
- Clean out your closet, and sell what you can. Donate the rest for a tax deduction.
- Cut the cord—go cable free! Compare the cost per month of cable service vs. Netflix, Amazon, or Hulu Plus: Each of those run around $10 per month, vs. $70 to $130 for basic or premium cable.
- Make sure to turn off lights and appliances that you are not using. Use a power strip—some devices, like television sets, stay "on" even though you've turned them off on the device.
- Cancel unused memberships or services. Do you have a gym membership that you never use? A magazine you never end up reading?
- Keep your car in good shape: Keep tires at the correct air pressure, and oil checked and replaced.
- Pay your bills on time and avoid late fees each month.
- Use an online bill payment service from your bank, or with each company—it will help keep you on schedule.
- If you use a bank or credit union, start a savings account and have the bank transfer a set amount into your savings into each month.
- If you use a money services center, have a set amount loaded on to your pre-paid debit card when you come in each month to pay bills or use another service.
- Only use the ATM of your own bank—otherwise you'll get charged up to $3.00.
- If your bank is charging you fees each month just for your checking or savings accounts, it's time to shop around for free accounts or alternative ways to manage your money.

The Saver Checklist

From AmericaSaves, this saving checklist includes the characteristics of successful savers, which includes debt management.

It can serve as a useful starting point for evaluating your savings preparedness.

- Check off your savings accomplishments to see how you're doing.
- Have a financial plan with savings and debt management goals.
- Don't rely on financial windfalls from gambling or winning the lottery.
- No high-cost debt or loans, and no credit card debt that is increasing.
- No credit card debt at all, or unpaid monthly balances.
- Affordable (or no) car and student loan debt payments.
- Save a portion of your income.
- In addition, save at least 5% of your income.
- Have an emergency fund to cover $500 of unexpected expenses.
- In addition, have enough in an emergency fund to cover three months of regular expenditures.
- At work, contribute regularly to a retirement account.
- Outside work, contribute regularly to an account for retirement.
- Outside work, make these or other savings deposits automatically.
- Own home with affordable (or no) mortgage payments.
- Own home and expect to pay off mortgage before retirement.

America Saves is a campaign managed by the non-profit Consumer Federation of America. It seeks to motivate, encourage, and support low- to moderate-income households to save money, reduce debt, and build wealth.

Build Your Emergency Fund

Establishing an emergency fund should be a top priority for everyone.

Maintaining emergency savings may be what makes the difference between those who manage to stay afloat and those who sink in debt or worse. If you keep a minimum of $500 to $1,000 (or more) in savings for emergencies, you'll be able to meet unexpected financial challenges, and not have your life fall apart.

Why should you set aside an emergency fund?

Here are just a few reasons:

- Car repair
- Clothes for a new job, or for school
- Home repairs
- Sudden doctor visit
- Dental work
- Parking or speeding ticket, or tow
- Emergency visit to relatives
- Tiding you over in-between jobs
- Utility deposits, or an unexpectedly high bill

Not only will you be able to handle an emergency, but you'll also have peace of mind. You won't have to constantly worry about what to do if this or that situation comes up.

What exactly is an emergency fund?
It's a small amount of money, usually in a savings account (or under the mattress, or in a jar, or in a stack of prepaid debit cards). The important point is that you do not have easy access to it—no opportunities to drain it a dollar at a time. Saving for an emergency fund starts with small, regularly scheduled amounts that build the fund up over time.

Start building your emergency fund with a specific goal in mind. A general rule of thumb is to save enough to cover four to six months' worth of expenses. But don't get distracted and discouraged if you can't save that much yet. It's much better to focus on having enough to cover expenses when setting your savings goal, not on replacing your entire income.

Having an emergency fund also keeps you from being forced to take out high-interest loans that you may not be able to afford.

A Federal Reserve Board survey showed that low-income families with at least $500 in an emergency fund were better off financially than moderate-income families with less than this amount, or with no emergency fund.

The best, and easiest place to keep your emergency fund:
A traditional bank or credit union savings account.

If you don't have, or want, a bank account, think about these ideas:

- Pre-paid debit cards: add to one card, or "buy" a new one every month.
- Money orders: buy a new one each month—they don't expire.
- Cash: The easiest way to set aside money, but be sure to use a fireproof lockbox.

Risk: Remember that all of these last three have an element of risk: what if you don't remember where you put them? What if your house is burglarized? What if there's a fire? You have to take on another measure of responsibility.

Whatever savings account or method you choose, make sure you can access your emergency savings fund when you need it so you're prepared for the unexpected.

How to fund your emergency savings:
There are many ways, and the best tactic is for you to add small amounts to your fund slowly. Don't wait until you have $500 lying around to start your fund. Set aside some small amounts, and then get your fund started, in whichever way that makes sense for you.

Where does the money come from? Try these ideas:

- If you have a traditional bank account, set up an automatic transfer of a fixed amount into your emergency savings account.
- Save your pocket change—when you get home, put your change in a small-necked bottle (like a Sparkletts or Arrowhead large water bottle) so it won't be easy to get out. Every six months empty it out and put the accumulated change into your emergency fund.
- Use your tax refund or Earned Income Tax Credit to start your fund, or rapidly build it up.
- Use Christmas and other holidays as an opportunity to save money for your emergency fund—take a look at what you spent the previous year, and start planning now how to cut that amount in half for the current year. Shop discount stores, look for special coupons and discounts, and be alert for sales on the items you are looking for.

Read chapter *40 Easy Ways to Save* for more simple and painless ways to set aside money.

There are many people who are living so paycheck-to-paycheck that a flat tire would send them into bankruptcy. An injured child or a natural disaster could easily be handled with emergency funds.

At least one study has shown that financial worries beat out to-do lists and work stress as reasons for losing sleep. However, there's one sure way to avoid sleepless nights: keeping enough money saved to cover not only your bills, but also emergencies.

If the recession taught us anything, it's that saving for a rainy day is a good idea.

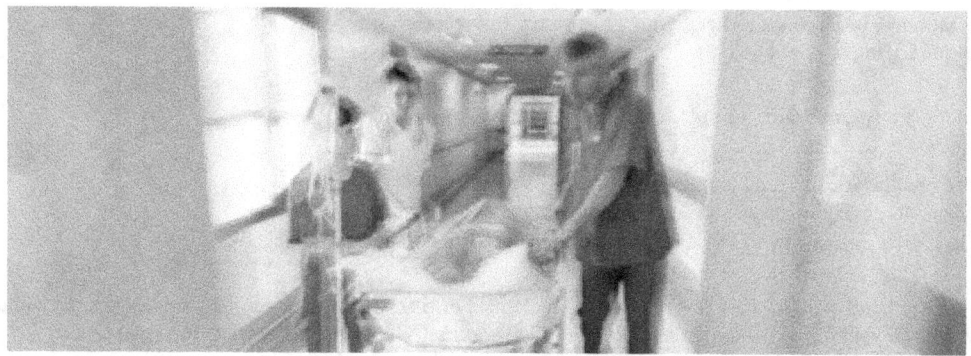

Plan to Save Long-Term

What is "long-term" saving?

Most in the financial industry consider any savings plan that is ten years or longer to be long-term, though consumers tend to think long-term is five years or more.

You are probably saying to yourself, "why do I need to save long-term—isn't doing the best I can to save every month good enough?"

Yes, there are some specific reasons you'll need to consider long-term savings:

- For retirement
- For college
- To buy a home
- To buy a small business.
- To buy a new car

What should you do with savings that you intend to be long-term?

In a word, invest. You'll have to think more carefully about what kind of saving plan (or financial investment product) you want to put your carefully set-aside money in. There are more options—plans, or products—for you to review, and you'll have to seriously think about what your goals are for your savings. How comfortable are you with risk, what interest do you want to make, and how often might you wish to access the funds?

Long-term savings plans have more flexibility, and there are more options to choose between than short-term savings plans.

Some things for you to consider:

Before you start investing: You should consider riskier long-term investment only after setting aside the equivalent of 3 to 6 months of income in an insured savings account for emergencies. When deciding how much is enough to set aside, consider your health and job security, and your families' needs. What amount available for immediate access makes you comfortable?

Your risk tolerance: You'll have to realize that with a long-term investment, such as in stocks and bonds, the value will go up and down from year to year. But in the long run, the average return (the profit on your investment) has been very positive. This is something you may or may not feel comfortable with.

63

Choosing an investment that fits your goal: If you are saving for retirement, you might want to go with a 401k or IRA or Roth IRA plan. To save for college expenses, most states offer tax-deferred or tax-exempt savings plans called 529 plans. If you are saving for a home down payment, you might want an ultra-safe plan, like a high-yield savings account.

How, and how often, you want to access your savings: Unlike a checking account, or a short-term savings account at a bank, you can't access these investment accounts as easily as walking up to an ATM. You CAN access them, but it will usually take some time and planning, and may involve penalties for early withdrawal.

How much interest you want to make: Realize that the most interest comes with the most risk, so you'll have to balance those two factors.

Service fees and easy access to information about your account: Compare several organizations: their fee structure, their product offerings, how they provide information about your account (and how timely it is), and if you'll have a live account representative to talk to (even if only by phone).

Finally:

- Consider what your needs are for your savings.
- Decide what your savings goal and purpose is.
- Do your due diligence and research on the pros and cons of the investments you are interested in, and in the companies you are considering investing with.
- Be sure to consider your emotional investment profile: your tolerance for risk, what company you feel comfortable with, if it feels okay that you won't have immediate access to your savings.

Investment Basics

You don't have to be a genius to be reasonably successful in investing. You just need to know a few basics, form a plan, and be ready to stay in for the long haul.

There is no guarantee that you'll make money. And you'll have to remember that there are no easy and fast ways to make lot of money. But if you get the facts about saving and investing and follow through with an intelligent plan, you should be able to enjoy the benefits of investment.

What kinds of investment products are there?
There are quite a few, and you need to research the benefits, risks, and fees for each.

Investment products include: stocks, bonds, municipal bonds, mutual funds, exchange-traded funds (ETFs), annuities, certificates of deposit (CDs), money market funds, commodities, hedge funds, real estate investment trusts (REITs), international investing. Sound confusing? Well, actually, it is!

HOW THE MARKETS WORK
The stock market is where buyers and sellers meet to decide on the price to buy or sell securities, usually with the assistance of a broker.

Public companies: A key part of the American economy that plays a major role in the savings, investment, and retirement plans of many Americans. If you have a pension plan or own a mutual fund, chances are that the plan or mutual fund owns stock in public companies. Like millions of Americans, you may also invest directly in public companies.

Brokerage accounts:
A cash account is a type of brokerage account in which the investor must pay the full amount for securities purchased.
A margin account is a type of brokerage account in which your brokerage firm can lend you money to buy securities, with the securities in your portfolio serving as collateral for the loan.

Stock purchases short and long: Having a "long" position in a security means that you own the security. Investors maintain "long" security positions in the expectation that the stock will rise in value in the future. The opposite of a "long" position is a "short" position. A "short" position is generally the sale of a stock you do not own. Investors who sell short believe the price of the stock will decrease in value. If the price drops, you can buy the stock at the lower price and make a profit. If the price of the stock rises and you buy it back later at the higher price, you will incur a loss.

TYPES OF ORDERS

A market order is an order to buy or sell a security immediately. This guarantees that the order will be executed, but does not guarantee the execution price. A market order generally will execute at or near the current bid (for a sell order) or ask (for a buy order) price.

A limit order is an order to buy or sell a security at a specific price or better. A buy limit order can only be executed at the limit price or lower, and a sell limit order can only be executed at the limit price or higher.

A stop order, also referred to as a stop-loss order is an order to buy or sell a stock once the price of the stock reaches the specified price, known as the stop price. When the stop price is reached, a stop order becomes a market order.

A buy stop order is entered at a stop price above the current market price. Investors generally use a buy stop order to limit a loss or protect a profit on a stock that they have sold short. A sell stop order is entered at a stop price below the current market price. Investors generally use a sell stop order to limit a loss or protect a profit on a stock they own.

EXECUTING AN ORDER

When you place an order to buy or sell stock, you might not think about where or how your broker will execute the trade. But where and how your order is executed can impact the overall cost of the transaction, including the price you pay for the stock.

Trade execution isn't instantaneous: When you push that enter key, your order is sent over the Internet to your broker--who in turn decides which market to send it to for execution—it does take time. And prices can change quickly. Investors may not always receive the price they saw on their screen or that their broker quoted. By the time your order reaches the market, the price of the stock could be slightly—or very—different.

Your broker has options for executing your trade: Just as you have a choice of brokers, your broker generally has a choice of markets to execute your trade.

Your broker has a duty of Best Execution: Many firms use automated systems to handle the orders they receive from their customers. In deciding how to execute orders, your broker has a duty to seek the best execution reasonably available for its customers' orders.

Should you "hire" yourself?
If you take the do-it-yourself route, go slowly and cautiously. Start by making sure your legal affairs are in order—you have a will and you have protected yourself from liability through appropriate insurance. Next make sure you set aside money for an emergency fund, money you can access quickly without fouling up an investment plan.

If you find a successful and experienced investor who is willing to be your mentor, consider entering that sort of relationship. But always use your common sense and remember that you are the boss.

If you want to hire an investment manager or advisor, choose carefully. Seek references from friends and relatives. Ask for references from lawyers and accountants. And an excellent rule of thumb: Never invest in anything that you don't understand.

Savings Financial Products

Product: Savings Account

Minimum Initial Deposit: Usually $25 - $100 but make certain monthly fees are not charged for small balances.

What It Is: A deposit account held at a bank or other financial institution that provides principal security and a modest interest rate.

Yield: Usually .2 - .5%

Safety: Government-insured

Access to Funds: Immediate

Where to Purchase: At any bank, thrift, or credit union

How to Make Deposits: Through tellers, ATMs, or automatic monthly transfer from checking account.

Other Features: At many institutions, minimum balance of $100-500 is required to avoid monthly fees or automatic transfers of $5 - $25 a month.

Product: Online Savings Account

Minimum Initial Deposit: As low as $1 at some institutions.

What It Is: Financial institutions that do not have traditional "brick and mortar" branches, and instead function as direct banks. These banks offer online savings accounts that pass on some of the reduction in overhead to depositors in the form of higher interest rates.

Yield: Usually .2 - .5%

Safety: Government-insured

Access to Funds: Immediate; 2 - 3 business day delay in transferring funds from your online account to an outside account or merchant.

Where to Purchase: At the online bank itself.

How to Make Deposits: By transferring money from a checking account, or through direct deposit.

Other Features: Confirm that the online institution is insured.

Product: Certificate of Deposit (CD)

Minimum Initial Deposit: At most institutions, at least $500 to $1,000

What It Is: Certificates of deposit (CDs) are investments that let you earn a fixed rate of interest for a specified period of time, usually between three months and 15 years.

Yield: Usually 1 - 2%

Safety: Government-insured

Access to Funds: Immediate, but interest penalty for early withdrawal.

Where to Purchase: At any bank, thrift, or credit union.

Other Features: Certain financial institution will notify you when CD matures.

Product: U.S. Savings Bond, Series EE

Minimum Initial Deposit: As low as $25 ($50 for payroll deduction).

What It Is: A government-issued bond that offers a fixed rate of interest over a fixed period of time. They cannot be easily transferred and are non-negotiable. This is an appreciation bond, in that its full value isn't realized until after 5 years. Early redemption comes with penalty.

Yield: Usually 1.5%

Safety: Government-insured

Access to Funds: After first 12 months, immediate access but loss of 3 months interest.

Where to Purchase: From the U.S. Treasury, banks.

How to Make Deposits: www.Treasurydirect.gov allows periodic deposit or checking account deductions to purchase bonds.

Other Features: Must cash in after 30 years or no more interest earned. They are not subject to state or local income taxes.

Product: U.S. Savings Bond, Series 1

Minimum Initial Deposit: As low as $25.

What It Is: A government-issued bond that inflation-indexed; it is sold at face value, and you can buy up to $10,000 (face value) in any calendar year. Series 1 Bonds offer a fixed rate of interest, adjusted for inflation. They cannot be easily transferred and are non-negotiable.

Yield: As low as $25

Safety: Government-guaranteed

Access to Funds: After first 12 months, immediate access but loss of 3 months interest.

Where to Purchase: Through http://www.treasurydirect.gov—where savers can buy electronic (no paper) savings bonds with checking account deductions, 24/7, and banks.

How to Make Deposits: EASY SAVER program allows periodic payroll deposit or checking account deductions to purchase bonds.

Other Features: Must cash in after 30 years or no more interest earned; has inflation protection.

Product: Money Market Account

What It Is: A money market fund is a type of mutual fund that is required by law to invest in low-risk securities. These funds have relatively low risks compared to other mutual funds and pay dividends that generally reflect short-term interest rates.

Yield: Usually .1 - .3%

Safety: Unlike a "money market deposit account" at a bank, money market funds are not federally insured.

Access to Funds: Immediate

Where to Purchase: Brokerages, banks

Other Features: Investor losses in money markets have been rare, but—they are possible.

Product: U.S. Treasury Bills and Notes

What It Is: **Treasury bills** are short-term government securities with maturities ranging from a few days to 52 weeks. Bills are sold at a discount from their face value. **Treasury notes** are government securities that are issued with maturities of 2, 3, 5, 7, and 10 years and pay interest every six months. **Treasury bonds** pay interest every six months and mature in 30 years. **TIPS** are marketable securities whose principal is adjusted by changes in the Consumer Price Index. TIPS pay interest every six months and are issued with maturities of 5, 10, and 30 years. Treasury securities are considered one of the safest investments: they are backed by the U.S. government.

Yield: Usually 1.5%; Treasury bills mature in less than a year; Treasury notes mature between two and 10 years.

Safety: Government-insured

Access to Funds: After first 12 months, immediate access but loss of 3 months interest.

Where to Purchase: From the U.S. Treasury, brokerages.

How to Make Deposits: www.Treasurydirect.gov allows periodic deposit or checking account deductions to purchase bonds.

Other Features: Must cash in after 30 years or no more interest earned; face value of bond twice the purchase price ($50 bond costs $25).

Product: Corporate Bonds

What It Is: Corporate bonds are bonds issued by companies. Companies issue corporate bonds to raise money for a variety of purposes, such as building a new plant, purchasing equipment, or growing the business. In return for your investment, they agree to give you interest on your money and eventually pay you back the amount you lent out.

Yield: If you are buying bonds from a stable government, your investment is virtually guaranteed, or risk-free. The safety and stability, however, come at a cost. Because there is little risk, there is little potential return. Bond prices rise and fall inversely to rising and falling interest rates.

Safety: The company that issued the bond could suspend interest payments, or even go belly up. State, local, or Federal government security does not back these companies.

Access to Funds: If you need your money before the bond matures, you may not get back all of your original investment.

Where to Purchase: Brokerages

How to Purchase: You may have to pay a commission to buy bonds.

Other Features: A corporate bond does not give you an ownership interest in the company—unlike when you purchase the company's stock.

Product: Municipal Bonds

What It Is: Municipal bonds are debt securities issued by states, cities, counties and other governmental entities to finance capital projects, such as building schools, highways or sewer systems, and to fund day-to-day obligations. Investors who buy municipal bonds are in effect lending money to the bond issuer in exchange for a promise of regular interest payments, usually semi-annually, and the return of the original investment, or "principal."

Yield: The date when the issuer repays the principal, the bond's maturity date, may be years in the future. Short-term bonds mature in one to three years, while long-term bonds won't mature for a decade.

Safety: The more creditworthy the municipality, the less it will pay in interest; they will usually pay more than government securities, money markets, or CDs. Risks include: Call risk, in which the issuer retires the bond before its maturity date; Credit risk, in which the issuer may experience financial problems that make it difficult or impossible to pay interest and principal in full; Inflation risk, in which inflation increases, reducing purchasing power; Interest rate risk, in which the bond's price will move up as interest rates move down and it will decline as interest rates rise, so that the market value of the bond may be more or less than the par value (fixed face value); Liquidity risk, in which investors won't find an active market for the municipal bond, potentially preventing them from buying or selling when they want and making pricing more difficult.

Access to Funds: The municipality issuing the bond could suspend interest payments, or even go belly up. They are not backed by state, local, or Federal security.

Where to Purchase: Brokerages

Product: Mutual Funds

Minimum Initial Deposit: The price that investors pay for mutual fund shares is the fund's approximate net asset value (NAV) per share plus any fees that the fund may charge at purchase, such as sales charges, also known as sales loads.

What It Is: A mutual fund is a company that pools money from many investors and invests the money in stocks, bonds, short-term money-market instruments, other securities or assets, or some combination of these investments. Each share represents an investor's proportionate ownership of the fund's holdings and the income those holdings generate.

Yield: Mutual funds are not guaranteed or insured by the FDIC or any other government agency—even if you buy through a bank and the fund carries the bank's name. You can lose money investing in mutual funds.

All mutual funds have costs that lower your investment returns: from .25% to 2.5% or more.

Safety: Mutual funds are not guaranteed or insured by the FDIC or any other government agency—even if you buy through a bank and the fund carries the bank's name. You can lose money investing in mutual funds.

Where to Purchase: You can purchase shares in some mutual funds by contacting the fund directly. Other mutual fund shares are sold mainly through brokers, banks, financial planners, or insurance agents.

Product: Annuities

What It Is: An annuity is a contract between you and an insurance company that is designed to meet retirement and other long-range goals, under which you make a lump-sum payment or series of payments. In return, the insurer agrees to make periodic payments to you beginning immediately or at some future date.

Yield: What you receive will vary depending the type of annuity you set up: on the performance of the investment options you have selected; returns based on changes in an index, such as the S&P 500 Composite Stock Price Index; or a specified rate of interest during the time that your account is growing. The insurance company also agrees that the periodic payments will be a specified amount per dollar in your account.

Safety: An annuity is as safe as the insurance company backing it; consider the risk ratings of the annuity provider as part of the due diligence surrounding the investment decision. The likelihood of losing your entire principal is pretty remote if you do your homework before signing the annuity contract.

Access to Funds: Withdrawal with penalty

Where to Purchase: Brokerages, insurance companies

Other Features: You will pay for each benefit provided by your variable annuity. Be sure you understand the charges. Carefully consider whether you need the benefit.

Product: Stocks

What It Is: The stock market is where shares of publicly listed companies are traded. The primary market is where companies offer shares to the general public in an initial public offering (IPO) to raise capital for their business. When you purchase stock, you become a part owner of the business. This entitles you to vote at the shareholders' meeting and allows you to receive any profits that the company allocates to its owners. These profits are referred to as dividends.

Yield: The yield you will realize depends greatly on the economy, and partly on the management of the companies you invest in. Be conservative and never invest in anything you do not understand.

Access to Funds: Your broker will have to find a buyer for the stock you wish to sell, so it could take a few days to a few weeks.

Where to Purchase: Brokerages

Product: IRA

What It Is: IRAs are investment accounts that are designed to provide you a tax-advantaged way to save for retirement. The special IRS status given to IRAs also comes with some limitations; such as how much you can contribute, when you must begin taking distributions, and what happens when you take your distributions too soon.

Yield: You choose your investments, including other types of investments like mutual funds, ETFs, and bonds to earn a higher rate of return.

Safety: You are accepting risk for a potentially higher return.

Access to Funds: Limited, and with penalty for early withdrawals.

Where to Purchase: Brokerages, banks

Product: Roth IRA

What It Is: An individual retirement plan that bears many similarities to the traditional IRA, but contributions are not tax deductible and qualified distributions are tax-free.

Yield: You choose your investments, including other types of investments like mutual funds, ETFs, and bonds to earn a higher rate of return.

Safety: When you invest your money into stocks, bonds, mutual funds, and ETFs you are accepting risk for a potentially higher return.

Access to Funds: Non-qualified distributions from a Roth IRA may be subject to a penalty upon withdrawal.

Where to Purchase: Brokerages, banks

Product: 401k

What It Is: A 401(k) Plan is a defined contribution plan that is a cash or deferred arrangement. Employees can elect to defer receiving a portion of their salary, which is instead contributed on their behalf, before taxes, to the 401(k) plan. Sometimes the employer may match these contributions.

Yield: You choose your investments, or investment plans with the 401k advisor. Usually they will steer you to a moderate plan—depending on your age—that will yield moderate earnings.

Safety: It's as safe as your investment choices—if the market goes down, your stocks in your 401k portfolio will go down as well.

Access to Funds: Non-qualified distributions may be subject to a penalty upon withdrawal.

Where to Purchase: Through your employer.

Other Features: Employees who participate in 401(k) plans assume responsibility for their retirement income by contributing part of their salary and, in many instances, by directing their own investments.

Personal Finance *for* Real People

Selecting, Managing, & Using Credit

Be a Responsible Borrower

We all know what it feels like to run short of funds occasionally: An unexpected expense might pop up, like a car repair, or money you expect to come in that just doesn't—at least not in time. What do you do then?

Hopefully, you've saved some money for emergencies, but not all of us can do that. What are your options?

Before we examine what to do, let's first take a look at your current situation. Is this truly a one-time occurrence, or do you keep getting stuck? If this is a regular situation, you need to examine how to avoid this pattern. You need to brush up your financial skills, take an honest look at your expenses and income, and set a realistic budget. Include in your budget an emergency fund for these tight spots, and set aside money for car repair, medical care, and other sudden and unexpected expenses.

But in this case you do have an expense coming up, and you don't have the funds to cover it. You can't borrow from your family, your overtime didn't come through, and you don't have enough money on hand. Now what? You can take a short-term, or cash advance, loan from a responsible lender.

Be a responsible borrower:

- Take out a loan only for the amount you absolutely need. I know it's tempting to get a little extra, but this is not a "treat yourself" situation. This is a "making ends meet" situation.

- Make sure you have a plan to repay the loan promptly. If you are just waiting for a check to arrive, then fine. But if you have to request overtime, or get some extra work, start planning that now.

- What if you get stuck and have trouble paying back your loan?
    - If you have to renew your loan, don't do it more than once or twice. Those charges start adding up!
    - Talk to your lender! Work out a payment plan, and discuss your options. Financial service centers are here to make this a successful transaction for you—not to drive you into the ground. Stop in and talk to any customer service representative.
    - Don't take more advances from additional lenders. If you can't pay back your first advance then you're simply digging yourself a hole you can't get out of by taking out multiple advances. In many states it is illegal to have more than one open cash advance. If your lender offers to give you more than one advance at a time, they are breaking the law.
    - If you have to, get another short-term, part-time job to pay off your debt. Depending on your skills and equipment, you could do additional handyman work, housecleaning, childcare, driving, etc. Check the Part-time and Gigs sections on Craigslist. If you have a computer at home, sign up for Amazon Mechanical Turk, an online site for task work suited to your specific skills. And talk to friends

and family—someone may need help with a one-time job.

Short-term and cash advance loans are just that—loans for a short period of time. They shouldn't be used as an income substitute. They are convenient and easy, but you will pay a fee for that convenience. Remember to manage your loan fees so that you don't pay any more than you absolutely need to.

Be Smart When Borrowing

There are many excellent reasons to borrow money: for an emergency, to purchase a car or house, for education, or just to tide you over for a bit.

But remember that credit costs money. Before you take out that loan, make sure you understand just what that borrowed money will actually cost, and also understand what options are available to you.

You want to stay in control of your credit and loans, not have them control you.

Interest rates:
When you borrow money, the lender—whoever it is—will charge you interest on your loan. Your loan interest rate will vary depending on a number of factors.

Short-term vs. long-term:
Debt (what you owe on your loan) falls into two categories, short and long-term. Long-term debt is what you incur when you take out a loan to purchase a house, for example, or a car. The interest rate on long-term loans is much lower than on a short-term loan, but of course you are making payments for a much longer time. Short-term debt is due anywhere between 30 days or a few months. The annual interest rate on short-term debt can be much higher—frequently 20 percent and up.

Calculating interest:
Lenders have different ways of calculating interest, and this can have a big impact on how much you'll spend over the life of the loan. Get acquainted with these methods—you'll need to identify them in the fine print of a loan contract. Your interest calculation may be based on one of the following:

- **On your Adjusted Balance:** This is the amount you owed at the beginning of the billing period minus any credits or payments made during that period. New purchases are not included in this amount.
- **On your Average Daily Balance:** Probably the most common method—this adds your balances for each day and then divides that total by the number of days in the billing period, minus any credits or payments made during that period. New purchases might or might not be included.
- **On your Previous Balance:** This bases your interest charge on the amount you owed at the end of the previous billing cycle.

Understand your credit card:
Remember that using your credit card is exactly like taking out a small loan to make that purchase. Read through your credit card contract and make sure you understand all the features and fees:

- Your Annual Percentage Rate (APR), if your rate is fixed or variable
- Annual fee, late fees, and over-limit fees
- How your interest rate is calculated
- What Grace Period you have before interest starts accruing on new purchases
- How your Rewards are calculated (Rewards credit cards typically charge a good-sized annual fee, so make sure the reward is useful to you, and that the benefit will cover the cost of the annual fee.)

Choose your lender:

- Do your research, and be especially careful if you are looking for a short-term, or micro-credit, loan.
- Go to a lender with a physical storefront. Online lenders are more expensive, and you can't talk face-to-face with a real person. Nor do you have the security of knowing where they do business.
- Research and be clear on the company's lending policies. These should be available online, in their location, and in their contracts.
- Read the policies carefully, so you know what is expected of you.
- Is the lender a member of an overseeing, responsible financial association? Are they members of a Financial Service Providers association? You should be able to read the business and lending standards they abide by on their website.
- Do some checking on the company. Google them to see if any complaints pop up, or check them through the Better Business Bureau, where you'll be able to see if they are properly licensed and if any complaints have been lodged against them.
- **Alert:** Be aware of garnishee orders, which allow credit providers to deduct repayments from your salary, if you have defaulted on your original debt repayment arrangement.

A few final guidelines:

- Borrow only what you need.
- Remember that short-term loans and credit cards are not simply additional income.
- As a rule of thumb don't borrow more than 20 percent of your income (not counting your rent or mortgage payment) or you could run into trouble repaying your loan or paying off your credit card.
- Read through any loan agreement, including credit cards, before signing.
- Make sure you know just what your loan will cost you in total.
- Have a plan for paying off your loan and total debt.

Use Credit Cards Wisely

- Know when your payment is due: Mark it on your calendar, set an alarm on your phone, or keep a checklist. Mark about seven (or more) days earlier, when you will be actually making the payment.
- Pay your bills on time.
- Make at least the minimum payment due.
- Try to make more than the minimum payment.
- Don't make a larger purpose unless you can pay it off immediately, or at least have a plan to do so.
- Do NOT exceed your credit limit.
- Know what your account balances are. Try to keep them below 25% of your credit limit—this will help your credit rating.
- Have a plan for paying off your balance, even if it's high.
- Check your credit report each year.
- Know your credit score.
- Definitely have credit cards, if you can pay them off each month. But don't have too many. Open accounts only if you need to.
- Shop for the best credit card offer, and read the terms.
- Never get a cash advance from a credit card.
- In most cases, you can pick your own payment due date—you can time it for when you get paid.
- Don't close old accounts, unless they have a steep annual fee or closing fee.

Different Types of Credit

Many people don't understand that all credit is not the same. There are several categories of credit, each with a different purpose: auto loans vs. home mortgage vs. credit cards. But they have one thing in common: They combine to make up your credit score, so it's important to be aware of your various kinds of credit at all times.

New Credit
You want to open new accounts because it establishes credit. However, if you open a lot of new accounts it makes lenders nervous—they think that you can't manage your financial life, and that you can't pay off your debt. Securing new credit lowers the average length of your credit score—it counts for 15% of your FICO score.

Types of Credit:

- Secured debt: Loans with collateral attached, such as a home mortgage or auto loan.
- Unsecured debt: Nothing has been put up for collateral; this is the category that credit cards fall into.
- Revolving debt: Debts that can be paid off, and then borrowed from again and again, like a credit line from a bank.
- Installment debt: Debts that must be paid off over a length of time with set monthly payments; student loans are an example.

How "Payday" Loans Work

Just what exactly IS a payday loan?

The answer is simple: It's more accurate to call it a **small short-term unsecured loan**, designed to get a customer through a short, tight-money patch. It's usually less than $500, and is extended for between 3 to 31 days. Even the most organized person can have an emergency—a medical crisis, a car repair, or utility bill—and need quick access to cash, or just something to tide them over until payday.

The loan is not necessarily tied to a customer's pay date, although frequently customers choose to repay their loans once they get their paychecks. These advance loans (like most loans) do rely on the consumer having previous payroll and employment records.

What does a customer need to provide in order to secure a payday loan? The borrower must usually be a resident of the state in which they are securing the loan. The customer will need to bring with them: their current government photo ID, their most recent pay stub or benefit statement, their text-capable telephone, or their most recent telephone bill.

What if the customer wants to extend the loan past its due date—"rollover" the loan? Some states do not allow any client to rollover the transaction principle by paying the transaction fee. Even if it is legal, this practice would very much be discouraged. In the long run, it does not really help the customer—in fact, it only gets them into a larger problem.

Can a customer with another short-term loan outstanding also get a payday loan? Most financial service centers will not extend credit to anyone with an existing payday loan, or similar 32-day-or-less credit transaction, from any storefront, online lender, bank or credit union.

Can a customer ever have multiple loans? Reputable financial service centers will never allow multiple transactions that occur at the same time. It is possible for a customer to take multiple, separate, loans spaced throughout the year—just not more than one at a time. Many lenders voluntarily provide a payment plan to any individual after four consecutive transactions to discourage repeat borrowing.

Are there additional fees? Each financial service center may differ, but many will not (and should not) charge upfront fees or additional excessive fees if a client has insufficient funds to pay the transaction in full by their due date.

Keep in mind that each state has its own rules and restrictions.

High-quality financial service centers provide many financial services to working families, from bill-paying services to tax planning and filing, from check cashing to U.S.P.S postal services, from money transfers to short-term loans. They care about their customers: Their customers are regular people who are unwilling or unable to utilize traditional banking services, or find it more convenient to take care of their financial needs in one place, with the same person. Many customers live paycheck to paycheck, and don't have the luxury of a 401-k, an understanding employer, a trust fund, or family members with money to loan.

We believe in financial education that regular, hardworking people can understand, and that applies to their life situations.

Rebuild Your Credit

Whether you have a bankruptcy in your past, or have just gotten yourself into a bad credit situation, sooner or later you are going to want to start thinking about rebuilding your credit score.

There's no such thing as a quick fix to a less-than-wonderful credit score, however. You will have to work on improving your credit gradually and over time. Be patient, stick to your plan, and you will see improvement.

A credit score is a living thing: always changing depending on your actions. Those actions can cause your credit score to steadily improve (or decline).

Examine the damage:
First, find out exactly what your credit reports look like, and what your credit history is.

Order and review your credit reports to make sure all the information included is correct. You are entitled under law to a free copy of your credit report each year from each of the three major credit reporting agencies:

- Equifax, Experian, and TransUnion. Request your reports at http://www.AnnualCreditReport.com.

Your credit report includes: Companies that have extended credit to you; the amounts of your loans and credit limits; your payment history; who has requested a copy of your credit report; your employment history and your addresses.

Make sure all items are correct. Things to look out for: Did a credit card company make a mistake about when you made your payments? Is your address correct in all cases, and is your name spelled correctly? Are all the credit accounts listed ones you took out? Has someone requested your credit report whom you don't recognize?

If you find any errors, report them to the agency—they must correct these at no charge to you.

Negative credit marks must fall off your credit report after a minimum of seven years (ten years for some bankruptcies, liens, or penalties). Review your reports to make sure there are no marks older than that. Again, if there are, contact the agency—they must correct those.

If you can, find out what your FICO score is.

Where you are right now:
Now that you know your history and how credit agencies perceive you, it's time to take a look at your current situation.

Review your debts, if you have any, and make a plan to pay them off as aggressively as you can. Pay down your loans, especially your credit cards: Make your payments regularly, and get your loan balance below 10-25% of your credit limit. Try to have an account or two where you owe nothing.

Manage your late payments or debts that went to collection: If you're normally a good customer, ask the company to erase that one late payment record. See if you can "re-age" your account by making steady payments for a determined period of time. Dispute items marked as "collection" if that's not what happened.

Protect your existing credit. Pay on time, and pay at least the minimum amount due. Set up automatic payments if you have trouble remembering when to pay your bills.

If you have credit cards that you rarely use, and that are not carrying a balance, make a small purchase every few months (and promptly pay it off), to keep those accounts open. Using your credit cards once in a while (and paying them off that month) ensures that all your credit (and good credit behavior) continues to get reported to the credit bureaus.

The "DON'Ts":

- Don't apply for new credit until you have made significant progress on resolving your bad credit history.
- Don't take cash advances from your credit cards—this can be seen as a sign of financial distress, as will transferring balances between credit cards. Don't ask your credit card company to lower, or increase, your credit limit.
- Don't revert to bad behavior. Make sure that you are not repeating any behaviors that got you into a bad credit situation in the first place.
- Don't outspend your income. If you have trouble with this one, create a budget and be ruthless about not exceeding it.

The "DOs":

- Do pay your bills on time.
- Pay at least the minimum due on all your bills, and keep to your payment schedule.

Start building for the future:
Now is when you want to start thinking about what you can do to improve your credit score.

- Pay your bills on time (are you sensing a theme here?).
- Use no more than 15 - 25% of your credit limits. This is your utilization ratio, and going higher than that can ding your credit score. If you use your credit card frequently (and pay it off each month), try making a few payments throughout the month to keep your utilization ratio below 20% at any given time.
- Establish a separate emergency fund, so you won't have to resort to your credit cards.
- Wait to apply for new credit. Even though you are now on the right credit path, be careful about applying for new credit. Yes, you will want to at some point, but you need to time it well, and make sure you can handle

it. Applying for new credit can knock points off your credit score, and will affect your score for the next year. So go slowly, and be aware of just where your credit score is.

It takes time.
Remember that repairing and improving your credit score, and your ability to get a loan, will take time. The exact amount of time depends on what your specific financial situation has been—if you've had delinquencies or bankruptcy, it will take longer.

But be patient and keep at it—a good credit score is achievable for everyone!

Your Credit Score

Your credit worthiness is based on your credit score. How do you figure out what your current credit score is, and why should you care?

What your credit score is based on: Your credit score is a number that comes from an analysis of your credit reports from several agencies. The major credit reporting bureaus are Experian, TransUnion, and Equifax. Each of these agencies tracks your credit and payment history, from outstanding loans (including credit cards), your payment record, your late payment record, the amount of debt you have relative to your income, your job stability and other factors. They tabulate all that information and provide it in a credit report to you, or to those want to examine your credit worthiness.

You are entitled to a yearly free copy of your credit report from each of the three main credit-reporting agencies. These can be obtained at www.AnnualCreditReport.com at no charge, once every 12 months.

Your credit score is calculated usually by another agency; they look at your complete information (provided by the bureaus) and determine your credit risk and worthiness. The FICO score is the most common, and it may be used in conjunction with other information or scores. This one final number is the distillation of your entire financial situation.

The FICO score number ranges from 300 (bad credit) to 850 (fabulous credit). Most credit-worthy people have a score in the 700s. The lowest score that is still credit-worthy is 640, but that has been trending up to sometimes as high as 740 for some companies and in some situations.

You may get a copy of your credit score, but there is a small charge for it, usually around $10. You can get this as an add-on to your credit report request, also at www.AnnualCreditReport.com.

Why should you care what your credit score is?
Obviously, if you ever want to purchase something on credit or take a loan, your credit score will determine whether you can get a company to approve your loan. This is true for buying a home and taking out a mortgage, getting a credit card, and buying a car. Realize, though, that your credit score and credit reports will also affect the interest rate you receive from your lender, the amount your insurance costs you, your ability to rent a place to live, and even to get a job. Yes, they all look at your credit reports.

You will want to review your credit reports to make sure all the information included is correct. Your credit report includes: Companies that have extended credit to you; the amounts of your loans and credit limits; your payment history; who has requested a copy of your credit report; your employment history and your addresses. Make sure all items are correct. Things to look out for: Did a credit card company make a mistake about when you made your payments? Is your address correct? Are the credit accounts listed ones you took out? Has someone requested your credit report that you don't recognize?

Examining your credit reports is key to preventing identity theft—and identity theft is a very painful and quick way to send your credit score plummeting.

How to build your credit score:
If your credit score is on the low end, don't despair. A credit score is a living thing, always changing depending on your actions, and those actions can cause your credit score to steadily improve. Some suggestions:

- **Get a credit card:** Even if you can't qualify for a regular credit card, take out a secured credit card (you deposit an amount of money to be used for your credit line), one that reports to all three credit bureaus.
- **Take out a small personal loan:** Your credit score goes up if you show you can handle different kinds of credit, from a credit card to actual loans. You may already have a student loan or a car loan; but if not, get a small personal loan (from a company that reports to the three credit bureaus) and pay it off reliably.
- **Pay your bills on time:** They all get reported to the credit bureaus. Set up automatic payments if you have trouble remembering.
- **Pay down your loans, especially your credit cards:** Make your payments regularly, and get your loan balance below 10-25% of your credit limit. Try to have an account or two where you owe nothing.
- **Know your credit limits and keep your credit cards active:** Make sure you are familiar with your credit card and loan terms, and that your credit card's credit limit is reported accurately in your credit report. Use your credit cards once in a while (and paying them off that month) so that all your credit (and good credit behavior) continues to get reported to the credit bureaus.
- **Manage your late payments or debts that went to collection:** If you're normally a good customer, ask the company to erase that one late payment record. See if you can "re-age" your account by making steady payments for a determined period of time. Dispute items marked as "collection" if that's not what happened.

What not to do:

- Make late payments, or skip payments.
- Ask a creditor to lower, or increase, your credit limit.
- Transfer balances between creditors.
- Apply for more credit if you don't need it.

Remember that repairing and improving your credit score, and your ability to get a loan, will take time. The exact amount of time depends on what your specific financial situation has been—if you've had delinquencies or bankruptcy, it will take longer.

But be patient and keep at it—a good credit score is achievable for everyone!

Alternative Credit Scores

If you are one of what's often referred to as "underbanked," have a whisper-thin credit record, or if you have no credit history, you are probably already aware of the issues and problems that can come with having a low credit score or credit rating.

How do people wind up with a low credit score?
Usually a low credit rating comes from one of two situations:

- You have had financial difficulties in the past: Declared bankruptcy, defaulted on loans or credit cards, defaulted on medical bills, etc.
- You have simply not accumulated enough financial information in the accepted places in order to develop a traditional credit score.

What makes building a credit score difficult?
Traditional credit scores are built on a small set of data, making it harder if:

- You have no credit cards.
- You've only ever had and used one credit card.
- You don't use your credit cards regularly.
- You've only taken out one or two smaller loans

Are you one of the "underbanked?"
If you haven't heard this term before, it refers to those who have short or non-existent credit histories, and those who do not use traditional bank services. If that describes you, know that you are not alone: 26 million people in the U.S. have no credit history with the major credit reporting companies. That's about 10% of the American population!

Other demographic groups often considered "underbanked" include immigrants, who often have difficulty transferring their financial information between countries, and Millennials, who are relatively new in the job market and new to credit.

The rise of the alternative credit score
With so many people "underbanked," the financial services industry is taking notice. Banks, lender and seller recognize that there's a need to help underbanked people build a useful credit score.

Just what is an alternative credit score?
This new type of credit score compiles and tracks your payment history for regular expenses like rent, utilities, internet, telephone, insurance, student loan, and even subscription services. These expenses are not usually included in major credit agencies' reporting, but they can show a credit-worthy payment history.

Alternative credit is not only legal, but growing daily. If you provide a lender with proof of non-traditional payment history (alternative credit score and rating), the lender is required by law to factor it into their credit evaluation.

What is alternative credit based upon?

You've most likely been making trackable payments of one kind or another for most of your adult life: Rent payments, utilities, telephone, insurance, and internet access. You may also be paying monthly for streaming services like Netflix or Hulu, or for cloud apps and storage such as Dropbox or Office 365.

By linking those accounts to a tracking provider, regular payments will be factored into your alternative credit score. You'll then have something concrete to give potential lenders.

Who will accept an alternative credit score?

In fact, more than 8,500 companies throughout the U.S. use alternative credit reports, and more are using them each year.

There are, however, specific businesses that are especially interested in using nontraditional credit reports, including:

- Car dealerships
- Jewelry stores
- Electronics retailers
- Furniture stores
- Property managers and landlords
- Financial services providers
- **Why should you use an alternative credit score?**
  It's a great way to proactively improve your credit score. Once you have built up your alternative credit score, other, more traditional, credit providers will see your payment track record and be more inclined to offer you credit, and potentially at better terms.

Where do you start?

One company that offers this service is **PRBC**, https://www.prbc.com/, the world's largest provider of non-traditional data to the credit market. Sign-up is free and you can use their tools to set up your account tracking to get your free alternative credit score. PRBC verifies your bills and payments automatically and in real time once you link your accounts to their secure database. You can also manage and organize your bills and accounts in one place, even setting up bill payment reminders.

Of course, there are additional companies that provide alternative credit services; https://rentalkharma.com/ is one.

Choosing an alternative credit company

Check to see what each company's fees are, what their security protocols are, exactly where they will be drawing your payment information from, and what services they offer.

Is getting an alternative credit score worth the effort?

Yes, it is. With alternative credit, you *can* create a positive impact on your credit ratings and credit score. By starting to build your alternative credit score you'll be building the path to improved economic security, more housing opportunities, more and better employment prospects, and greater purchasing power.

Selecting a Credit Card

What kind of credit card you choose depends on how you plan to use it, and what you qualify for. Here's a quick rundown of the types of credit cards available:

Balance transfer credit card: If you are currently paying off card balances on multiple credit cards, you might find it helpful to consolidate your debts into one monthly payment. Some may even offer a low introductory rate for 12 to 18 months so you can spend that time paying off your old balances.

Low interest credit card: Good if you typically carry over a balance from month to month.

Rewards/cash back credit card: Helpful if you'll use your credit card often to maximize your rewards or cash back earned. Not for the person who doesn't pay their credit card off each month, and it may also have a pricey yearly fee. It is likely only be available to consumers with excellent credit.

Airline credit card: Only if you fly frequently and plan on using your card to pay for travel expenses, and if you fly a single airline. Also may have a yearly fee, and a time limit on points and miles earned.

Secured credit card: The card to start with if you have no credit history, or if you are recovering from a foreclosure or bankruptcy. You'll have to provide a security deposit, usually a few hundred dollars. Be sure to pay this one off each month, to build up your credit-worthiness.

Those are the types of credit cards available. Now, how do you prepare yourself to choose one, or to get the best one possible?

Get a copy of your credit score. That's what the credit card company will be looking at. Also, it's not a bad idea to check your credit report and clean up any issues that show up on it.

Do your research: Depending on the type of card you are going for, you'll have to research slightly different things, but these remain consistent:

- Is there an annual fee, and what is it?
- What is the APR? Is that likely to change at any time?
- What credit line are you likely to get?
- If it's a rewards or airline card, examine the details of the program.
- How secure is the card? What are the company's security measures?
- Does it have added conveniences (paying your bill and looking up your transactions online, getting your past billing history, etc.)?

- What is the grace period (the time you have to pay your monthly payment without accruing interest)? Or does it even have one? If they have one, it's usually 21 to 30 days.
- Make sure it has a standard monthly billing cycle.
- Read the fine print. It's tiny, it's boring, but it has important information you need to know.

Now you're prepared to get that good credit history started!

Credit Card Comparison Worksheet

Review your options before applying for a specific credit card: You want to know all the fees and terms involved, and figure out what suits your needs.

CREDIT CARD COMPARISON

Evaluate different credit card applications comparing finance charges, interest, late fees, closing costs, annual fees, etc. Credit Card information: www.creditcardcomparison.com. Store Cards and Pay Day Lenders search individually on internet.

	Type of Credit & Company	APR (%)	Annual Fee	Other Fees	Balance Transfer	Finance Charge	Grace Period	Other
Example	Visa Signature, Capital One – No Hassle	0% for 9 mo, 13.9% after	None	Cash adv. 3% Late fees $29-35	No fees	$0.50	20 days	Earn double miles on purchases, Fly on any airline, No blackout dates, Seat restrictions
Credit Card								
Credit Card								
Store Card								
Store Card								
Pay Day Lender								

Get Rid of Your Debt

Did you know that the average American household has more than $15,000 in credit card debt alone? Perhaps your own debt is smaller (or larger!), but it still needs to be paid off—keeping your debt going costs you a lot of extra money.

Debt does seem overwhelming, and you probably wonder how on earth you will ever be able to pay it off, but there are relatively painless steps you can take to work your way through the process.

Make a budget:
Before you can even begin to address your debt—or any other financial issues—you have to know exactly where you are financially. How much money comes in, and how much goes out? When the money goes out, where does it go? Take some time to work on your budget and actuals, and fill in as many categories as apply to you.

Make a list of your debts; be sure to include the amount you owe and what your interest rate is.

Now examine your budget:
Where can you cut expenses? Once you have your expenses entered by category, you'll see some opportunities to save some money: Take your lunch to work, not eating out so often, curtailing impulse buying, going without cable for a while, etc.

Now is also the time to stop using your credit cards. Don't pile on additional charges until your old ones are paid off! Take your cards out of your wallet, and delete them from any online accounts.

Pay off your most expensive debt first:
If you have credit card debt, focus on the card with the highest interest rate first. This one is costing you the most additional money. Increase your payments on this debt, and continue to pay the minimum payments on your other credit cards. Once that card is paid off, move down the list to the card with the next-highest interest rate.

Pay more than your minimum payment:
If you only pay the minimum payment due each month, it will take you years (and a boatload of expensive additional interest) to pay off your debt. Try paying double your minimum payment, or try making payments twice a month (or even weekly). You will be amazed at how this accelerates your progress!

If you have a home mortgage, this is also an excellent way to shorten the life of your loan. Pay two mortgage payments a month, add extra to your payment, or even just round up your payment to the next even hundred. Just check your loan terms to make sure that additional payments will be applied to the principal (your original loan amount).

Use balance transfers:
This is a worthwhile short-term tactic to save money on accumulating interest, but you must be careful and pay attention. If you have a credit card that is offering a zero-interest balance transfer, consider moving your high-interest credit card balance over. Things to watch out for: That zero interest will only apply for a certain length of time, so make sure you can pay it off before that date; also make sure you understand any fees involved.

Apply any unexpected windfalls to your debt:
This is really a pain-free approach. Did you get a tax refund, or a bonus at work? Apply those to paying off your debt. Additionally, if you get a raise, apply that extra amount to your debt payment.

Sell household items you no longer want or need:
Do you have quality goods gathering dust that you just don't need or want anymore? Sell them on Craigslist or on eBay. Just remember to use the proceeds to pay down your debt.

Extra work:
If you have the opportunity to do some short-term additional work, you will have that much more to apply to your debt. Ask around; check Craigslist and other job sites, volunteer for holiday hours or overtime. Or perhaps you have a hobby that you can turn into a part-time business (repair work, crafting goods, art). It all adds up!

Make sure you stick to your goals:
Don't let previous "spendy" ways derail your path to being debt-free. Keep an eye out for impulse purchases and sneaky small expenditures like that daily morning latte. Keep checking your budget, and enter your actual income and expenses so you always know just what your current financial picture is.

Celebrate!
Once you have that debt paid off, reward yourself for your hard work, but within reason. Buy that new outfit—but on sale!

Debt Payment Plan Worksheet

Debt	
Total Amount	
Minimum Payment	
Interest Rate	

Date		Starting Balance	Payment	Remaining Balance

Work with Creditors

If you have a large amount of debt that you just can't manage to pay back on time, don't just stick your head in the sand and hope it will all go away. Now is the time to reach out to your creditors and ask them to work with you. After all, they want at least some or most of their money back—if you are forced to declare bankruptcy, they lose it all. You may feel uncomfortable talking to them, but it's better than the alternative.

This is called debt settlement, or debt negotiation.

What's possible:
There are several options available in which your creditor can either give you more time, or help you reduce your debt.

- Settle a debt by getting the creditor to accept a lower amount, if you pay a lump sum up front.
- Negotiate lower payments, either temporarily or permanently.
- Extend your payment period—get more time to pay off your debt.

Review your situation and set some goals:
Before you reach out to your creditors, understand your financial situation over-all, and your financial situation with each creditor. Know if you'll be able to afford to offer a lump sum partial payment to settle the situation. Understand how much it will cost you to extend your payments.

Know whether your debt is secured (as in when you buy a car or house) or unsecured (credit card debt). Keep in mind that unless you work with the creditor, they can eventually repossess your house or car.

Set goals for each creditor:

- Try to get a creditor to settle for 50% of the debt or less. Start lower and work your way up to 50%.
- For one creditor, you just need a little more time (be specific—do you need 3 months, a year?)
- For another, you need their cooperation to reduce your debt.
- Or, you may be able to offer a lump sum (less than the total of the debt) to settle the debt.

How to handle the conversation:
Your creditor DOES want to know if you are in a hardship situation, and you need to tell them about it. Don't go into too many details, but use a few sentences that sympathetically describe your situation, and that you can use with each creditor.

Examples of how to describe your situation:

- "I was ill with X, and unable to work for X months. Now I'm trying to get caught up and get my finances back in order."
- "I've been laid off, and am looking for a job, but it's taking a while. I just don't have the money to pay right now, but I'd like to work out a plan with you."
- "I lost my investment/nest egg/home, and I'm having trouble keeping up. I'm considering bankruptcy. Do you have any suggestions on how I can avoid that?"

Tell the creditor your situation, what steps you are taking to remedy it, and propose a specific solution.

Hint at the possibility of bankruptcy. Regardless of the actual likelihood of filing for bankruptcy, a subtle suggestion to the creditor that bankruptcy is a likely future event may encourage the creditor to lower their settlement offer.

Don't get angry, overly dramatic, or wildly exaggerate. Remember that you are the one who got yourself into this situation, not the creditor. If you lose your temper, you will just make it harder to negotiate with the creditor. Now, if the representative you are speaking with IS actually abusive, rude, and not helpful, tell them that you are recording the phone call. And if you have to talk to them again, DO record the call, or ask to speak to their supervisor.

Ask your creditor detailed questions, and make sure you understand all your alternatives. If the creditor threatens to sue you for non-payment, calmly ask them, "What exactly does that mean? When and how would I be notified? Would there be a grace period to allow me to come up with a payment? Would you take the money from my bank account, or do I need to send a payment?" The more information you have about your situation, the better. The more you show your creditor that you are seriously considering your situation, the more likely they will be to work with you.

Don't settle your debt with a home equity loan, a loan using your car as collateral, or your retirement savings.

If you can have cash available to settle the debt in a lump sum and can immediately transfer it, the creditor will be much more likely to consider that option.

Follow up your first detailed creditor conversation with a letter. Attach some kind of proof to hold up your story: a copy of your disability benefits statement, a budget work sheet, medical bills, job interview responses, references, or other paperwork that backs up your validity.

You promised a letter with documentation; sit down immediately and write it, and then go right to the post office. Make sure to include your full name and account number, address and phone number, and address it to the correct employee or department.

Recap your situation in brief paragraphs, the agreed-upon resolution (if applicable—if not, what you are offering), and a final statement of how you are committed to keeping the account in good standing. Make copies of the letter and any paperwork, then send the entire package via certified mail, return receipt requested.

Maintain regular contact—it will help you avoid having to re-explain your situation, and reassures creditors that you are sincere in your efforts to get financially back   on track.

Suggestions for negotiating with creditors and collection agencies:

- Be sure you are talking to the right person. When you first call, the person you will get is a lowly customer service rep.
- Ask if they have to ability to lower your interest rate, modify your payments, reduce your debt—and of course, they won't. Then ask to be transferred to a manager who has the authority to discuss this with you.
- Don't lie. You will get caught if you lie. Period.
- Don't share unnecessary details. The creditor doesn't really care about the many details that got you in this situation. Don't tell a long story.

What else to do:

- Keep a file: Make sure you take detailed notes whenever you speak with someone. Write down whom you talked to, their title if you can get it, and the date and time you talked. Keep all this information in a file folder for each creditor. Keep copies of all correspondence. All you want to do at this point is not answer calls and throw away all your mail, but, understandable as that is, it won't help you in either the short or long run.
- Get the settlement or payment agreement in writing before you pay anything. That way you have proof that the issue was settled, even if the creditor makes a "mistake" and sells your debt to a collection agency.
- Don't get to the point where you are forced to deal with collection agencies. Always, always work with the creditor first. Collections do greater damage to your credit report than late payments.
- Consult with a bankruptcy attorney (the first visit is usually free) to see just what your situation is, if you can or cannot declare bankruptcy, and the information you would need to gather. They may also be able to tell you what your creditors are and are not allowed to do to collect.
- Beware of debt consolidation companies. They charge a hefty monthly fee, and in most cases do not help you get rid of your debt or handle your creditors.

Stay strong, and work your way through each debt, in whichever way is most appropriate. You can do it!

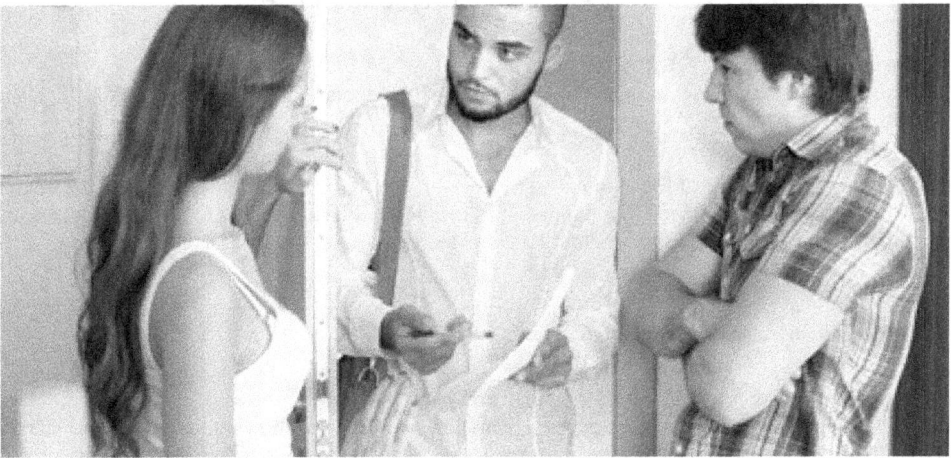

Know Your Rights with Debt Collectors

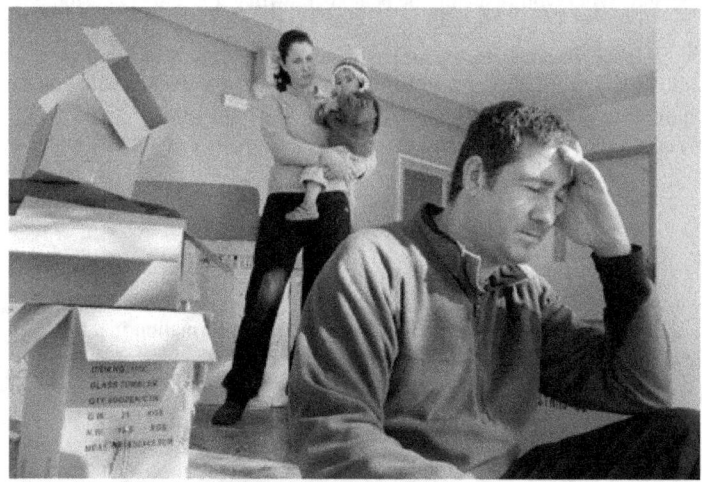

You owe money on your credit cards, you haven't made a payment in a while, you didn't pay attention to our previous section on working with your creditors, and now you are being hounded by debt collection agencies. Sometimes you suspect that they are trying to scare you into paying them, and you wonder if anything they say is true.

Thankfully for everyone, the federal government created the Fair Debt Collection Practices Act (FDCPA). It puts limits on the tactics collection agencies use, but it also allows them to try to collect against debt—the debt you so happily ran up on your shiny new credit card.

The FDCPA may not cover everything, but it does put limits on how far debt collectors can go to try to get that debt paid.

In the FDCPA's terms, a debt collector is someone who regularly collects debts owed to others. This includes collection agencies, lawyers who collect debts on a regular basis, and companies that buy delinquent debts and then try to collect them.

Here are the main points you need to know about your rights under the Act:

What debts are covered by the FDCPA:
Personal, family, and household debts, including what you owe on a personal credit card account, auto loans, medical bills, and your mortgage.

If your debt is outside the statute of limitations—as little as three to four years in some cases, you are not required to pay up. However, you should honor your obligations when you're financially able to do so. A negative mark resulting from a delinquent account can hang out on your credit report for 7 years or more.

What debts are not covered:
The FDCPA doesn't cover debts you incurred to run a business.

Can a debt collector contact debtors at any time or any place?
No. A debt collector may not contact you at inconvenient times or places, such as before 8:00 am or after 9:00 pm, unless you agree to it. And collectors may not contact you at work if they're told (orally or in writing) that you're not allowed to receive personal calls there.

Debt collectors can contact you by phone, letter, email, or text message to collect a debt, as long as they follow the rules and disclose who they are. No matter how they communicate with you, it's against the law for a debt collector to pretend to be someone else—like an attorney or government agency—or to harass, threaten or deceive you.

When and if you do talk to a debt collector, record the call, and let them know you are recording it.

How you can stop a debt collector from contacting you:
If a collector contacts you about a debt, you may want to talk to them at least once to see if you can resolve the matter—even if you don't think you owe the debt, can't repay it immediately, or think that the collector is contacting you by mistake.

If you decide after contacting the debt collector that you don't want the collector to contact you again, tell the collector—in writing—to stop contacting you.

Sending the letter:
Make a copy of your letter.

Send the original by certified mail, and ask to get a return receipt so you'll be able to document that the collector received it (and the collector knows that you know this).

Once the collector receives your letter, they may not contact you again, with two exceptions: a collector can contact you to tell you there will be no further contact, or to let you know that they or the creditor intend to take a specific action, like filing a lawsuit.

Sending this letter to a debt collector does not get rid of the debt, but it should stop the relentless contact. The creditor or the debt collector can still sue you to collect the debt.

Can a debt collector contact anyone else about your debt?
If an attorney is representing you about the debt, the debt collector must contact the attorney, rather than you.

If you don't have an attorney, a collector may contact other people—but only to find out your address, your home phone number, and where you work.

Collectors usually are prohibited from contacting third parties more than once. Other than to obtain this location information about you, a debt collector generally is not permitted to discuss your debt with anyone other than you, your spouse, or your attorney.

What does the debt collector have to tell the debtor about the debt?
The debt collector must send a written validation notice telling you how much money is owed within five days after they first contact you.

The notice also must include the name of the creditor to whom you owe the money.

It must also tell you how to proceed if you don't think you owe the money.

You don't think you owe any money—can a debt collector keep contacting you?
If you send the debt collector a letter stating that you don't owe any or all of the money, or asking for verification of the debt, that collector must stop contacting you.

You have to send that letter within 30 days after you receive the validation notice.

A collector can begin contacting you again if they send you written verification of the debt, like a copy of a bill for the amount you owe.

What practices are off limits for debt collectors?

Harassment:

- Debt collectors may not harass, oppress, or abuse you or any third parties they contact.
- Debt collectors may not:
  - Use threats of violence or harm.
  - Publish a list of names of people who refuse to pay their debts (but they can give this information to the credit reporting companies).
  - Use obscene or profane language.
  - Harass you by calling numerous times a day about your debt.

False statements:

- Debt collectors may not lie when they are trying to collect a debt.
- Debt collectors may not:
  - Pretend that they are attorneys or government representatives.
  - Falsely claim that you have committed a crime.
  - Claim that they represent, operate, or work for a credit reporting company.
  - Misrepresent the amount you owe.
  - Pretend that papers they send you are legal forms if they are not.
  - Pretend that papers they send to you are not legal forms if they are.
- Debt collectors also are prohibited from claiming that:
  - You will be arrested.
  - Your property or wages will be seized, garnished, attached, or sold unless they are permitted by law (in a legal judgment) to take that action and that they sincerely intend to do so
  - Legal action will be taken against you, if doing so would be illegal, or if they don't intend to take the action.
- Debt collectors may not:
  - Give false credit information about you to anyone, including a credit reporting company.
  - Send you anything that looks like an official document from a court or government agency if it's not that.
  - Use a false company name.
- Unfair practices. Debt collectors may not engage in unfair practices when they try to collect a debt.
- Debt collectors may not:
  - Attempt to collect any interest, fee, or other charge on top of the amount you owe, unless the contract that created your debt, or state law, allows it.
  - Deposit a post-dated check early.
  - Take or threaten to take your property unless it can be done legally.

- Contact you by postcard.

Paying your debt:
If you legitimately owe the amount claimed by the creditor, and wish to make a deal to pay, never give a collector your checking account number over the phone. Collectors routinely take more money than they say they'll take.

- Pay only by money order.
- Never pay until you have an agreement in writing stating your payment will resolve the debt in full.

Control what debts your payments will be applied to:
If a debt collector is trying to collect more than one debt from you, they must apply any payment you make to the debt you select. As well, a debt collector may not apply a payment to a debt you don't think you owe.

Garnishment:
If you don't pay a debt, a creditor or a debt collector can sue you to collect. If they win, the court will enter a judgment against you. The judgment states the amount of money you owe, and allows the creditor or collector to get a garnishment order against you, directing a third party, like your bank, to turn over funds from your account to pay the debt.

- Wage garnishment happens when your employer is required to withhold part of your paycheck to pay your debts.
- Your wages usually can be garnished only as the result of a court order.

Don't ignore a lawsuit summons, which you will receive in the mail. If you do, you lose the opportunity to fight a wage garnishment, and judgment will be granted against you.

Can federal benefits be garnished? Many federal benefits *cannot* be garnished, including:

- Social Security Benefits
- Supplemental Security Income (SSI) Benefits
- Veterans' Benefits
- Civil Service and Federal Retirement and Disability Benefits
- Military Annuities and Survivors' Benefits
- Federal Emergency Management Agency Federal Disaster Assistance

Federal benefits *may be* garnished if you owe:

- Delinquent taxes
- Alimony
- Child support
- Student loans

What to do if a debt collector has violated the law:
You have the right to sue a collector in a state or federal court within one year from the date the law was violated.

If you win the suit, the judge can require the collector to pay you for any damages you can prove you suffered because of the illegal collection practices, like lost wages and medical bills.

The judge can require the debt collector to pay you up to $1,000, even if you can't prove that you suffered actual damages.

You also can be reimbursed for your attorney's fees and court costs.

A group of people also may sue a debt collector as part of a class action lawsuit and recover money for damages up to $500,000, or one percent of the collector's net worth, whichever amount is lower.

Remember, however, that even if a debt collector violates the FDCPA laws when trying to collect a debt, the debt does not go away if you owe it.

What to do if a debt collector sues the debtor:
If a debt collector files a lawsuit against you to collect a debt, respond to the lawsuit, either personally or through your lawyer, by the date specified in the court papers to preserve your rights.

Where to report a debt collector for a violation of the law:
Report any problems you have with a debt collector to:

- Your state Attorney General's office
- The Federal Trade Commission
- The Consumer Financial Protection Bureau
- Many states have their own debt collection laws that are different from the federal Fair Debt Collection Practices Act. Your Attorney General's office can help you determine your rights under your state's law.

Remember also that if you pay even so much as one penny against an old debt that's not legally active anymore, the entire debt comes back to life—legal or not—even if it had been outside of the statute of limitations.

Bankruptcy Basics

Bankruptcy is a complex and emotional event that requires much thought and effort. The process takes at a minimum several months, and there are many steps to go through.

Filing for bankruptcy can help an individual, or a couple, by discarding debt or making a plan to repay debts. A bankruptcy case normally begins when the debtor files a petition with the bankruptcy court. A bankruptcy petition may be filed by an individual, by spouses together, or by a corporation or other entity.

All bankruptcy cases are handled in federal courts, and there are different types of bankruptcies:

Chapter 7 or Chapter 13: Individuals file for bankruptcy, depending on the specifics of their situation.

Chapter 9: Municipalities—cities, towns, villages, taxing districts, municipal utilities, and school districts file to reorganize.

Chapter 7 or Chapter 11: Businesses file to liquidate/reorganize.

Chapter 12: Family farmers and fishermen file to secure debt relief.

Chapter 15: Filings involving parties from other countries.

We strongly suggest you seek the advice and assistance of a qualified bankruptcy lawyer for your bankruptcy, or even if you are just considering it. The first meeting is usually free. A bankruptcy has long-term financial and legal consequences of which you need to be aware.

If you need help finding a bankruptcy lawyer, check with:

- The American Bar Association's Legal Help website
- Your own state's Bar Association
- Legal Aid (Legal Services Corporation)
- Those who can't afford a lawyer may qualify for free legal services.

What exactly is a bankruptcy discharge?
A bankruptcy discharge releases the debtor from personal liability for certain specified types of debts—the debtor is no longer legally required to pay any debts that are discharged by the court. The discharge is a permanent order prohibiting the creditors of the debtor from taking any form of collection action on discharged debts, including legal action and communications with the debtor, such as telephone calls, letters, and personal contacts. You'll

receive your copy of the discharge in the mail. The legal copy of your discharge is what you will copy and send to any creditors or debt collectors still trying to collect on any of your debts.

The steps of filing for bankruptcy:

- You'll meet with your attorney, who will review your case.
- You'll collect information on ALL your debts, and fill them out on the form your attorney gives you. Be sure to include anything and everything. Do NOT attempt to hide assets.
- Your attorney will submit your petition.
- You'll attend an approved course of financial counseling—usually one or two sessions, which may also be offered online.
- You may meet with the bankruptcy judge or clerk (not a long meeting, and not private), who will quickly review your petition, and let you know if any other paperwork or information is needed.
- You'll receive your bankruptcy discharge a few months later.

What debts cannot be discharged?
Your attorney will know, but generally non-dischargeable debts include:

- Student loans
- Pre-existing property liens
- Certain tax claims
- Debts you did not list on your petition
- Child support or alimony
- Government fines or penalties

Can creditors object?
Your creditors will receive notice from the court that you are planning to declare bankruptcy, and that the debt owed to that creditor will be discharged. The creditors are given a deadline to object to the discharge.

Trying to collect a debt after the discharge:
The first thing you should do is send the collector, registered and return receipt, a copy of your discharge papers with a letter explaining that their debt has been discharged.

If a creditor still tries to collect on a discharged debt, you can file a motion with the court: Report the attempt and ask to reopen the case. The court will do so to protect the discharge that they approved, and that is recorded. The discharge is a permanent injunction prohibiting creditors from taking any action to collect the discharged debt, including filing a lawsuit.

Can filers for bankruptcy get fired from their jobs?
Employers are prohibited by the government from firing employees who have declared bankruptcy, because they were a debtor, were insolvent, or because they failed to pay a debt. Employers and governmental units are also prohibited against discrimination during the hiring process, revoking or declining to renew a license, franchise, etc.

Losing your bankruptcy discharge papers:
You can get another copy of your discharge by contacting the clerk of the bankruptcy court that handled your bankruptcy. There will be several fees involved.

Your credit rating and report:
Remember that your bankruptcy will show up on your credit report, lower your credit rating, and stay on your credit report for 7 years or more.

Take this action seriously, do your homework, and find an attorney you can trust.

Personal Finance *for* Real People

Banking & Banking Alternatives

Do You Need to Use Traditional Banking Services?

We've been brought up to think that traditional banks are the place to go for anything financial, especially as a place to keep and withdraw your money. Is that really still true? Let's look at the pros and cons.

Traditional Bank Checking Accounts
A checking account is probably the first thing you think of when you think of banking services. Every bank and credit union offers a range of checking account services, and they usually charge for them. Those monthly charges can range from fairly minimal—under $20—to higher amounts. They can also be free if you keep a minimum balance in your account, or if you also have a savings account with a minimum balance. Those minimum balances will differ from bank to bank, and from account type to account type, but they are usually around $1,000 or more. The message here is: Be sure to shop around, be clear on the rules of your accounts, keep your paperwork, and read the fine print.

One much-complained-about feature of bank checking accounts is their hefty overdraft fee. Those fees have increased, and can very quickly add up to a serious amount, as much as between $50 and $100 for a single overdraft and bounced check(s).

Checking Account Alternatives
What do you use your checking account for? For most of us, it's to pay bills. But thanks to modern technology, there are several alternatives to writing out a paper bank check and mailing it.

Most utilities and other services have electronic bill-pay options, and you can frequently use a credit or pre-paid card to pay electronically.

You can also drop off your payment at a utility's office, or come in to a financial services center to pay most of your monthly bills in one place. In fact, some centers may offer a bill-pay service—it's fast, easy, and secure, with no checks or stamps required. You can pay your monthly utility bills with just one stop in a location. You may even be able to pay many car payments and mortgages.

Traditional Bank Savings Accounts
There are many ways to set aside your money for savings, including traditional bank savings accounts. You may be able to get a free savings account if you also have a checking account at that bank, or if you keep a minimum balance in your account. Interest rates are usually very, very low. Also available: Online saving accounts, which are a little more flexible—but make sure the institution is federally insured.

Other options include U.S. Savings Bonds, CDs (Certificates of Deposit), and Money Market Accounts. These accounts tend to be much less flexible, with less convenient access to your account and money—but they do offer higher interest rates. CDs and Money Market Accounts may have a higher initial deposit required, as well.

Savings Account Alternatives
Why not use prepaid debit cards as savings tools? Totally flexible, always handy, and no monthly fees! Prepaid debit cards can be used as one, or several, savings accounts. Use one to set aside money for the holidays, one for vacation savings, or one to set aside funds for unexpected expenses. Save for college expenses, or any other purpose. Set up a schedule to add money to it, or add as is convenient for you. Read the fine print, and check on minimum deposits (most do not require that) and maximum amounts you can put on the card.

Your financial services center may offer a special pre-paid debit card that includes an interest-paying savings account.

Of course, then it's up to you to make sure your pre-paid debit card is kept safe and secure!

What About Convenience?
It does seem sometimes that there's a traditional bank on just about every corner, so it could make sense that it would be easier and more convenient to use them for your services. But now that online services are the standard, it may actually more convenient to manage your finances from home.

And if you are not comfortable using online services, there are many physical locations where you can pay bills, drop-off payments, and take care of other tasks, from financial services centers to Wal-Mart to supermarkets and more.

How you set up your finance handling, from paying bills to saving money, really depends on what you are comfortable with, who your trust, how much money you have to manage, and how flexible you want that money to be.

Confused? It CAN be confusing! Just stop by any financial services center and they'll be happy to explain their services, and help you decide what options work best for you.

Bank Fees: Here to Stay

You've probably noticed all the talk of new and additional bank fees in the news; or maybe you've experienced it firsthand—a new bank fee for a service that used to be free. Unfortunately, that is the new norm—bank fees are here to stay.

Banks, too, were hit hard by the financial crisis, and especially by new regulations (aimed at NOT having another crisis). With many of their previously profitable enterprises having been restricted, the banks' new business model is to replace that lost revenue by creating additional fees, ranging from $4 to $40, for as many services as possible.

How can you minimize these extra fees?

First, carefully examine all communication from your bank, and read the fine print. Pay attention to see if they are instituting any new fees, and see if you need to change your accounts (keeping a minimum balance, not using actual bank tellers, or banking online, for example).

Don't overdraw your checking account: Those fees have increased, and can very quickly add up to a serious amount.

Only use your ATM card at your own bank's ATMs: Most banks charge a fee for using another bank's ATM, even if it's part of the same "network."

Don't make a late payment to your credit card account. Again, those fees have greatly increased, and are very profitable to the banks and credit card companies.

If you've made just one late payment, or can't get out of a new additional fee, talk to your bank. They don't advertise it, but frequently you can get them to waive a fee one time, especially if you've been a reliable customer.

It's not necessarily true that you'll get a better deal if you combine all services at the same bank. It DOES pay to shop around and even divide up the services you need.

Reconsider what services you really need from a bank, or if you need a bank at all. Don't pay for services you are not using! If you only write one or two checks a month, do you really need a checking account? Many financial service centers offer a bill paying service, check cashing, money orders and money transfers, and prepaid debit cards, all perfectly suited for everyday life.

For full banking services, price-shop at smaller local banks and at credit unions; both will likely offer better deals and lower fees.

In today's world, "buyer beware" is truer than ever. Don't assume, and always ask questions. You worked hard for your money—don't waste it on bank fees!

More Than One Way to Pay Bills

You probably know the old saying: The two sure things in life are death and taxes. But monthly bills are also a sure thing, no matter who you are, or what you do. We all have to deal with them each month: utility bills, credit card bills, rent or mortgage payments, insurance bills, and loan payments.

It used to be true that there were only two ways you could pay your bills:

Writing a check, and mailing it in, or going to your creditor's physical office and paying in person, sometimes only in cash.

Today, though, there are many more ways you can handle your bill payments. You'll be surprised at how many there are!

Pay by check or money order, and send it through the mail: This is the old standard, and works if you have a checking account with a bank or credit union. If you don't have a bank account, you can send in a money order. The drawback to this method is that your account isn't credited until your check arrives, via USPS, and your check clears. Not good if you are a last-minute type of person, or if you are waiting for a deposit to clear so your check won't bounce.

Pay by check or money order, and drop off at collection stations: You can still pay by check or money order, but you don't have to wait for USPS to deliver it—you also save the cost of a stamp. You can drop off your payment (sealed in its addressed envelope) at places like

- Supermarkets
- Big-box stores like Wal-Mart
- Banks
- Shopping centers
- City Halls
- Military bases
- The utility itself, if it's local
- Your local financial services center

Visit a financial services center. Pay your bills via Western Union, or purchase money orders to mail in your payments. At a financial service center, the money order fee is usually extremely competitive—certainly less than a bank—and they probably have envelopes and stamps at the ready.

Pay through Western Union: Just about any payment can be made through Western Union. Many clients come in to their financial services center every month and pay cable, phone, water, and electric (some even do their mortgages and car payments) through Western Union. You can also go to Western Union's website (https://www.westernunion.com/us/en/bill-pay/app/billpay-start) and make bill payments online; or you can make payments by phone.

Pay by check, money order, cash, credit or pre-paid debit cards at your utility's office: Your utility may have additional locations where they can process cash and credit/debit card payments for your accounts.

Set up an Automatic Bill Payment account directly with your creditor. In this case, you make an agreement with your creditor to have your monthly payment taken automatically out of your bank account each month. You will need to make sure that there's enough in your account to cover this, and that you know how much the withdrawal will be (you don't want any surprises!), and what date on which it's going to be withdrawn.

Set up Online Bill Paying with your bank or credit union. If you have a bank account, this offers a number of options:

- Set up your list of creditors, utilities, businesses, and individuals. Then select and manage your payments online, all in one place.
- Have bills sent to your bank, and paid automatically on their due date (or before).
- Manage your account and payments via the bank's mobile app.
- Payments are usually guaranteed by the bank to arrive no later than the due date. Be sure to check what your bank's terms are for this. You will need to allow five business days for the payment to arrive.
- Ask about any fees involved! If you don't meet certain requirements, there may be a monthly or transaction fee involved.

Pay online directly with your creditor or utility. You'll log on, find your account, enter your payment information (bank account, credit or debit card), and make your one-time payment.

Pay by phone directly with your creditor or utility. You'll call your creditor, enter your account information, then your payment information, and make your one-time payment. This has the advantage of having your account credited within 24 hours or sooner. Good for procrastinators! Ask if there's a fee involved in using this method.

Pay by Digital Channel: Interestingly, you can now pay some cable company bills through their digital channel. You'll need to set it up initially, using your credit card. After than you should be able to just pay your monthly bill on the appropriate channel.

Prepay your account: Some utilities will allow you to prepay your account. Put extra money into your utility account, and your next bill or bills will be drawn from that. Good if you are going to be away from home for more than a week. Check your utilities to see what their policies for prepayment are.

Thing to remember:

- Whenever you do business with a company—such as a bank or utility—there may be fees involved. Always ask if there is a fee, and what it is. Believe it or not, some utilities may charge a fee for accepting a cash payment.
- Know what the terms of your bank checking account are, and if there any fees for using a bill-pay service.
- There may be a small fee for purchasing money orders. Money orders are available at a wide variety of locations, from the post office, to convenience stores, to supermarkets, to banks, and of course, at your financial services center. Fill in the payee information and sign the money order immediately upon purchase.

- There may also be a small fee for using Western Union services.
- Be sure to get a receipt for all payments you make in person, especially cash payments.
- If you are using your credit card to pay bills, make sure that you are not carrying those amounts over and accruing interest. That will make an already painful monthly payment that much more expensive.
- If you are concerned about online security, you can use a pre-paid debit card to make payments. You'll be limited on the amount of damage a hacker can do. Make sure you know if there are fees for purchasing and reloading your card.
- If you are REALLY concerned about online security, or just don't trust a bank, then paying by money order or Western Union will be best for your peace of mind.
- Never mail cash to pay a bill!

Pre-Paid Debit Cards: The Advantages

Pre-paid debit cards don't get much love from the mainstream financial press, and yet they've proven to be popular, and are increasing in use and availability. In 2015, pre-paid debit cards were loaded to the tune of $118.09 billion, a 6.1% increase over the previous year. That amount is expected to keep increasing by 5 - 6% per year.

What's the truth about pre-paid debit cards? How can you use them wisely and take steps to protect yourself?

First, understand the difference between a bank debit card and a pre-paid debit card—they are *not* the same.

A **debit card from your bank** is used as a "draw" on your checking or savings accounts; is limited in funds only by the amount you have in your accounts at the time; and is subject to regular bank fees, including checking account, overdraft and ATM fees.

A **pre-paid debit card** is not attached to a bank—you do not need to have a checking account to get and use one; there may or may not be small fees (although celebrity prepaid cards have much higher activation fees—beware!) to set one up and use it; it can be loaded with whatever amount you choose. Neither bank debit cards nor pre-paid debit cards are subject to financial information oversight as credit cards are, so it is up to you to make sure you understand what you are getting, and to protect yourself and your money.

What Are the Advantages of a Pre-Paid Debit Card?
You don't have to qualify for it as you would for a credit card, but you can use it in most places you would use a credit card, sometimes even internationally.

You don't need a bank account to get one.

No monthly bills or late charges!

It's safer to carry than cash.

And you can still use it to withdraw cash from the card if necessary.

You can use it to shop on the internet without needing a credit card.

It can be easily reloaded with funds, via the internet, phone, or ATM.

You can use it as a savings account, even keeping funds on different cards for different purposes. You can also give it as a gift (a good choice to give a student for school expenses).

You can also use it as a way to budget and to control your spending: There's a definite limit on what you can spend, and you can't rack up debt, unlike a credit card.

Pre-paid debit card fees are generally lower in total than those fees imposed by banks on checking accounts with their accompanying debit and ATM cards.

Most financial services centers do offer pre-paid debit cards.

At some financial services centers, with your pre-paid debit card, you maybe be eligible for a NetSpend Savings Account: No minimum deposit, and it pays 5.00% interest (Annual Percentage Yield)—one of the highest interest rates in the country. Load your card with funds from your savings account, or use it to deposit funds. And it's FDIC insured.

Pre-Paid Debit Cards: Protecting Yourself

Previously we talked about the advantages—and they are many—of pre-paid debit cards. Now, we need to think about cautions regarding the cards: How can you use a pre-paid debit card and protect yourself and your money?

How to Protect Yourself
Make sure you know what fees, if any, are involved. These can vary widely from company to company.

Is it cheaper to have funds direct deposited onto the card? Is there a fee for a customer service call? Or a fee for paper documents or to check your balance? Is there a monthly service fee, and how can you avoid that? Compare set-up or activation fees. Be sure to review and know your card's fee structure, and account for those fees when thinking about your card's available balance.

Where to go if you have a problem? Frequently there may be a fee to call customer service. Can you talk to someone in person to avoid that fee? Or where would you send a letter?

Know what ATMs you can use without incurring a fee.

Your pre-paid debit card will not necessarily establish your good credit, although credit bureaus are looking at adding that information in the future.

Remember that a pre-paid debit card is essentially the same as cash, and can be stolen. Take care of it as you would actual cash or a credit card.

Use a strong password and keep it safe. When you key it in, be aware of your surroundings and shield the keypad.

Track your debit card spending. This will keep you within your budget, help you avoid unnecessary fees, and let you anticipate expenses.

Be cautious if your pre-paid debit card automatically draws from your savings account—you don't want to unknowingly start draining your savings. Many financial centers offer pre-paid debit cards, and you may be eligible for a NetSpend Savings Account: No minimum deposit, and it pays 5.00% interest (Annual Percentage Yield)—one of the highest interest rates in the country. Load your card with funds from your savings account, or use it to deposit funds. And it's FDIC insured.

What Is a Credit Union?

What is the difference between a credit union and bank? You have no doubt seen credit union buildings around, or seen their ads. They sound like banks, but they don't have the word "bank" in their name—just what are they?

Credit unions are not-for-profit organizations that are in business to serve their members (unlike banks, which are *for*-profit organizations). The governing board at each credit union is elected by its members to manage the credit union for the benefit of the members. Profits made by credit unions are returned back to members in the form of monetary credits (dividends), reduced fees, higher savings interest rates, and lower loan interest rates.

Federally chartered credit unions are regulated by the National Credit Union Administration and insured by the National Credit Union Share Insurance Fund, which is backed by the full faith and credit of the United States government. Before you join a credit union, check to see that they are indeed insured by the NCUSIF—they must display the official NCUA insurance sign in their offices.

If a credit union does not have the word "federal" as a part of its name and is not headquartered in Arkansas, Delaware, South Dakota, Wyoming, or the District of Columbia, then it is probably a state-chartered credit union, and the state supervisory authority where the credit union's main office is located will usually be the regulator.

Credit unions are like banks in that members have checking and savings accounts. They also provide loans, and other financial services.

On average, credit unions offer higher saving rates and lower loan rates. This could help your savings grow faster and your loan cost less. Credit unions also tend to charge lower fees, require lower deposit balances and offer better service.

Who can join a credit union?
Just about anyone—you just have to fall into the credit union's targeted group:

- **Employer:** Many employers sponsor their own credit union, or help sponsor a regional credit union.
- **Family:** If a family member is part of a credit union, you may be able to join as well.
- **Geographic location:** A credit union may choose to serve anyone who lives, works, or attends school in a specific geographical location or area.
- **Membership in a group:** If you are a member of a group, you may be eligible to join a credit union—this could include a labor union, a school, a place of worship, an employer, or a homeowners association.
- **Military:** If you are a current or former member of the military, you may be eligible to join a credit union such as the **Navy Federal Credit Union** (https://www.navyfederal.org).

As an example, to join the **CU Hawaii Federal Credit Union** (https://www.cuhawaii.com), you must fall into one of the following groups:

- You live on the Island of Hawaii.
- You regularly work, attend school, worship, perform services, or participate in associations headquartered on the Island of Hawaii.
- You belong to an organization headquartered or maintaining a facility on the Island of Hawaii.
- You are a family member of a CU Hawaii member (you don't have to live in the same household).

Small and local business support

Because they are locally based, and because frequently local businesses are members, credit unions are more focused on supporting their local small businesses. This can be in the form of more consideration for small business loans, auto loans, and even home mortgages, as well as other community support such as financial education. A local business will also get more personal attention at a credit union than at a national bank.

Is a credit union right for you?

Over 98 million Americans belong to a credit union. Is joining one right for you? Here's a quick list of what they offer:

- Personal service
- Local and community interest
- Ability to vote on leadership
- Not-for-profit
- Fewer fees than a nationals or regional bank
- Direct deposit
- Financial education
- Multiple branches
- Electronic banking and ATMs
- Overdraft protection
- Loans: mortgage, home equity, small business, and auto

Credit unions are a safe place to have a checking account, to save, and to borrow at reasonable rates. You can find a credit union near you **at the National Credit Union Administration** (www.ncua.gov).

Personal Finance *for* Real People

Don't Be Afraid of Tax Time

Easy Tax Preparation Tips

Are you dreading tax time? There's no real way we can make it fun, but we can make it easier, and less stressful.

First, get help
Free tax help is available in every state. That's right—free!

Volunteer organizations have staff that are trained and approved by the IRS, and are available to help you wade through your tax filings. What do you need to know? Check with the organizations listed below to see if you qualify (free tax prep is focused on lower to moderate income workers), and if you need to make an appointment. You can save up to $150 just by getting this service for free. They'll also make sure that you file for your Earned Income Tax Credit (EITC)—a windfall that many people don't realize they qualify for, and don't claim.

Second, get organized
Make your taxes easier by gradually getting started on your tax prep and getting yourself a little organized. It will take less time with your tax preparer, and might end up saving you money. If you are really organized, you can e-file your tax return as early as January 30.

Find Free Tax Help

- The IRS website offers an easy way to look up VITA (Volunteer Income Tax Assistance) sites throughout the country (http://www.irs.gov/individuals/find-a-location-for-free-tax-prep).
- You can also look up TCE (Tax Counseling for the Elderly—for those who are 60 and older) sites using the same VITA locater tool. In addition, AARP (www.aarp.org) can help you locate a TCE Tax-Aide site.
- The IRS offers free tax counseling for military families, also through the VITA program. For more information, check their website (https://www.irs.gov/businesses/filing-extensions-and-tax-return-preparation-assistance-for-military-personnel-stationed-abroad-or-in-a-combat-zone). VITA tax counselors for the military are specially trained on military tax issues.
- Community colleges and libraries frequently have volunteers available to help you with your taxes several days a week after the beginning of February.
- Goodwill Industries usually offers tax clinics, but be sure to check for their availability.
- United Way: If you made a combined income of less than $66,000, you can prepare and e-file your tax returns (federal and state) on the MyFreeTaxes website (www.myfreetaxes.com).

And of course, your local financial services center may offer a service to help you with your tax preparation, at a lower cost than other tax preparers. Make sure they are EITC specialists.

Tips to Get Organized

Even if you are able to take advantage of one of the above services for free tax help, you will still need to show up with your tax information organized and in order. Keep these following tips in mind:

- If you did any freelance or consulting work, make sure you've filled out the W-9 form and returned it to that company. If you had any other income (alimony, other self-employment, etc.) start pulling together the documentation for that, too.
- Gather together your paycheck stubs. You'll want to check them against your W-2 when it arrives. Check the amounts and check your Social Security number.
- If you have bank accounts, check to see if you have all your bank statements. If not, start finding them now (hopefully you'll be able to download online).
- Check that you have your social security cards for each member of your family, including any new family additions. If not, start the process to get them now. If you need to replace a missing card, you can get started at the Social Security website (www.ssa.gov).
- Make sure that you and your spouse have current photo IDs (driver's license, etc.), and that you bring them with you to your appointment. Again, if you don't, or can't find it, get started now to replace it.
- Consider if you had any work-related expenses last year. Hopefully you saved those receipts—start gathering them together, or print out receipts for purchases made online. Did you buy a uniform for a job; use your home computer for work; or buy tools for work? Did you have to travel for work, to a customer or to a meeting? If you drove your car for work (and weren't reimbursed by your employer) start calculating the distances you traveled.
- If you have a home office or workspace, you'll need to figure out how much of your utilities your home office uses. Start gathering your utility bills from last year. If you can't find all of them, you may be able to get your information from the utility's website.
- Now is also a good time to check through your receipts, credit card, or bank statements to see if there are any purchases you made for work, or for charitable donation, that you might have forgotten.
- Did you make any charity donations last year? Or purchase something that you donated to a charity (canned food for a food bank, for example)? Or did you donate clothing or other items to a charity? Start figuring out just what all that adds up to, and getting all the receipts together.
- The amount of medical and dental bills you can claim as a deduction must exceed 10% of your adjusted gross income, if you are under 65, 7.5% if you are over 65 (check most recent tax laws at http://www.IRS.gov to confirm these numbers). It's worth gathering together receipts for what you have spent and asking your tax preparer. Don't forget prescriptions, chiropractic treatments, dental treatments, and insurance co-pays.
- Do you pay childcare, school tuition, have a student loan, or receive financial aid for education? Start putting together those documents.
- You will also need copies of last year's tax returns, and any real estate taxes you may have paid; plus complete birth dates for you, your spouse, and your dependents.

By starting to get organized now, you'll be sure not to forget anything come tax time. You don't want to miss any deductions you can claim!

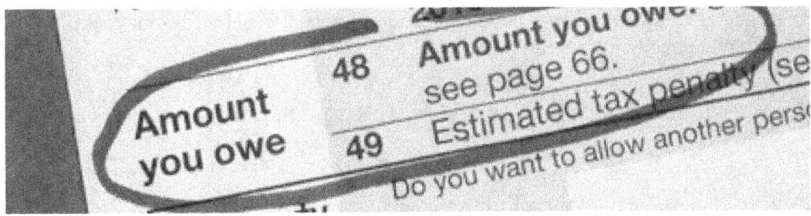

Earned Income Tax Credit: A Windfall

EITC = Earned Income Tax Credit. It doesn't sound very exciting, but it could potentially mean an extra refund at tax time—and sometimes a very significant refund.

The EITC was designed to assist low-to-moderate income families, and is considered to be the nation's largest and most successful anti-poverty and work-incentive program. Over $40 billion in EITC benefits are paid out each year to eligible taxpayers. But each year millions of people, between 15% and 25% of those eligible, don't file for their EITC, leaving billions of refund dollars unclaimed. In one single state, workers fail to claim $30 to $40 million in EITC benefits.

The Earned Income Tax Credit (EITC) is a refundable tax credit that was designed for lower-income working families (although you don't need to have children to qualify). That means it's a credit against the taxes you owe to the IRS for your work in the previous year.

Here's how it works: Let's say you made $38,000 this year, and the total amount of taxes you owe (which may already have been deducted from your paycheck) is $4,000, and let's say you have two qualifying dependents. The IRS will allow you to apply your EITC credit of over $5,000 to your owed taxes. That means you would get a payment, or "refund" of $1,000 plus. And that's on top of any normal income tax refund you might already be receiving.

How do you get this tax credit and refund? First, you must have a Social Security number, and you must file a tax return.

Second, you must have "earned income" of less than $48,340 (for 2018) a year ($53,930 if you are married and filing jointly) if you have three (or more) qualifying children; $45,007 ($50,597 married filing jointly) with two qualifying children; $39,617 ($45,207 married filing jointly) with one qualifying child; $15,010 ($20,600 married filing jointly) with no qualifying children. The more qualified (meeting the IRS's requirements) dependents you claim (up to three), the greater the tax credit amount. Your tax credit could be as much as $6,318 if you have three or more qualifying dependents, compared to $510 if you have no qualifying dependents.

Your stated "earned income" must come from employment, self-employment, long-term disability benefits, or non-taxable combat pay. Your investment income is limited to approximately $3,000 for the year.

What doesn't count as "earned income?" You cannot use income from the following to qualify for the EITC: Interest and dividends, retirement income, Social Security payments, unemployment benefits, alimony, child support, or pay for work while an inmate in a penal institution.

You must have lived in the U.S. for at least half of the tax year, and have been a U.S. citizen or resident alien for the entire year.

You must provide proof of residency documentation when you sit down with your tax preparer (school records, medical records, child care records, etc.).

There are special EITC rules for members of the military, ministers, members of the clergy, those receiving disability benefits, and those impacted by disasters.

Check the IRS website, www.IRS.gov, for current income levels and more details.

Don't forget to also check on other tax credit programs, such as the Child Tax Credit.

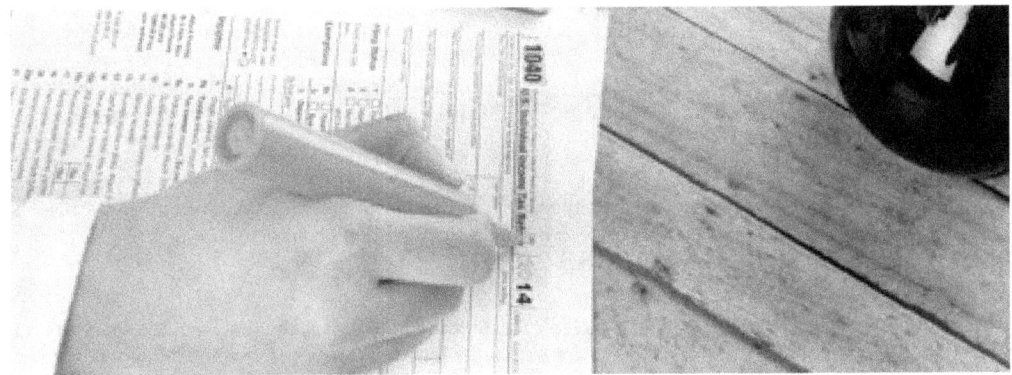

When You Owe Back Taxes

Over the last few years, the IRS has instituted a more lenient attitude and additional programs to help people pay their back taxes and their current taxes. But when I say "lenient," I mean less draconian. They still want you to pay all your taxes (and penalties), but they are more amenable to offering programs that will help you do so.

Like so many problems in life, it's best if you just bite the bullet and deal with your tax issues up front. Don't put your head in the sand, don't pretend it doesn't exist, don't put off thinking about it, and don't think the IRS will forget about you.

But know that you are not alone (which may be one reason the IRS is working with taxpayers): Americans who are behind on their taxes are estimated to be anywhere from 8 to 20 million people.

What to do first

First, you *will* need to file a return, even if you haven't for quite a while. This is the first step. It's scary to bring yourself to the attention of the IRS, but it's better for you in the long run. File, even if you can't pay your taxes yet.

But what if you haven't filed a tax return in several years?

Call the IRS. You'll need to give them your current information: name, address, Social Security number, employer, and current salary. Then, you'll have to commit to a certain date by which you will have filed all your delinquent returns. If you find during the process that you might not make this date, stay in touch with the IRS. Call them and request an extension.

The IRS will provide you with your account summaries: What returns are still outstanding and what have been filed, what you currently owe, and if any refunds were applied to your owed taxes.

Now, work out the tax returns for each year skipped. If you don't have W-2s or pay stubs for those years, do your best to estimate.

After you've caught up with your tax filings, the IRS will let you know what your owed tax amount is, plus any penalties and interest. If you had a significant life event, you may be able to convince the IRS to reduce your penalty amount: If you had a death in the family, mental illness, alcoholism or very serious illness, bad accountant advice, military service. Be prepared to back these up with documentation.

Consult a professional

Are your taxes complicated? Start with an experienced tax accountant. If they can't help, look for a tax attorney. Interview two or three of the most experienced in your city. You want a firm that specializes in IRS tax controversy and IRS collection resolutions.

Look out for, and beware of, firms that offer you pennies-on-the-dollar, firms that only exist online or at 800 numbers, even if they promise great things. There is no easy fix for your situation, and such firms—who may even have been prosecuted and fined—will just take your money and do nothing.

You know what you owe—now what?

What NOT to do
The IRS would greatly prefer it if you would just take out a loan, or use your credit cards, to pay your taxes. That's because they get their money right away. But if you are in a financial position where you are unable to pay taxes, then taking a loan or charging up credit card debt (if you are even able to) are not going to help your financial situation. Also, don't take money out of your IRA or 401k or other retirement fund.

Instead, use one of the two main programs the IRS has for getting you back on track:

Monthly installment payments
If you think you can eventually pay your owed taxes, this is your best option. It's the easiest and quickest way to get a plan worked out. Go to the IRS website and fill out the online payment agreement application. You'll find out right away if you are eligible, what your payments will be, and how long it will take. According to the IRS, if as an individual you owe $50,000 or less (taxes, penalties, interest), and can pay the entire amount within six years, you will be able to get a payment agreement.

Don't meet the criteria for an online agreement? Check the Payment Plans and Installment Agreements on the IRS website for how to proceed—you may well still be able to work out a payment plan.

Don't surprise the IRS—stick to your payments and stay in communication! If you find you cannot make a payment, be upfront with them. Call the phone number on your notice, and discuss it with them. They may let you skip the current due payment as long as you make the next one. If you simply stop payments, they will take action and could very well seize your property and bank accounts and/or put a lien on your paycheck.

Offer in Compromise
The IRS has expanded and streamlined this program, which allows you to reach a settlement for your debt for less than what you owe. Before you get excited about this option, know that the IRS takes this very seriously. They will require a full accounting of your financials, and they must be convinced that you won't be able—at all—to pay your tax debt without severe financial hardship. Read more about this program on the IRS website under Offer in Compromise. If you think this might be an option for you, use the Offer in Compromise Pre-Qualifier to verify your eligibility.

Generally speaking, to use either of these plans, you must be up-to-date in your tax filings (remember what we said to do first!).

Realize that the IRS could fine you up to $25,000 for each tax year you owe returns for, or put you in jail for a year. Much more likely though, if you come forward voluntarily and are honest about your situation, they will work with you. The IRS is more interested in getting your tax payments than in punishing you.

The task does seem daunting, especially if you have to sort out several years' worth of financial information and tax returns. But take it one step at a time, seek advice if necessary, and you will get through it!

Tax Prep Checklist

W-2s	
Job 1	
Job 2	
Job 3	
1099s	
Job 1	
Job 2	
Job 3	
Paycheck Stubs	
Bank Statements	
Social Security Cards	
Photo ID	
Business Expense Receipts	
Business Travel Receipts	
Home Office	
Home Office Size	
Home Size	
Home Utilitites	
Charitable Donation Receipts	
Medical Expenses	
Child Care Expenses	
Education Expenses	
Student Loan Interest	
Education Financial Aid	
Mortgage Interest	
Investment/Savings Interest	
Other	

Personal Finance *for* Real People

Handle the Unexpected

Prepare for Unexpected Expenses

We know unexpected expenses happen to everyone; why is it so hard for us to prepare for them, to make these events planned for, rather than let them be disastrous bombshells?

Whatever the reason, it's true: we leave these at the bottom of our lists of things to take care of.

There are events and expenses that can reasonably be expected, and then there are those that COULD happen, but are unlikely. Let's focus more on the everyday reality-based unexpected events and expenses.

Unexpected expenses you *should* you plan for:
Truly unplanned and unexpected expenses can happen everywhere and in any category. Areas where unplanned expenses occur can include:

- Car repair (we've all been there!)
- Illness and medical treatments, serious dental treatments
- Death of a family member
- Losing your job
- Weather-related damage, from your house to your car, to simply not being able to get to work or to the market.

Expenses that only *seem* unexpected; in fact you can expect them every year:

- Higher utility bills during the winter and summer
- Annual insurance premiums
- Regularly occurring medical treatments or doctor visits
- Holiday gifting
- Home repairs
- School expenses
- Taxes

How can you plan these expenses into your life, so that you are not blindsided when they occur?

Set up an emergency fund. Include them in your monthly and yearly budget. How to do it:

Make a list of your possible unexpected expenses. Is your car older? Plan a certain amount for car repair. Will you possibly need to go to the doctor or the dentist? What about new eyeglasses? What about clothing, equipment, or permits you might need for work? Include them in your list. Don't forget about family events: vacations, airfare, holiday and birthday gifts, and single occurrences like quinceaneras or bar or bat mitzvahs.

Now take a look through what records you have for the previous year: statements, receipts, etc., and look for any other surprise expenses: school fees, bank fees, computer or equipment repair, etc.

Add up the amount you spent on all these, and then divide that total by the number of paychecks you receive during the year (are you paid monthly, weekly, or twice a month?).

That amount is how much you should set aside each pay period for reasonably expected "unexpected" expenses.

If it seems impossible to set aside $100 a month, or whatever your number is, start slightly slowly. Set aside perhaps $50 for the first couple of months, and then gradually increase the amount. See where you can cut other expenses to make up for it: bring your lunch to work a few times a week, skip the movies, or have a shopping moratorium for a month.

You can also pad your regular budgeted expenses. Is your rent $850 a month? Budget and set aside $900. Do you think gas will cost you $75 a month? Set aside $100. At the end of the month, or the year, you'll have an extra nest egg you can put into your emergency fund.

Set aside this money, your emergency fund, into a separate account. You can keep it in cash in an envelope where you won't see it every day; put it on a prepaid debit card each pay period, and set those aside; or start another bank account to deposit it in. The goal is to take it out of your everyday finances so you won't accidentally spend it—or be tempted to spend it.

For expenses that are truly hard to predict, take a long look at your personal situation.

How secure is your job? Have you heard rumors about the company selling, or that sales are way down? This will be your clue to start preparing for a time without employment, and to start looking around for another job.

How is your health? Has your doctor or dentist told you to expect a change in medication, a specific treatment or test, or a root canal? Check your insurance coverage at re-enrollment time, and make sure you know what your coverage is. Set aside money in your emergency fund for the difference, what you'll have to pay out of pocket.

What's your family situation? Do you have celebratory life events coming up (significant anniversaries, etc.)? How healthy are your parents? As unpleasant as it is to think about, will you need to prepare for their end of life?

Where do you live? Are you in a specific weather event zone? Is your home older and needing repair (roof leaks and holes, patio shoring up, plumbing issues).

Take all the factors that apply to you and your family into consideration, and decide on an amount that would make you feel comfortable were any (or several) of these events to occur. Establish goal levels to reach: Maybe you first want to reach an emergency fund of $500, but gradually increase it to $1,000 or more. Take it at a pace that is comfortable for you, but don't slack.

Be consistent about setting aside money into your   emergency fund.

Manage Your Budget Shortfalls

Previously, we've covered the basics of setting up a budget for your expenses, and how to calculate your monthly income.

But what do you do when you have an unavoidable temporary income shortfall?

Of course, you *could* simply not pay your bills, bounce checks, and have your landlord threaten you with eviction. Not a pretty picture, and though it might seem easier at the time, it ends up being an expensive way to handle the problem.

Your utility companies will add a fine to your bill and eventually cut your service—and when you get the service turned back on, you'll probably have to pay an additional deposit.

If you bounce a check, your fee will be a minimum of $35, PLUS another fee from the bank where your check was deposited, PLUS another fee from your bank if you don't cover your check in the required time frame.

So, what's a better solution if you don't already have money set aside for an emergency?

Consider a short-term cash advance to tide you over and see you through this rough patch. Perhaps you're saying, "Yes, but a cash advance costs money!" And that's true, but it's not even CLOSE to what you'll pay in fees if you bounce checks or don't pay your bills.

Small loans are easy to apply for, and offer quick access to cash much more cheaply than the bank fees you would otherwise incur. Generally, fees run between 11% and 15%. If you get an advance for $100, that fee is then between $11 and $15—much less than the cost of bouncing a check, and with none of the hassle or credit damage.

A small loan advance is a good, short-term, alternative to a traditional loan. Quick access to cash can help pay the rent, fix the car, handle a sudden out-of-pocket medical emergency, or pay an overdue utility bill. If you need extra cash until payday, a small loan is the quickest and most secure way to get fast cash.

Of course, your financial goal is not to depend on loans; your goal should be to set up your budget in such a way that you don't get into a situation where a loan is necessary. But don't get discouraged if once in a while you do need a loan in a crisis—you are still improving your financial skills, and a sudden emergency can happen to anyone!

You Need More Than a Cash Advance or Payday Loan—Now What?

We've all had those BIG emergency situations: You have a sudden medical need that must be taken care of *now* (hello, root canal!); your car needs $2,000 in repairs or it won't be operable; or you need to replace your washer and dryer. Or maybe, because of previous unforeseen expenses, you can't quite make this month's rent.

Or let's say you can't pay off that cash advance you got last month unless you get another one. That fee of $15, $30 or $60 seems reasonable on the first advance, but these fees add up and can easily reach an APR of over 300% if you continually use this service.

Are you tempted to get more than one cash advance or get additional payday loans online? Don't do it! You'll only get yourself into a debt crisis that you'll have serious problems getting out of.

If any of these examples describes your own money crisis, let's take a look at what your options are—only you will know what works best for you and your situation.

SHORT-TERM LOANS

A short-term loan is a loan amount generally from $500 on up, and can be taken for several months, all the way up to five or six years (though most are for fewer). The good news is, there are plenty of companies willing to give you a short-term loan. The bad news is, most of those have very high interest rates.

Try first with your bank or credit union, if you belong to either. If you don't have accounts with either, consider joining a credit union. You'll be able to get a more competitive interest rate (probably between 5% and 20%). The next resource you have would be a financial services company or lending company (with interest rates between 15% and 30%); frequently they will act as a conduit between you and financial lenders.

Both banks and credit unions have federal programs specifically for short-term loans under $1,000: The FDIC launched the Small-Dollar Pilot Program in 2008; The National Credit Union instituted the Short Term Small Loan Program in 2010.

Short-term, or personal, loans can be unsecured; you just sign the paperwork and the money is yours. Or they can be secured loans; you have something of value that acts as a guarantee for the loan: savings account, automobile, real estate, etc.

If you take out a loan through a bank or credit union, you can have your payments automatically deducted from your checking account (usually you'll receive a lower interest rate for doing so).

A loan through a bank or credit union will also improve your credit score—as long as you repay in full, and on time.

The interest rate you will be charged for your short-term loan depends on a few factors: The amount of the loan, your credit score, if you have collateral, the length of time you will take to pay back the loan, if you already have a relationship with the lender, and who you secure the loan from (banks and credit unions will have lower interest rates than lending companies).

OTHER OPTIONS

Personal line of credit: Again, through a bank or credit union. A line of credit is like applying for a loan and having it at the ready, before you actually need it. When you need to, you draw on it, sort of like a credit card or checking account (except that you have to pay it back!). The interest rate should be reasonable.

Credit card cash advance: If you have a credit card, this is a no-fuss, easy way to get money fast. The problem? Very high interest rates: 25% to 30%. And unless you pay it off relatively quickly, it can ding your credit score.

Secured credit card: Like the personal line of credit, this is an option you have to plan for in advance. This type of credit card requires the user to provide a cash deposit (usually between $300 and $500), which serves as collateral and determines the credit line. When you are in a bind, you can use it for part or all of your unexpected expense, or you may be able to do a cash advance.

Military Aid: If you, or a member of your family, have served in the military, you may have other options for financial aid. Military relief organizations offer grants or interest-free loans to military personnel and their immediate families. There are relief organizations for each branch of the military (The Navy Marine Corps Relief Society [http://www.nmcrs.org], for example), and state organizations.

Borrowing from family or friends: Not always the best option, but if you have a good relationship, and you pay the loan back promptly (and with a modest interest amount), it might work for you.

Borrowing from a retirement account: If you are lucky enough to have a 401k retirement account through your employer, you may be able to borrow a portion of it—check with your employer.

Talk to your creditors: Your utility companies may be willing to accept delayed payments, freeing up that money for you to use for your emergency.

Pawn shops: If you have something of value that you won't need for a while (jewelry, for example), you'll be able to get a collateral-based loan. But check on their finance charges up front!

WHAT TO KNOW WHEN YOU APPLY

Have your ID ready. You will need to provide government issued ID. You may also be asked for a recent utility statement to provide proof of residency. Make sure you know your Social Security number, and your Driver's License (or state ID) number.

Credit check. Your credit score may very well matter. You can still find short-term loans without a credit score check, but you will pay a much higher interest rate, and the loan amount will be smaller. If it's required, the lender will run a credit check.

You'll need your bank account information. Frequently, lenders will prefer to direct deposit your loan into a bank account. If you don't have a bank account, check with the lender up front to see what other options are available—they may just issue a check. Though not all lenders will want to see it, it would be good to have a recent bank statement available.

Employer verification. In some cases the lender may want to verify your employment and/or your income, either directly with your employer, or just by seeing your last paycheck stub. Have your employer contact information and your most recent paycheck stub available. If you are unemployed but receiving benefits, have that information handy.

Email and telephone contact information. Some lenders may prefer a landline phone number for your contact number. Use a reliable and private email address—your work email is probably not the best one to use.

Read the fine print. For some loans, you may be charged an application fee or other finance charges. Or, there may be a prepayment penalty if you pay off the loan early. Be sure to carefully examine the terms of the loan before you sign!

In a perfect world, you would be well prepared for a rainy day and for unexpected expenses. But you are not alone: Recent studies have shown that 40% of Americans would have a hard time putting together $2,000 in a hurry to handle an emergency. Review your options, make sure the one you select works for you and your situation, and that you will be able to repay the loan.

Are You Ready for an Emergency?

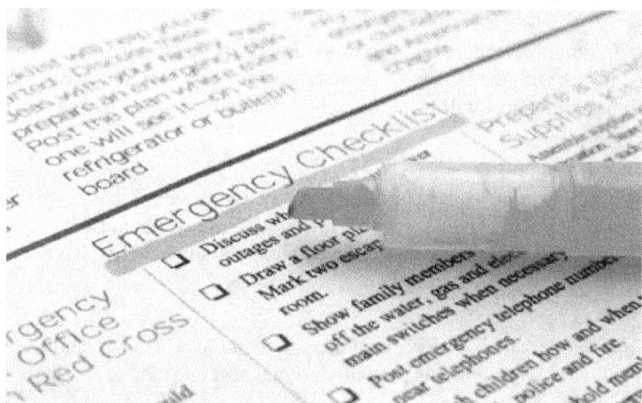

The beginning of the year is a great time to think about those once-a-year tasks: Changing the batteries in your fire alarms, getting papers sorted for tax prep, checking your insurance policies.

It's also a good month to review your emergency plans. Even if you live in a tropical paradise, you still have to file taxes, get insurance, be prepared for a fire, power failure, car trouble, and natural disasters.

Make sure you're prepared:

- Check and replace batteries in your smoke detectors, flashlights, and radios. An emergency wind-up radio is not dependent on either batteries or electricity. Check that your fire extinguishers are current.
- Have *at least* a half-tank of gas in your car.
- Do a household-hazard check: Are there flammable items that need to be secured, things that might fall, furniture you might trip over in the dark, tree branches that might break a window or impede exit? Keep small emergency lights in a few spots around the house.
- Learn how to shut off gas, water, and electricity.
- Have a plan for your pets: Carriers, leashes, food, bowls, prescriptions, immunizations records, and arrange lodging in case you must go to a shelter.
- Set up your email account so you can check it on the web from another location.
- Practice an emergency exit drill, from home and work.
- Establish an emergency contact plan for your family.

Stock emergency supplies at home, at work, and in your car:

- Put together a go-kit: Flashlight, radio, batteries, candles/matches, cash in small denominations, copies of important documents and identification (keep in a plastic bag), phone numbers (don't rely on your cell phone), personal hygiene items (toilet paper, soap/shampoo, feminine hygiene, diapers, tissues, toothbrush, comb), maps, extra keys to house and car, snack items, water, prescription medication, sturdy shoes, rain gear, hat, gloves, change of clothes, extra prescription glasses and repair kit, towel, pocket knife, utility knife, duct tape, plastic bags (all sizes), sewing kit, mirror, dust mask, paper/pens, wrist watch/clock, whistle, recent photos of family and pets.
- Emergency medical kit: Disposable gloves, sterile dressings and bandages, Ace bandages, antibiotic ointment, antibiotic towelettes, eye-wash solution, scissors, tweezers, matches, aspirin, anti-diarrhea medication, prescription medication.
- Stockpile a reasonable amount of emergency food and water (one gallon per person per day) to last at least three days, and remember to check expiration dates. Rotate fresh items in, if they are supplies you use normally. Food items should be easy to open, and not require heat or refrigeration.

- Car kit: Window punch, jumper cables, fire extinguisher, flares, electrical/duct tape, emergency tire inflator, blankets, tarps, sleeping bags, cell phone charger, tools, hatchet, nylon rope, shovel, bolt cutters, camp lantern, and water.

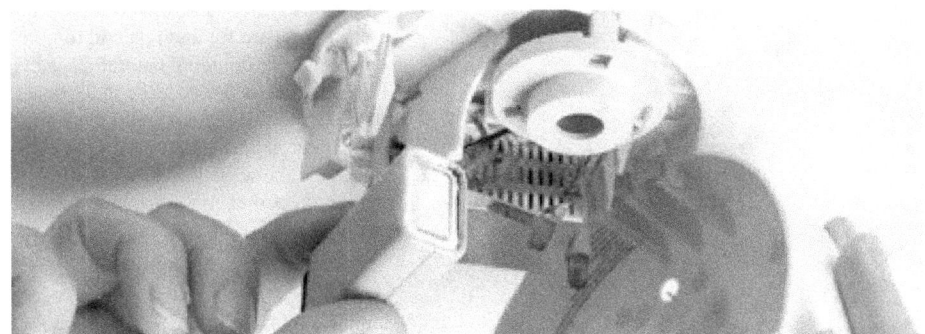

FEMA Emergency Supply List

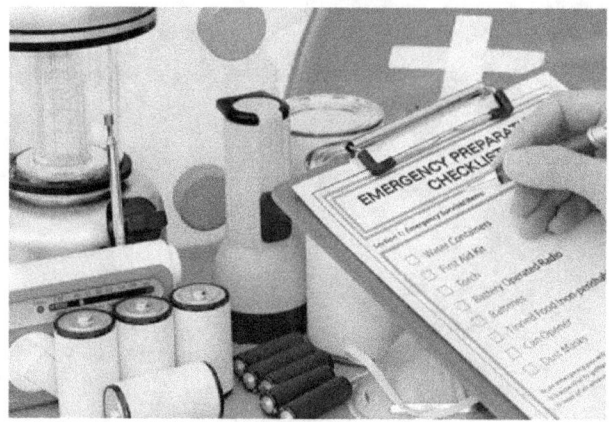

Through its Ready Campaign, the Federal Emergency Management Agency educates and empowers Americans to take some simple steps to prepare for and respond to potential emergencies, including natural disasters and terrorist attacks. *Ready* asks individuals to do three key things: get an emergency supply kit, make a family emergency plan, and be informed about the different types of emergencies that could occur and their appropriate responses.

All Americans should have some basic supplies on hand in order to survive for at least three days if an emergency occurs.

Following is a listing of some basic items that every emergency supply kit should include. However, it is important that individuals review this list and consider where they live and the unique needs of their family in order to create an emergency supply kit that will meet these needs. Individuals should also consider having at least two emergency supply kits, one full kit at home and smaller portable kits in their workplace, vehicle or other places they spend time.

Recommended Items to Include in a Basic Emergency Supply Kit:

- Water: One gallon of water per person per day for at least three days, for drinking and sanitation
- Food: At least a three-day supply of non-perishable food
- Can opener for food (if kit contains canned food)
- Battery-powered or hand crank radio and a NOAA Weather Radio with tone alert, and extra batteries for both
- Flashlight and extra batteries
- First aid kit
- Whistle to signal for help
- Dust mask, to help filter contaminated air
- Plastic sheeting and duct tape to shelter-in-place
- Moist towelettes, garbage bags and plastic ties for personal sanitation
- Prescription medications and glasses
- Infant formula and diapers
- Pet food and extra water for your pet
- Wrench or pliers to turn off utilities
- Important family documents such as copies of insurance policies, identification and bank account records in a waterproof, portable container
- Cash or traveler's checks and change
- Emergency reference material such as a first aid book or information from http://www.ready.gov.

- Sleeping bag or warm blanket for each person. Consider additional bedding if you live in a cold-weather climate.
- Complete change of clothing including a long sleeved shirt, long pants and sturdy shoes. Consider additional clothing if you live in a cold-weather climate.
- Household chlorine bleach and medicine dropper: When diluted nine parts water to one part bleach, bleach can be used as a disinfectant. Or in an emergency, you can use it to treat water by using 16 drops of regular household liquid bleach per gallon of water. Do not use scented, color safe or bleaches with added cleaners.
- Fire extinguisher
- Matches in a waterproof container
- Feminine supplies and personal hygiene items
- Mess kits, paper cups, plates and plastic utensils, paper towels
- Paper and pencil
- Books, games, puzzles or other activities for children
- Local maps

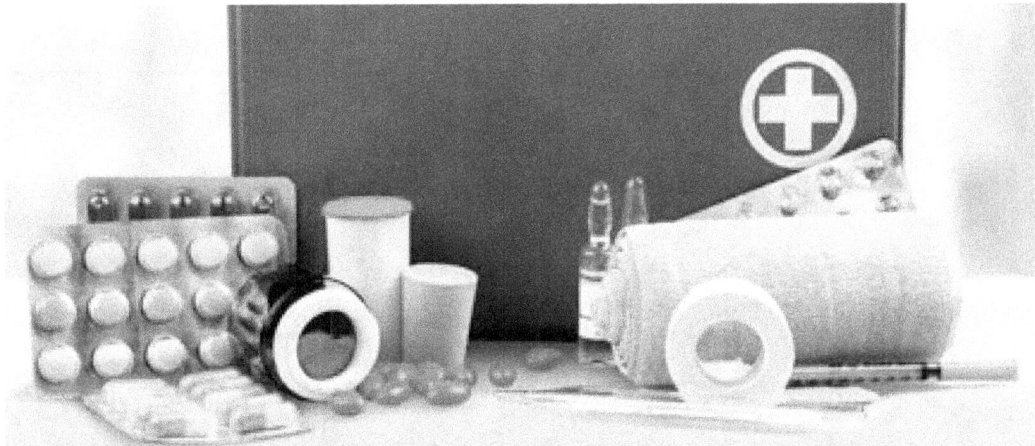

Personal Finance *for* Real People

When You Need Help

How Food Stamps Work

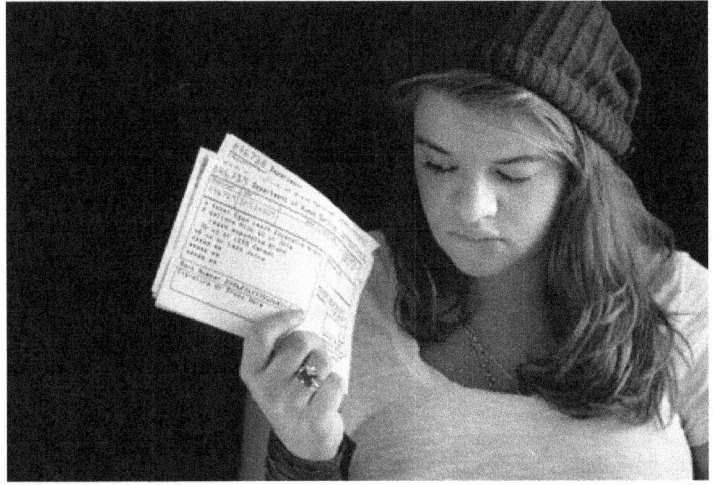

The federal food stamps program (or SNAP: Supplemental Nutritional Assistance Program) is always in the news. It's good, it's bad, the program doesn't supply enough, it supplies too much and gets abused, etc.

But here's what you should know: The federal and state governments have set aside funds for those individuals and families who simply don't make enough money to cover all their (modest) living expenses AND get enough nutritional food to eat.

If you've been in that situation—and over 46 million of your fellow-Americans have—it's nothing to be ashamed of. The programs are there to be used. They're there to be used *by you,* if you need them. They can provide a lifeline during a temporary setback, or help supplement income from a low-paying job. They'll help you to provide healthier food for your family.

The SNAP program is administered by the USDA, and by your state. Find information and more details about SNAP and other assistance programs on their website, www.fns.usda.gov/snap/supplemental-nutrition-assistance-program-snap.

Who can receive SNAP benefits?
There are three primary criteria:

- You must be a U.S. citizen, and all household members must have a Social Security number.
- Your household's "countable" resources cannot exceed $2,000. Countable includes cash and money in bank accounts, but does not include a home or property. If one member of your household is over 60, you are allowed a $3,000 countable resource limit.
- Your household's combined gross monthly income (that is your income from all sources before any deductions are taken out) must equal no more than 130% of the Federal poverty guidelines. AND your household's net income must be no more than 100% of the Federal poverty guidelines. For these purposes, "net" means your household's total gross income minus government approved deductions for childcare, housing costs, and other approved expenses.

Also:

- Households where all members receive, or are authorized to receive TANF or SSI cash assistance, are categorically eligible for SNAP.
- If you are able to work, you may have to meet certain work requirements.

During the recession, SNAP benefits were expanded. A new category of recipients was added: Broad-Based Categorical Eligibility (BBCE). This new category expands SNAP benefits to low-income families with high expenses, and to families whose gross incomes are slightly higher than the 130% Federal Poverty Limit normal gross income test.

This can all be very complicated to figure out! Your best bet is to go into your local benefits office or Social Security office, sit down with a representative, and work it through. Each state has its own application form; check to see if your state has an online form here: https://www.fns.usda.gov/snap/apply.

What are Federal poverty guidelines?
These guidelines are a measure of income level issued annually by the Department of Health and Human Services. Federal poverty levels are used to determine your eligibility for certain programs and benefits, such as Medicaid and SNAP.

How much can you receive?
It all depends on your household's combined income, your family size, and your resources. Your assistance is calculated using your specific qualifications. The lowest-income families with the lowest resources will obviously need, and receive, the most assistance. Benefits can range greatly, from under $200 per month up to $500, depending on number of people in the household and their financial status.

How can you apply for SNAP benefits?

- Download an application from your state's website.
- At your local State benefits office.
- At your Social Security office: They'll help you fill it out, and send it in for you.

What you'll need with you when you apply:

- Name, address and phone number
- Date of birth, Social Security number
- Gender, ethnicity, marital status, citizenship
- Monthly household income
- Monthly household expenses such as rent/mortgage, utilities and phone
- The same information on others in your household
- Household members' employer information
- Non-employment income sources
- Expenses for child/dependent support and medical services
- Household members' resources such as bank accounts, CDs, mutual funds and cash
- Children's information if you need assistance for children
- You may also need to supply documentation, so bring whatever paperwork you can.

How long will it take before you receive benefits, and how will they arrive?
If you are approved, you'll receive an approval letter through the mail. It's probably best to figure on the process taking anywhere between four business days and three weeks. It all depends on how complicated your application is, and how backlogged the system is.

You'll receive your benefits loaded onto an Electric Benefit Transfer card (other benefits can get deposited to your card as well, if you have any). You can use your SNAP benefits at **authorized** food retailers, such as groceries, markets, and convenience stores, through their Point of Sale (POS) machines and Automated Teller Machines (ATMs).

What can you buy with SNAP benefits?
You **CAN** buy foods for the household to eat, such as:

- Breads and cereals
- Fruits and vegetables
- Meats, fish and poultry
- Dairy products
- Seeds and plants that produce food for the household to eat

You **CANNOT** buy:

- Beer, wine, liquor, cigarettes or tobacco
- Pet foods
- Soaps, paper products
- Household supplies
- Vitamins and medicines
- Food that will be eaten in the store
- Hot foods

Still confused, can't get to the benefits office, or need some extra help?
You can also seek help and advice from local non-profit groups that offer assistance with negotiating the paperwork and how to get the most nutritional bang for your buck.

WIC: Another nutritional services program
WIC (women, infants, children) is another, more specific, assistance program. It includes supplemental foods, free lunch programs for kids, nutrition education, breastfeeding assistance, and health and social services referrals. Eligible are: women who are either pregnant, breastfeeding, or postpartum; and infants and children under the age of five. They must meet income guidelines and have a medical or nutritional risk.

Remember: The SNAP (Food Stamp) and other assistance programs are there to be used. They're there to be used *by you,* when and if you need them. They won't solve all your problems, or even fill all your family's food needs, but they *will* help.

Women, Infants, and Children Program

Another place for assistance that you might not know about is the Women, Infants, and Children Program, or WIC.

WIC is a federally funded health and nutrition program for women, infants, and children. WIC helps families by providing nutrition education, issuing checks for healthy supplemental foods, and making referrals to healthcare and other community services. Participants must meet income guidelines and be at least one of the following: pregnant, a new mother, a mother with an infant, or families with a child or children under the age of five.

In California, for example, 84 WIC agencies provide services locally to over 1.3 million participants each month at over 600 sites throughout the state.

You can search for an office at your location on the USDA website, www.fns.usda.gov/wic/women-infants-and-children-wic.

What can you get at WIC?

- Special checks to buy healthy foods from WIC-authorized vendors: milk, eggs, bread, cereal, juice, peanut butter, and much more. You can see the authorized shopping guide for California, as an example, here: www.cdph.ca.gov/Programs/CFH/DWICSN/Pages/WICFoods/CAWICFoodListDatabase.aspx, and you can pick up your own state's guide when you apply.
- Information about nutrition and health to help you and your family eat well and stay healthy.
- Support and information about breastfeeding your baby.
- Help in finding health care and other community services.

Who meets the income guidelines?

- A low-income parent or guardian who is the sole provider of children under age five who are at nutritional risk and who are at or below 185 percent of the federal poverty level.
- Income levels range from an annual gross income of $29,637 for a single mother with one child (or pregnant with one child), to $75,647 annual gross income for a family of eight. Check on your own state's Department of Health website for current and state income levels.

How do you shop with WIC?

- Make sure the store you shop in displays the WIC logo, either the logo for your state, or the national logo.
- Bring your signed WIC ID folder with you.

- Use your checks starting on the "First Day to Use" and no later than the "Last Day to Use."
- Look at "What to buy" on your check. Choose WIC authorized foods (brands and formats) using your WIC *Authorized Food List Shopping Guide.*
- Group your WIC foods by each check—each check will list what you can purchase with that check. You may redeem more than one check at a time.
- Tell the cashier right away that you are using WIC checks.
- Give your WIC ID Folder and checks to the cashier.
- The cashier then fills in the *Exact Purchase Price* area on the check while you are at the register.
- After the purchase price has been entered, you'll sign your WIC checks in front of the cashier.
- You must buy the full amount of formula printed on the Infant Formula WIC Checks. You may, however, choose to buy less of the other foods listed on the check.
- The WIC Fruits and Vegetables Check has a printed dollar value. If your purchase costs more than the amount on the check, you may pay the extra amount.
- You will not receive change from any WIC check transaction.
- You should be able to use your WIC check at your local farmers market.

If you have any problems redeeming your WIC checks at the store:

- Ask to speak with the store manager.
- If you are not satisfied, contact your local WIC agency at the number listed on the front of your WIC ID Folder.
- Or, contact your state WIC Program.
- Save your store receipt.
- Report the following information:

  - Date
  - Time
  - Store name
  - Names of the store staff involved
  - Details of the situation

A few things you won't be able to buy:

- Products with any added sugars, whether "natural," artificial, regular sugar, or corn syrup.
- Chocolate milk, goat's milk, buttermilk, acidophilus milk, condensed milk
- Greek yogurt, yogurt with mix-ins, artificially sweetened yogurt, drinkable yogurt
- Canned fish packed in oil, tuna kits
- Food from the salad bar or deli
- Decorative vegetables or fruits
- Bagged salad kits
- Herbs and spices

Stretch your WIC dollars further:

- Check store ads and websites for sales.
- Create a weekly meal plan based on food prices.
- Make a shopping list.

- Use grocery store club cards.
- Use store and manufacturer coupons.
- Buy store or generic brands.
- Take advantage of "buy one, get one free" specials.
- Buy fresh fruits and vegetables that are in season.
- Pay attention as foods are scanned to make sure you are charged the correct shelf price.

Above all, don't hesitate to utilize the WIC services and food dollars: WIC is there for your use, and is fully funded. Their goal is to help give your young family a healthy start in life!

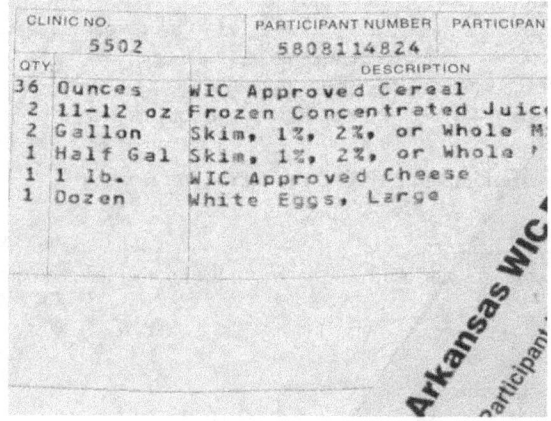

Are You Eligible for Disability Benefits?

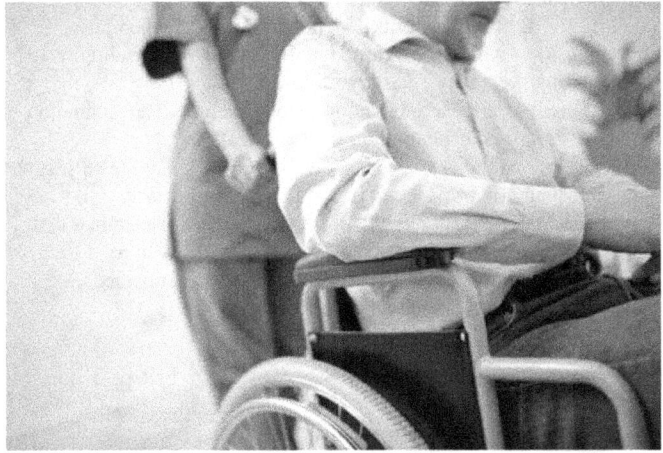 Disability benefits are administered through Social Security. You can both start your application for benefits, and manage your benefits online on the SSA website, www.ssa.gov/benefits/disability. You can also call at 1-800-772-1213, or apply in person (but make an appointment first).

Studies show that just over 1 in 4 of today's 20-year-olds will become disabled before reaching age 67. While we spend a great deal of time working to succeed in our jobs and careers, few of us think about ensuring that we have a safety net to fall back on should we become disabled. This is an area where Social Security can provide valuable help to you.

Who can apply for disability benefits?

- You must be age 18 or older.
- You are not currently receiving benefits on your own Social Security record.
- You must first have worked in jobs covered by Social Security—jobs in which deductions for Social Security were deducted from your paycheck.
- You are unable to work because of a medical condition that is expected to last at least 12 months or result in death.
- You have not been denied disability benefits in the last 60 days. If your application was recently denied for medical reasons, the Internet Appeal is a starting point to request a review of the medical determination we made.

What is Social Security's definition of being disabled?

- You cannot do work that you did before.
- Social Security decides that you cannot adjust to other work because of your medical condition(s).
- Your disability has lasted or is expected to last for at least one year or to result in death.

Social Security pays only for *total* disability. No benefits are payable for partial disability or for short-term disability.

Do you qualify for disability benefits?

- Check with Social Security for the most recent earnings requirements.
- You must have worked long enough—and recently enough—under Social Security to qualify for disability benefits.

- Social Security work credits are based on your total yearly wages or self-employment income. You can earn up to four credits each year. For example, you earn one credit for each $1,260 of wages or self-employment income. When you've earned $5,040, you've earned your four credits for the year.
- The number of work credits you need to qualify for disability benefits depends on your age when you become disabled. Generally, you need 40 credits, 20 of which were earned in the last 10 years ending with the year you become disabled. However, younger workers may qualify with fewer credits.
- If you are not currently working, Social Security will send your application to the Disability Determination Services office that will make the decision about your medical condition.
- For each of the major body systems, Social Security maintains a list of medical conditions that are so severe they automatically mean that you are disabled. If your condition is not on the list, Social Security will have to decide if it is of equal severity to a medical condition that *is* on the list. If it is, it will be determined that you are disabled. You can check the list on the SSA website under Medical/Professional Relations.
- Certain cases that usually qualify for disability can be allowed as soon as the diagnosis is confirmed. Examples include acute leukemia, Lou Gehrig's disease (ALS) and pancreatic cancer.

Information you must have with you when you apply for disability benefits.

- Your Social Security number and proof of your age.
- Names, addresses and phone numbers of doctors, caseworkers, hospitals, and clinics that took care of you and the dates of your visits.
- Names and dosages of all the medications you are taking.
- Medical records from your doctors, therapists, hospitals, clinics and caseworkers, which you already have in your possession.
- Laboratory and test results.
- A summary of where you worked and the kind of work you did.
- Your most recent W-2 form or, if you were self-employed, a copy of your federal tax return.

You've been approved! What benefits will you receive, and when?

- Your first Social Security benefit will be paid for the sixth full month after the date Social Security finds that your disability began.
- Social Security benefits are paid in the month following the month for which they're due—so you'll receive May's payment in June.
- The amount of your monthly disability benefit is based on your lifetime average earnings covered by Social Security.
- Social Security will automatically enroll you in Medicare after you get disability benefits for two years. The two parts of Medicare in which you are enrolled are hospital insurance and medical insurance.
- If you get Medicare and have low-income and few resources, your state may pay your Medicare premiums and, in some cases, other Medicare costs for which you are normally responsible such as deductibles and coinsurance. You'll need to check with your specific state.

Your disability application has been declined! What can you do?

- If your application was declined it will have been for one of two reasons:

  - Denied for medical reasons: You couldn't meet the disability requirements, or couldn't provide enough documentation to support your claim.

- Denied for financial or other reasons: You didn't earn enough income that qualified for Social Security coverage.

- Appeal the decision. There is an appeals process, and Social Security will help you through it. Find more information on the SSA website under Appeal A Decision, and under the Appeal Process.

Other disability programs

- Supplemental Security Income pays benefits based on financial need. It is designed to help aged, blind, and disabled people, who have little or no income; and it provides cash to meet basic needs for food, clothing, and shelter. You can find more information on the SSA website under Supplemental Security Income.
- There are also a number of special rules, called *work incentives*, which provide continued benefits and health care coverage to help you make the transition back to work. You can find out more information about the multiple programs under the Work Incentives section on the SSA website.

Did you know that 56 million Americans live with disabilities? Disability is something many read or hear about happening to others, but no one thinks it will happen to them. However, disability could happen at any moment in our lives. Social Security's disability program has played a substantial role in supporting needy individuals.

Other Services Your State May Offer

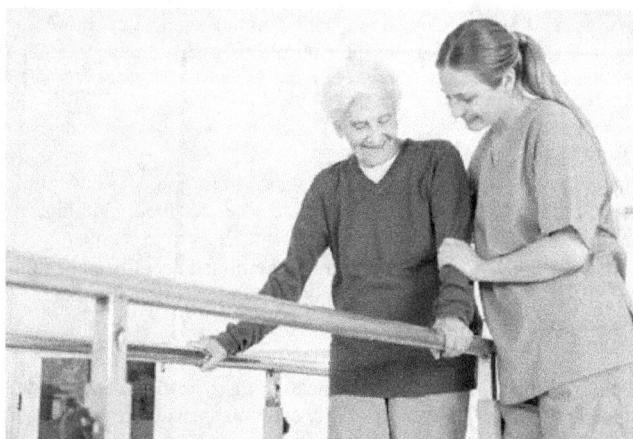

Chances are you don't know even a portion of the many services your state offers for people in need.

These services are in addition to the benefits of Social Security, Disability, Medicare, WIC, and SSI offered by the federal government.

We'll take a look at just some of what California offers, but look for similar programs in your own state.

A selection of California state agencies:

- The California Arts Council offers grants, artist calls, jobs, and internships.
- California Commission on Disability Access (CCDA)
- The California Department of Aging (CDA) administers programs that serve older adults, adults with disabilities, family caregivers, and residents in long-term care facilities throughout the state.
- California Department of Child Support Services works with parents and guardians to ensure children and families receive court-ordered financial and medical support.
- California Department of Education If your child needs extra help or assistance, or has been a victim of discrimination or harassment, check the California Department of Education website.
- California Department of Social Services This is a workhorse of a department, handling everything from foster children to a home-aide registry to in-home support services and more. CalWORKS is a cash aid program for low-income families. CAPI provides monthly cash benefits to aged, blind, and disabled non-citizens who are not eligible for SSI solely due to their immigrant status. The Assistance Dog Special Allowance Program (ADSA) provides $50 per month to eligible persons who use a guide, signal, or service dog to help them with needs related to their physical disabilities.
- California Health and Human Services Agency provides a wide range of services in the areas of health care, mental health, public health, alcohol and drug treatment, income assistance, social services and assistance to people with disabilities.
- The California Victim Compensation Board (CalVCB) provides compensation for victims of violent crime who are injured or threatened with injury.
- Community-Based Adult Services/Adult Day Health Care provides services to older persons and adults with chronic medical, cognitive, or mental health conditions and/or disabilities who are at risk of needing institutional care.
- Department of Consumer Affairs Consumers learn how to protect themselves from unscrupulous and unqualified individuals.
- The Department of Fair Housing and Employment protects Californians from employment, housing and public accommodation discrimination, and hate violence. The DFEH is the largest state civil rights agency in the country.
- Center for Disease Prevention and Health Promotion provides programs that support healthy behaviors at multipurpose senior centers, at congregate meal sites, through home-delivered meal programs, and reduces

the risk of chronic diseases among California's older adults by teaching techniques and strategies that delay and/or manage chronic health conditions.

- Family Caregiver Support Program
- Health Insurance Counseling and Advocacy Program
- Legal Assistance
- Long-Term Care Ombudsman Program
- Medi-Cal (Medicaid) Free or low-cost health coverage for California residents who meet eligibility requirements.
- Multipurpose Senior Services Program
- Health Facilities and Nursing Home Guide Search for a nursing home in California that best suits your family member's needs.
- Nutrition Services Nutrition education and home-delivered meals.
- Paid Family Leave Where and how to file.
- Retired Senior Volunteer Programs and other senior volunteer opportunities: Senior Corps is a network of programs that tap the experience, skills, and talents of older citizens to meet community challenges with Foster Grandparents, Senior Companions, and RSVP (Retired and Senior Volunteer Program).
- Senior Community Services Employment Program
- Senior Information and Assistance Program
- The State Council on Developmental Disabilities (SCDD) ensures that people with developmental disabilities and their families receive the services and support they need.
- Supportive Services Program provides funding for a variety of supportive services programs for older adults.
- Unclaimed Property Search

Assistance Programs that Really Help

In addition to state and federal government assistance and aid programs, there are many non-profit and charitable aid programs that may be available to you, from free business advice from retired businesspeople, to free meals or clothes, or help with utility bills.

Programs may differ in your state, but there are sure to be either these or similar programs available.

The American Red Cross provides home comforts and critical services on military bases and in military hospitals around the world; supports military families during deployments and emergencies; and continues serving veterans after their service ends. In a disaster, the Red Cross is the first in to provide medical care, shelter, and other services to victims of tornadoes, hurricanes, floods, earthquakes and other disasters.

Homes for Our Troops builds mortgage-free, specially adapted homes nationwide for severely injured, post-9/11, veterans.

Operation Homefront assists military families during difficult financial times by providing food assistance, auto and home repair, vision care, travel and transportation, moving assistance, essential home items, and rent-free transitional housing for wounded veterans and their families. They also award mortgage-free homes to wounded veterans, provide school supplies, holiday meals for military families, and more.

Animal Control and Shelters: Your local Animal Control department most likely offers low-cost vaccinations, works with a local groomer for low-cost grooming needs, and can refer you to a participating vet for discounted spaying and neutering.

Big Brothers Big Sisters of America programs are designed to match children ages 5 through 17 with mentors in professionally supported one-to-one relationships.

Covenant House assists homeless kids coming to Covenant House in crisis. Immediately and without question, their basic human needs are met--a nourishing meal, a shower, clean clothes, medical attention, and a safe place away from the dangers of the street.

Goodwill Industries serves persons with disabilities or other vocational disadvantages, and local businesses seeking qualified employees, by providing education, skills training, work experience and job placement services. As well, Goodwill stores are excellent sources of inexpensive clothing, toys, furniture, and housewares.

Catholic Charities has grants to help pay for funeral costs, as well as emergency rent help, food, assistance with paying utility and heating bills, health care, and more.

Other organizations that may help pay for funeral costs include your own church, if you attend one; American Red Cross; Veterans' Benefit Administration and each branch of the military for members of the armed forces; the Federal Emergency Management Association; the Railroad Retirement Board; your state's Department of Health; and your state's Office of Victims of Crime.

Community Action Agencies in your state can help with rent assistance, utility bills, medical bills, health care, mortgages, student and other loans, debt counseling and more.

Jewish Federations of North America: Most of the 300 non-profits that are part of the Jewish Federations provide social services and some form of emergency assistance to all qualified low income individuals and seniors in the region, regardless of their religion, age, gender, or culture. Some sites may limit assistance to only Jewish members of the community. Locations may have financial assistance for basic needs such as rent, utilities, food, or medications. Other sites will not offer direct financial aid but may instead offer referrals to non-profits or charities that they partner with. You can get applications for and help with assistance programs, including LIHEAP, public housing, SNAP Food Stamps, section SSI, disability, and more. Receive guidance with government entitlement eligibility, documentation, applications, help enrolling, and recertification including Medicare, Social Security, SSI, Medicaid, and Food Stamps if needed.

Low Income Home Energy Assistance Program assists low-income families with energy costs.

There are many organizations that shelter victims of domestic abuse. They may also provide reentry assistance: transitional housing, training, job search, counseling, and professional clothing. Some are local like Shelter from the Storm in California's Coachella Valley. HelpGuide offers a good overview of the domestic violence situation, including warning signs, how to leave, protecting yourself, where to get help, legal issues, and other resources. WomensHealth provides a list of resources for battered and abused women by state.

Meals on Wheels America's website lets you search for programs in your area.

There is sure to be a food bank in your area, as well. Search for "food bank" with your state name, and multiple resources will come up, usually including a state association of food banks. In California, for example, The California Association of Food Banks website lets you search for a food bank near you, as well as search for other food assistance.

There are many charitable and government options for you, no matter what your needs are. The lists in our articles are a place to start, but don't be limited by them. Do a website search for the issue you need help with, and places that will help are sure to come up.

How Social Security Works

The good news is that applying for Social Security retirement is easier now than it's ever been: You can complete your application online in about 15 minutes or so. If your case is complicated, or you simply have questions, you can also make an appointment at your local Social Security office. *Do* make an appointment, though—the lines at Social Security can be as bad as the lines at the DMV!

Requirements to apply for Social Security retirement benefits:

* You are at least 61 years and 9 months old.
* You are **not** currently receiving benefits (such as disability) on your own Social Security record.
* You want your benefits to start no more than four months in the future. Your application cannot be processed before that time.

Information that you'll need to supply:

* Date and place of birth
* If you were born outside the United States or its territories:
    * Name of your birth country at the time of your birth (it may have a different name now)
    * Permanent Resident Card number (if you are not a U.S citizen)
* Marriage and divorce:
    * Name of current spouse
    * Name of prior spouse (if the marriage lasted more than 10 years or ended in death)
    * Spouse(s) date of birth and SSN (optional)
    * Beginning and ending dates of marriage(s)
    * Place of marriage(s) (city, state or country, if married outside the U.S.)
* Names and dates of birth of children who:
    * Became disabled prior to age 22
    * Are under age 18 and are unmarried
    * Are aged 18 to 19 and still attending secondary school full time
* U.S. military service:
    * Type of duty and branch
    * Service period dates
* Employer details for current year and prior two years (not self-employment):
    * Employer name

- Employment start and end dates
- Self-employment details for current year and prior two years:
  - Business type
  - Total net income
- You can view your Social Security Statement online on the SSA website.
- Direct deposit information:
  - Domestic bank (USA)
    - Account type and number
    - Bank routing number
  - International bank (non-USA):
    - International Direct Deposit (IDD) bank country
    - Bank name, bank code, and currency
    - Account type and number
    - Branch/transit number

Other things to know:

- Your full retirement age:
  - Depending on your date of birth, your full retirement age (for Social Security purposes—more information on the SSA website—may be between age 66 and 67. This could affect the amount of your benefits and when you want the benefits to start.
- When you can start benefits:
  - You may start receiving benefits as early as age 62 or as late as age 70.
- Benefits are reduced for age:
  - Your monthly benefits will be reduced if you start them any time before your full retirement age.
- Working while you receive benefits:
  - If you elect to receive benefits before you reach full retirement age, you should understand how continuing to work can affect your benefits.
- Delayed retirement credits:
  - Delayed retirement credits may be added to your benefits if they start **after** your full retirement age.
- Life expectancy:
  - If you live to the average life expectancy for someone your age, you will receive about the same amount in lifetime benefits whether you choose to start receiving benefits at age 62, full retirement age, age 70 or any age in between.

Use the Social Security Retirement Calculator (https://www.ssa.gov/planners/calculators/) **to estimate your benefits**. The Retirement Estimator gives estimates based on your actual Social Security earnings record. Please keep in mind that these are *just* estimates. Social Security can't calculate your actual benefit amount until you apply for benefits.

And that amount may differ from the estimates provided because:

- Your earnings may increase or decrease in the future.
- After you start receiving benefits, they will be adjusted for cost-of-living increases.
- Your estimated benefits are based on current law. The law governing benefit amounts may change because, by 2034, the payroll taxes collected will be enough to pay only about 79 cents for each dollar of scheduled benefits.

- Your benefit amount may be affected by military service, railroad employment or pensions earned through work on which you did not pay Social Security tax.

What is the best age to start your benefits?
The answer is that there is no one best age for everyone and, ultimately, it is your choice. You should make an informed decision about when to apply for benefits based on your individual and family circumstances. Your monthly benefit amount can differ substantially based on the age when you start receiving benefits. If you decide to start benefits:

- *Before* your full retirement age, your benefit will be smaller but you will receive it for a longer period of time.
- *At* your full retirement age or later, you will receive a larger monthly benefit for a shorter period of time.

The amount you receive when you first get benefits sets the base for the amount you will receive for the rest of your life.

There are also some other things you may want to consider when you make that decision:

- Are you still working full-time?
- Do you come from a long-lived family?
- How is your health?
- Will you still have health insurance?
- Are you eligible for benefits on another person's Social Security record?
- Do you have other income to support you, if you decide to delay taking your benefits?
- Will other family members qualify for benefits with you on your record?

Can you work *and* receive Social Security?
You *can* work while you receive Social Security retirement (or survivors) benefits. When you do, it could mean a higher benefit for you in the future.

Each year Social Security reviews the records for all working Social Security recipients. If your earnings for the prior year are higher than one of the years used to compute your retirement benefit, your benefit amount will be recalculated. The increase is paid retroactive to January the year after you earned the money.

If you are younger than full retirement age and make more than the yearly earnings limit, your earnings may reduce your benefit amount. (If you were born between 1/2/1943 and 1/1/1955, your full retirement age is 66 years.)

- If you are under full retirement age for the entire year, $1 is deducted from your benefit payments for every $2 you earn above the annual limit. For 2016, that limit is $15,720.
- In the year you reach full retirement age, $1 is deducted in benefits for every $3 you earn above a different limit.

Note: If your earnings will be over the limit for the year but you will be retired for part of the year, there's a special rule that applies to earnings for one year. The special rule lets you get paid for a full Social Security check for any whole month you are considered retired, regardless of your yearly earnings.

When you reach full retirement age:

- Beginning with the month you reach full retirement age, your earnings no longer reduce your benefits, no matter how much you earn.
- Your benefit amount will be recalculated, leaving out the months when social Security reduced or withheld benefits due to your excess earnings.

If you work outside the United States, the rules for receiving benefits while you are working are different.

You can check on your Social Security application status on the SSA website (http://www.ssa.gov), and you'll be contacted if Social Security has any other questions for you.

Of course, check with Social Security when you are ready to file to make sure you have up-to-date information. And we haven't included more complicated issues such as survivor's benefits and other topics. The Social Security website may answer your questions, or you can just make an appointment, and go talk to a real person about your situation.

How Medicare Works

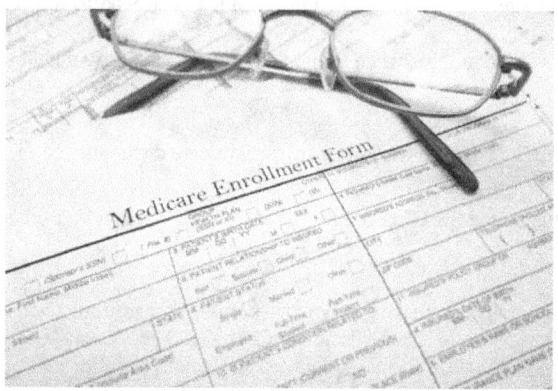

Just what exactly is Medicare?
Medicare is the federal government program that provides health care coverage (health insurance) for those who are 65 or older, or under 65 and who receive Social Security Disability Insurance (SSDI) for a certain amount of time. The Centers for Medicare & Medicaid Services (CMS) is the federal agency that runs Medicare. Medicare and Medicaid are in part funded by Social Security and Medicare taxes that are deducted from each person's paycheck; in part funded through premiums that are paid by people with Medicare; and in part funded through the federal budget.

Once you've become eligible for Medicare, you can enroll in Original Medicare, the traditional fee-for-service program offered directly through the federal government, or choose to enroll in a Medicare Advantage Plan, a type of private insurance offered by companies that contract with Medicare.

There are many choices to make, and it's important to really understand your Medicare coverage choices and to pick your coverage carefully. How you choose to get your benefits and who you get them from can affect your out-of-pocket costs and where you can get your care.

There are 2 main ways to get your Medicare coverage: Original Medicare or a Medicare Advantage Plan.

In Original Medicare you are able to go to nearly all doctors and hospitals in the country. Medicare Advantage Plans restrict you to approved networks—you'll be more limited in your choice of doctors and hospitals. However, Medicare Advantage Plans can also provide additional benefits that Original Medicare does not cover, such as routine vision or dental care.

Medicare Parts A and B
Medicare is divided into two main areas of coverage, Part A and Part B. Whether you have Original Medicare or the Medicare Advantage Plan, you will still pay monthly Part B and Part A premiums. Part A and Part B of the Medicare plans cover two different areas:

- Part A covers hospitalization and related costs
- Part B covers all other medical treatments
- Each Original Medicare and Medicare Advantage Plan must provide all Part A and Part B services.

Medicare Part A
If you or your spouse (living, deceased or divorced) paid Medicare taxes during at least 10 years of work, you won't have a premium to pay for Medicare Part A (hospitalization insurance). Medicare Part A covers inpatient hospital care, skilled nursing facility, hospice, lab tests, surgery, and home health care.

Medicare Part B

Most people pay a monthly premium for Medicare Part B, which was about $125 in 2018. Some people pay a higher premium based on their income, or if they don't enroll when they are first eligible. Medicare Part B (medical insurance) covers doctor and other health care providers' services, outpatient care, durable medical equipment, home health care, and some preventive services. You must already have Medicare Part A before you apply for Part B.

When can you sign up?

When you're first eligible for Medicare, you have a 7-month Initial Enrollment Period to sign up for Part A and/or Part B. For example, if you're eligible for Medicare when you turn 65, you can sign up during the 7-month period that begins 3 months before the month you turn 65, the month you turn 65, and ends 3 months after the month you turn 65.

- You can sign up for free Part A, if you're eligible, any time during or after your Initial Enrollment Period starts. Your coverage start date will depend on when you sign up. If you have to buy Part A *and/or Part B*, you can only sign up during a valid enrollment period.
- In most cases, if you don't sign up for Medicare Part B when you're first eligible, you'll have to pay a late enrollment penalty for as long as you have Part B and you could have a gap in your health coverage.

- Between January 1–March 31 each year
    - If you didn't sign up for Part A and/or Part B when you were first eligible, and you aren't eligible for a Special Enrollment Period, you can sign up during the General Enrollment Period between January 1 and March 31 each year.
    - Your coverage will then start July 1.You may have to pay a higher premium for late enrollment in Part A and/or a higher premium for late enrollment in Part B.
- Special circumstances (Special Enrollment Periods)
    - Once your Initial Enrollment Period ends, you may have another chance to sign up for Medicare during a Special Enrollment Period. If you're covered under a group health plan based on current employment, you have a Special Enrollment Period to sign up for Part A and/or Part B any time as long as you or your spouse (or family member if you're disabled) is working, and you're covered by a group health plan through the employer or union based on that work.
    - You also have an 8-month Special Enrollment Period to sign up for Part A and/or Part B that starts the month after the employment ends or the group health plan insurance based on current employment ends, whichever happens first. Usually, you don't pay a late enrollment penalty if you sign up during a Special Enrollment Period.
    - COBRA and retiree health plans aren't considered coverage based on current employment. You're not eligible for a Special Enrollment Period when that coverage ends.
    - You may also qualify for a Special Enrollment Period for Part A and Part B if you're a volunteer serving in a foreign country.

How do you sign up?

- Apply online at Social Security.
- Visit your local Social Security office.
- Call Social Security at 1-800-772-1213. TTY users should call 1-800-325-0778.
- If you worked for a railroad, call the RRB at 1-877-772-5772.

- Complete an Application for Enrollment in Part B (CMS-40B). You can also get this form and its instructions in Spanish.
- Remember, you must already have Part A to apply for Part B.
- You don't need to sign up for Medicare each year. However, each year you'll have a chance to review your coverage and change plans.

When will your Medicare coverage start?
If you sign up for Medicare Part A and/or Medicare Part B during the first 3 months of your Initial Enrollment Period, your coverage start date will depend on your birthday. Your coverage starts the first day of the month you turn 65.

Medicare prescription drug coverage
Medicare offers prescription drug coverage to everyone with Medicare. If you decide not to join a Medicare Prescription Drug Plan (Part D) when you're first eligible, or if you decide not to join a Medicare Advantage Plan (Part C)—like an HMO or PPO—or other Medicare health plan that offers Medicare prescription drug coverage, you'll likely pay a late enrollment penalty.

To get Medicare drug coverage, you must join a plan run by an insurance company or other private company approved by Medicare. Each plan can vary in cost and drugs covered.

Medicare Prescription Drug Plan (Part D): These plans (sometimes called PDPs) add drug coverage to Original Medicare, some Medicare Cost Plans, some Medicare Private Fee-for-Service (PFFS) Plans, and Medicare Medical Savings Account (MSA) Plans.

Medicare Advantage Plan (Part C): Like an HMO or PPO, or other Medicare health plan that offers Medicare prescription drug coverage. You get all of your Medicare Part A (Hospital Insurance) and Medicare Part B (Medical Insurance) coverage, *and* prescription drug coverage (Part D), through these plans. Medicare Advantage Plans with prescription drug coverage are sometimes called MA-PDs. You must have Part A and Part B to join a Medicare Advantage Plan.

- If your Medicare Advantage Plan (Part C) includes prescription drug coverage and you join a Medicare Prescription Drug Plan (Part D), you'll be unenrolled from your Medicare Advantage Plan and returned to Original Medicare.

Get help paying Medicare costs

- **Medicaid** helps with medical costs like nursing home care and personal care services for people with limited incomes. You may be eligible for extra help paying for Medicare prescription drug coverage (Part D), even if your income exceeds Medicaid income levels, under the spend down rules.
- **Medicare Savings Programs** in your state may help pay your Medicare premiums, your Medicare Part A and Medicare Part B deductibles, coinsurance, and copayments, and Medicare prescription drug coverage costs. You may qualify for the Qualified Medicare Beneficiary Program, Specified Low-Income Medicare Beneficiary Program, Qualifying Individual Program, or Qualified Disabled and Working Individuals Program, even if your income and resources are higher than the state limits.
- **PACE (Program of All-inclusive Care for the Elderly)** is a Medicare and Medicaid program that helps people meet their health care needs in the community instead of going to a nursing home or other care facility. PACE covers adult day primary care, dentistry, emergency services, home care, hospital care, laboratory/x-ray services, meals, medical specialty services, nursing home care, nutritional counseling,

occupational therapy, physical therapy, prescription drugs, Part D covered drugs, preventive care, social services, caregiver training, support groups, respite care, social work counseling, and transportation if medically necessary.

- **Medicare** may help pay the costs of Medicare prescription drug coverage if you meet certain income and resource limits.
- **The Supplemental Security Income (SSI)** program pays benefits to disabled adults and children who have limited income and resources. SSI benefits also are payable to people 65 and older without disabilities who meet the financial limits.

Lower your costs with assignment

Assignment means that your doctor, provider, or supplier agrees (or is required by law) to accept the Medicare-approved amount as full payment for covered services.

Make sure your doctor, provider, or supplier accepts assignment. Most doctors, providers, and suppliers accept assignment, but you should always check to make sure. Participating providers have signed an agreement to accept assignment for all Medicare-covered services.

Here's what happens if your doctor, provider, or supplier accepts assignment:

- Your out-of-pocket costs may be less.
- They agree to charge you only the Medicare deductible and coinsurance amount, and usually wait for Medicare to pay its share before asking you to pay your share.
- They have to submit your claim directly to Medicare, and can't charge you for submitting the claim.

Here's what happens if your doctor, provider, or supplier doesn't accept assignment:

- Non-participating providers haven't signed an agreement to accept assignment for all Medicare-covered services, but they *can* still choose to accept assignment for individual services. You might have to pay the entire charge at the time of service. Your doctor, provider, or supplier will submit a claim to Medicare for any Medicare-covered services they provide to you.
- They can't charge you for submitting a claim. If they don't submit the Medicare claim once you ask them to, call 1-800-MEDICARE.
- In some cases, you might have to submit your own claim to Medicare to get paid back.
- They can charge you more than the Medicare-approved amount, but there's a limit called *the limiting charge.* The provider can only charge you up to 15% over the amount that non-participating providers are paid. Non-participating providers are paid 95% of the fee schedule amount.
- The limiting charge applies only to certain Medicare-covered services and doesn't apply to some supplies and durable medical equipment.

Private contracts

A private contract is a written agreement between you and a doctor or other health care provider who has decided not to provide services to anyone through Medicare. The private contract only applies to the services provided by the doctor or other provider who asked you to sign it.

You don't *have* to sign a private contract. You can always go to another provider who gives services through Medicare. If you sign a private contract with your doctor or other provider, the following rules apply:

Medicare won't pay any amount for the services you get from this doctor or provider, even if it's a Medicare-covered service.

- You'll have to pay the full amount of whatever this provider charges you for the services you get.
- If you have a Medicare Supplement Insurance (Medigap) policy, it won't pay anything for the services you get. Call your insurance company before you get the service if you have questions.
- Your provider must tell you if Medicare would pay for the service if you got it from another provider who accepts Medicare.
- Your provider must tell you if he or she has been excluded from Medicare.
- You can't be asked to sign a private contract for emergency or urgent care.
- You're always free to get services not covered by Medicare if you choose to pay for a service yourself.

How Medicaid Works

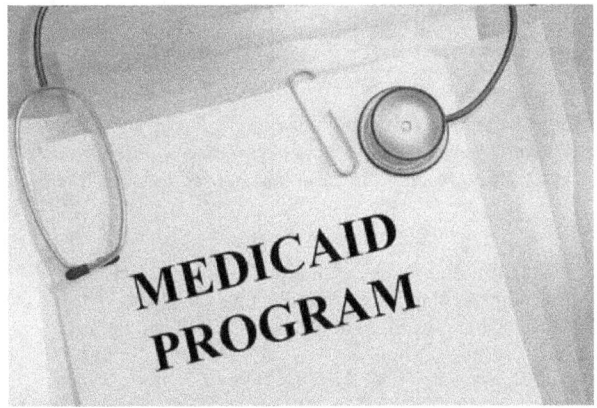

Not only is Medicaid available for low-income families and individuals, but there are two additional programs that can help: The Children's Health Insurance Program, and the Basic Health Program. We go into a little detail below, but explore your state's Medicaid website for more detailed information, and see how it applies to your own situation.

Medicaid
Medicaid, www.medicaid.gov, provides health coverage to millions of Americans, including eligible low-income adults, children, pregnant women, elderly adults, and people with disabilities. Medicaid is administered by states, according to federal requirements. States (who have signed up for Medicaid) and the federal government jointly fund the program.

Federal law requires states to provide certain mandatory benefits and allows states the choice of covering other optional benefits. Mandatory benefits include services like inpatient and outpatient hospital services, physician services, laboratory and x-ray services, and home health services, among others. Optional benefits include services like prescription drugs, case management, physical therapy, and occupational therapy. See a list of mandatory and optional benefits for Medicaid programs on the Medicaid website.

- In all states, Medicaid provides coverage for some low-income people, families and children, pregnant women, the elderly, and people with disabilities.
- In some states, Medicaid has been expanded to cover all adults below a certain income level.
- Medicaid programs must follow federal guidelines, but coverage and costs may be different from state to state.
- Some Medicaid programs pay for your care directly. Others use private insurance companies to provide Medicaid coverage.
- You may be eligible for extra help paying for Medicare prescription drug coverage (Part D), even if your income exceeds Medicaid income levels, under the spend down rules if you are medically needy.

Children's Health Insurance Program (CHIP)
The Children's Health Insurance Program, www.medicaid.gov/CHIP/index.html, provides federal matching funds to states to provide health coverage to children in families with incomes too high to qualify for Medicaid, but who can't afford private coverage. All states have expanded children's coverage significantly through their CHIP programs, with nearly every state providing coverage for children up to at least 200 percent of the Federal Poverty Level. In some states, CHIP covers pregnant women. Each state works closely with its state Medicaid program. In many cases, if you qualify for Medicaid your children will qualify for either Medicaid or CHIP.

Basic Health Program (BHP)
The Basic Health Program, www.medicaid.gov/basic-health-program/index.html, was enacted by the Affordable Care Act and provides states the option to establish health benefits cover programs for low-income residents who would otherwise be eligible to purchase coverage through the Health Insurance Marketplace.

It provides affordable coverage and better continuity of care for people whose income fluctuates above and below Medicaid and CHIP levels.

These critical health coverage programs serve millions of families, children, pregnant women, adults without children, and also seniors and people living with disabilities.

All states, the District of Columbia, and the U.S. territories have Medicaid programs designed to provide health coverage for low-income people. Although the Federal government establishes certain parameters for all states to follow, each state administers their Medicaid program differently, resulting in variations in Medicaid coverage across the country.

Beginning in 2014, the Affordable Care Act provides states the authority to expand Medicaid eligibility to individuals under age 65 in families with incomes below 133 percent of the Federal Poverty Level and standardizes the rules for determining eligibility and providing benefits through Medicaid, CHIP and the health insurance Marketplace.

Medicaid and CHIP Eligibility Levels
The 2018 Federal Poverty Level income numbers (below) are used to calculate eligibility for Medicaid and the Children's Health Insurance Program.

- $12,140 for individuals
- $16,460 for a family of 2
- $20,780 for a family of 3
- $25,100 for a family of 4
- $29,420 for a family of 5
- $33,740 for a family of 6
- $38,060 for a family of 7
- $42,380 for a family of 8

Federal Poverty Level amounts are higher in Alaska and Hawaii.

How Federal Poverty Levels are used to determine eligibility for reduced-cost health coverage:

- **Income between 100% and 400% of the Federal Poverty Level:** If your income is in this range, in all states you qualify for premium tax credits that lower your monthly premium for a Marketplace health insurance plan.
- **Income below 138% of the Federal Poverty Level:** If your income is below 138% FPL, and your state **has** expanded Medicaid coverage, you qualify for Medicaid based only on your income.
- **Income below 100% of the Federal Poverty Level:** If your income falls below 100% FPL, and your state **hasn't** expanded Medicaid coverage, you won't qualify for either income-based Medicaid or savings on a Marketplace health insurance plan. You may still qualify for Medicaid under your state's current rules.

How to apply for Medicaid
Find out if your state is expanding Medicaid and if you qualify based only on your income. You can also find out if you qualify for savings on a health insurance plan instead at http://www.Healthcare.gov.

- Even if your state hasn't expanded Medicaid and you don't qualify based on income alone, you should apply.
- Each state has coverage options that could work for you—particularly if you have children, are pregnant, or have a disability.
- There's no limited enrollment period for Medicaid or CHIP. If you qualify, coverage can begin immediately, any time of year.
- Medicaid and CHIP program names vary. Learn what they're called in your state at http://www.Healthcare.gov.

Apply for Medicaid and/or CHIP in one of two ways:

- **Through the Health Insurance Marketplace**
  - Fill out an application through the Health Insurance Marketplace.
  - If it looks like anyone in your household qualifies for Medicaid or CHIP, your information will be sent to your state agency. They'll contact you about enrollment.
  - When you submit your Marketplace application, you'll also find out if you qualify for an individual insurance plan with savings based on your income instead. Plans may be more affordable than you think.
  - Start a Marketplace application. Just choose your state, click "Continue," and select whether you want to use a quick Medicaid/CHIP screener or just start an application.
- **Through your state Medicaid agency**
  - You can also apply directly to your state Medicaid agency.
  - On the application page of the Medicaid website, select your state from the dropdown menu, and you'll find your state's Medicaid contact information.

What to do if you've been turned down or don't qualify for coverage:

- **If you've been turned down for Medicaid or CHIP coverage:**
  - You may be able to buy a private health plan through the Marketplace instead. You may qualify for savings based on your income through a premium tax credit and savings on out-of-pocket costs. Many people can find plans for $100 or less per month.
- **If your state Medicaid or CHIP agency said you're not eligible**
  - If your state agency decides someone in your household isn't eligible, you'll get a notice explaining this.
  - In most cases, the state will send your information to the Marketplace. The Marketplace will send you a notice explaining how to submit an application for a private insurance plan. The application will be pre-filled with information you gave the state agency.
- **If your state hasn't expanded Medicaid coverage**
  - If your state **hasn't** expanded Medicaid and your state agency said you're not eligible under its current rules, you may have fewer options for coverage. Depending on your income you may not qualify for savings on a private insurance plan.
- **If you don't qualify for either Medicaid or Marketplace savings**
  - You can get care at a nearby community health center and Planned Parenthood. The health care law has expanded funding to community health centers, which provide primary care for millions of Americans. These centers provide services on a sliding scale based on your income.
- **If you don't have any coverage, you don't have to pay the fee.**
  - Under the law, most people must have health coverage or pay a fee. But you won't have to pay this fee if you live in a state that hasn't expanded Medicaid and you would have qualified

if it had. This is called having an exemption from the fee. You can get an exemption when you apply for coverage in the Marketplace. Or you can apply for the exemption without having to fill out a Marketplace application.

If your income level rises:

If your expected yearly income increases so it's between 100% and 400% of the federal poverty level, you become eligible for a Marketplace plan with advance payments of the premium tax credit. In this case, you may qualify for a Special Enrollment Period that allows you to enroll in a Marketplace plan any time of year. You must contact the Marketplace Call Center **within 60 days** from the date your income changed to request this SEP. When you call, you'll need to attest that you:

- Weren't eligible for Medicaid when you first applied because you live in a state that hasn't expanded Medicaid
- Weren't eligible for a Marketplace plan with tax credits when you first applied because your income was too low
- Had an increase in expected yearly income that now qualifies you for a Marketplace plan with tax credits

You should apply for Medicaid coverage, even if your state hasn't expanded

Even if your state hasn't expanded Medicaid, you should apply for coverage to see if you qualify. Each state has coverage options that could work for you—particularly if you have children, are pregnant, or have a disability.

Learn how to apply for Medicaid on http://www.Healthcare.gov.

Welfare: Temporary Assistance for Needy Families (TANF)

Federal government benefit programs can help people with a low income cover basic expenses like food, housing, and healthcare.

Temporary Assistance for Needy Families (TANF), also known as welfare, is designed to help families recover from temporary difficulties and move forward.

Financial Assistance Welfare or Temporary Assistance for Needy Families (TANF) provides cash for a limited time to low-income families working toward self-sufficiency. TANF may also offer non-cash benefits such as childcare and job training. Supplemental Security Income (SSI) provides cash to low-income seniors and low-income adults and kids with disabilities.

How do you qualify for TANF?

- All programs have income limits, meaning that your income must be under a certain level.
- Most programs require you to be a U.S. citizen or eligible non-citizen.
- Many programs have other state requirements like family size and financial resources.
- Households that include an adult who is not exempt are allowed to receive TANF or TAONF cash benefits for a maximum of five years in their lifetime.
- A family must include children under the age of 19 and earn a total gross income under 185% of the 2006 Federal Poverty Level.
- Applicants must participate in the TANF work program.
- Some tribal groups operate their own TANF programs.
    - Each state or tribal territory decides the specific eligibility criteria for financial assistance or other benefits and services.
- Each state TANF program is operated differently and has a different name.

- You must be a resident of the state where you are applying.

Learn more about who is eligible and how to apply for these programs at http://www.Benefits.gov or your state's social, human, or health services office.

What help is available?
If you qualify, you can get help with food, housing, home energy, childcare, job training, and more.

How to apply:
To signup for temporary benefits, you can apply at your local or county social services agency. Call your state TANF office for your local contact information. https://www.acf.hhs.gov/ofa/help

Other Assistance and Federal Services

- **AARP** (www.aarp.org): Advocacy group American Association for Retired Persons
- **American Foundation for the Blind** (www.afb.org/default.aspx) is dedicated to addressing the critical issues of literacy, independent living, employment, and access through technology for the ten million Americans who are blind or visually impaired.
- **U.S. Department of Veterans Affairs** (http://www.va.gov)
- **U.S. Housing and Urban Development** (www.hud.gov) provides all kinds of housing information and services, including housing for seniors.

Personal Finance *for* Real People

Legal Matters

Should You Loan to Family?

What do you do when a family member has financial difficulties?

You may have taken all the steps to get your financial house in order, but it's possible that you have family members who have not been so careful. Or perhaps you have a family member who is suffering financial hardship through no fault of their own—death in the family, loss of a job, sudden medical bills, or major car repairs.

You want to help, but should you? You need to guard not only your money, but also your family relationships.

If someone in your family comes to you requesting a loan, think carefully and make sure you have a thorough and frank discussion with them. Ask specifically why they need the loan. If it's for something that will improve your family member's financial situation (like college tuition, or help with the purchase of a home), you will probably feel better about making the loan. But think carefully about lending to a family member who has a history of poor financial decisions. It could be very likely you will never see that money again, and you will have damaged your family's relationship. Ask for a credit report (they can get one for free each year). Be clear about your financial situation and what your expectations will be if you decide to make a loan.

Proceed only if you feel reassured and confident that your loan will be paid back on schedule.

Only lend what you can easily—and without hardship—afford. Check your budget and your expenses to double-check your financial situation.

Decide now what you will do if your family member doesn't pay you back, and you have to collect on the debt. Your choices can range from getting nothing back—just writing off the whole experience—to trying to collect it yourself, all the way to going to court. Best to make that decision now before you go any further. If you decide that you will do your best to collect on the debt, if necessary, be sure to document your process and keep meticulous records.

Put it in writing! It seems like an inconvenience and unnecessary, but making a loan agreement formalizes the loan, and makes it a loan, not a gift. The IRS will want to see the loan document if they question your taxes, as will your tax preparer. Don't make the loan if your family member doesn't want to put everything in writing—remember that it IS your money at stake here. Nolo, http://www.nolo.com, is a good source for standard promissory note templates and information.

In your loan agreement, spell everything out: Who is borrowing and who is lending, the amount of the loan, the interest rate, payment amounts and dates of payments, and penalties for late or missed payments, or default of the loan.

Be sure to find out what the tax implications are for a loan to a family member. In some cases you may need to charge a minimal amount of interest to avoid tax complications for both of you (and to make sure the IRS views it as a loan and not a gift). The minimum is usually the current applicable federal rate (AFR). Find out more about it from the IRS website (http://www.irs.gov) under Index of Applicable Federal Rates.

Remember that once you've granted the loan, the process is in your family member's hands. It's not up to you how they handle the money, how they handle their finances, or their relationships. Think about how non-intrusive a bank loan is—once you get the loan, all the bank cares about is having you meet the payment schedule. Do, however, keep your communication lines open.

Loaning to a family member is never an easy decision, for either of you. But by following some reasonable guidelines, you can avoid trouble and hard feelings down the road.

When to Take Over Your Aging Parents' Finances

Those of us with aging parents or relatives will someday face a delicate and emotional decision: When to step in and help with their money management.

It could be as simple as helping them with their health insurance, Social Security, or Veterans benefits and paying bills, or as complicated as managing financial accounts or a trust.

Welcome to the caregiver generation!

How do you know when to step in?

- Are you finding unpaid bills, or second notices on utilities?
- Are they donating (with money they can ill afford) to dubious charities?
- Are they making excessive purchases from television shopping networks, online, or buying lottery tickets?
- Are they entering "contests" that charge a fee?
- Have they been the victims of a scam?
- Are they making duplicate bill payments?
- Do they have high credit card debt?
- Is their house less than clean?
- Have they had a fall or a lengthy illness? Dealing with their own health issues leaves less room for concentrating on financial matters.

As with most things, it's best to start your preparations in advance. Some things to check off your list first:

- Find out about tax credits and deductions for which you might qualify if you are caring for an aging parent.
- See what assistance programs your parent might qualify for, such as transportation services for elders, utility discounts, discounted basic telephone service, and more.
- Does your parent have long-term care insurance?
- Review and organize your parent's financial accounts, and make sure you have all their account numbers and passwords/PIN numbers. Also make sure you have the name and number for any financial advisors, tax preparers, and legal help. Be sure to get information on *all* their credit cards.
- Gather their important records and store in a safe place: Their will, birth certificate, marriage and death certificates, divorce paperwork, tax returns, insurance and benefits documents, Social Security cards, mortgage records or property deeds, auto titles, bank cards.
- Find out if they have a safety deposit box, or a safe. Know where the key is, or what the combination to the safe is. For a safety deposit box, you will want to arrange to be a co-signer so you can access it.

173

- Write down (or photograph) your parent's prescriptions and doctors, and any ongoing health conditions.

Now that you know just what your elder's situation is, you can get started with a plan to move forward:

- First of all, be gentle and respectful. Handing over one's independence is emotional and difficult, at best.
- Set up Durable and Health Care Powers of Attorney, giving you the right to make decisions and care for an incapacitated parent, to handle their finances, cash their Social Security checks and sell their house, if necessary. For more information on these legal documents and more, http://www.Kiplinger.com,
- If your parent does not already have a will, consult with legal help to put that in place.
- Set up an income and expense budget. If you're not comfortable with this, consult with a money manager.
- Establish an automatic bill pay system, either with each company or through the bank.
- Consider having their mail forwarded to you.
- If your parent is not managing their money well, think about loading a prepaid debit card for them each month. That will give them a measure of independence, while still making sure the bills can get paid.
- Evaluate whether your parent needs in-home assistance, for anything from simple cleaning to health care.

Get help! You don't have to figure this out alone. You may have local resources you can utilize. Look for:

- Resources for Aging, Disability, and Caregiving
- Offices on Aging
- Departments on Aging and Elder Services

There are also national organizations you can reach out to:

- The National Association of Professional Geriatric Care Managers, or Care.com for care assistance.
- The National Association of Senior Move Managers for when your parent or relative needs to relocate.
- The National Association of Elder Law
- AARP

The Consumer Financial Protection Bureau publishes a series of guidebooks: The *Managing Someone Else's Money* guides. The guides help you to be a financial caregiver by walking you through your duties as a financial "manager," how to deal with scams, and where to go for help.

The upside is that the aging baby boomer generation rejects traditional ideas of aging. They see retirement as a more active lifestyle, value independence (even in assisted living circumstances), and embrace technologies that keep their minds active and help them to stay socially connected.

Remember that the best time to start this discussion is while your parents or elders are healthy, competent, and self-sufficient. Your parents probably taught you about money management and responsibility—now it's your turn to return the favor. Just keep them involved in the discussion, and try to make is as low-stress as possible.

What to Do When a Loved One Dies

The loss of a loved one can be an overwhelmingly emotional time; a time in which you just don't feel up to taking care of everything you know is just waiting for attention. All you want to do is grieve.

But there are tasks that need to be done, and sometimes you may be the only one with either the authority or willingness to do them.

For many, having a checklist helps them move through a task and get in to the next one, until you've gotten through the entire list of responsibilities. Your family situation may call for additional things you need to take care of, or more elaborate or simpler arrangements.

But this list will give you a place to start.

Immediately

- Arrange for organ donation, if that is what your loved one wished. There will be someone on the hospital's staff to guide you through the process.
- Notify all immediate family. Also, if you don't know what your loved one's wishes were for burial or for a service, another member of the family might know.
- What funeral arrangements did your loved one want, if any? Certainly take that into consideration, but also consider what you can afford, what's realistic, and what will make the family satisfied.
- Choose a funeral home, if that is what the family's plan is.
- Notify all other interested parties: close friends, extended family, and employers.
- Did your loved one have pets? Make sure someone is taking care of them at least for this immediate time period.
- Secure your loved one's property. If you can, remove all cash, credit card information, extra keys, and valuables from their house. Make sure the home is locked up and the windows are secure, and that their car is parked legally and is locked. If you can, notify the landlord or property manager, and trusted neighbor.
- Have their mail forwarded to you, or to whoever will be handling it. Also stop newspaper delivery.
- Find your loved one's will, the original signed copy.

Before the funeral

- If you are having a funeral, meet with the funeral director, and go through the arrangements. You may have to make decisions, but they are experienced at leading people through all the considerations.
- Do not, however, feel you have to get as expensive an arrangement as the funeral director might be encouraging you to select.

- If your loved one did not leave enough money to take care of funeral expenses, and you don't feel like you can shoulder all the expenses, talk to the rest of the family. They may be able to contribute varying amounts. Also consider organizations your loved one may have been a member of: a church, a synagogue, a union, a professional organization, or the military. Any of those may be able to help you.
- If you loved one is being buried in a cemetery, arrange for a headstone.
- Get the family to help with all the various responsibilities of a funeral and any gatherings afterwards. They can cook or arrange meals, babysit, take care of pets, be pallbearers, speak at the funeral, design a program, water plants, or do any necessary shopping.
- Arrange a post-funeral gathering for family and friends.
- Notify everyone about the date, time, and address for the funeral and the post-funeral gathering.
- Prepare an obituary, if that is something your loved one would have wanted. If writing is not your strength, enlist another family member or friend. Don't include the date of birth (this could lead to identity theft). Check with the newspaper for pricing and deadlines.

After the funeral

- Keep track of the people who have sent cards, flowers, gifts, or provided services. You will want to thank them, or send thank you cards now.
- Get duplicate death certificates—about a dozen. Your funeral director should be able to help you with this.
- Meet with a probate attorney; they will guide you through the execution of the will, with the probate process, and with any financial concerns.
- Contact a tax preparer. A tax return will need to be filed for both your loved one and the estate.
- In cooperation with your probate attorney, pay any outstanding bills as they come in.
- Organize your loved one's records and find important documents you will need: birth certificate; recent tax returns; home ownership documents and title; automobile ownership documents, title, and registration; birth certificates for any children; insurance policies; stock certificates; marriage certificates and divorce papers; Social Security card.
- Find any serious valuables, provide a list to the probate attorney, and lock them up.

Notifications

Most of the following will require either an official death certificate, or a photocopy of a death certificate.

- Notify the Social Security Administration. Don't cash or deposit any payments received after your loved one's death. Ask Social Security about increased benefits for any dependents or a surviving spouse, and the one-time payment to your loved one's survivor.
- Notify Medicare: There should be contact information on the back of their Medicare card.
- Notify their health insurance company, if they had one.
- Notify any appropriate insurance companies: life insurance, disability insurance, homeowners or renters, automobile, etc.
- If your loved one had accounts with any financial advisors and/or stockbrokers, notify them and change ownership of the account.
- Did your loved one have a safety deposit box? If they did not leave a key, password, or have a cosigner, then probate court will have to order the box opened.
- Notify all your loved one's credit card accounts, and close them.
- Notify all three credit-reporting agencies: Equifax, Experian, TransUnion.
- Notify the DMV and cancel your loved one's driver's license.

- Cancel any online accounts, such as Facebook, and email accounts.
- Notify the loved one's election board.
- Cancel membership in any appropriate organizations.
- Notify utilities, and decide a date to cease service.

After probate closes

- With your family, decide what should be done with your loved one's belongings, and assign people to handle each disposal task—giving items to a family member or friend, Goodwill or other organization, selling items of value, etc.
- If your loved one owned their home, decide if it's going to be sold or if another family member will live there (they will have to purchase it or rent it).
- Decide who will become responsible for any pets your loved one had. If no family member wants them, go to a humane society or rescue organization, not the animal shelter.

It's a difficult, long process, happening right at a time when you are emotional and vulnerable. Just take it one task at a time, delegate jobs, and rely on professionals, and you'll get through this.

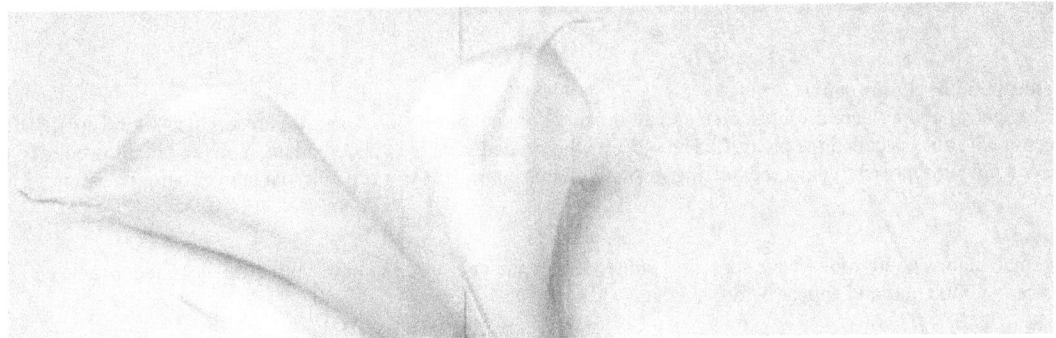

Handle Small Claims Court

Each state has its own small claims court system, and its own set of rules, procedures, and regulations. Be sure to research what's required in your own state before either appearing in small claims court, or pursuing a case in small claims court.

In general, here are some explanations and guidelines that are true in most states (but be sure to check your own state's requirements!). Your state may also have online materials or pamphlets you can pick up for more information.

What is small claims court?
It's a special court where disputes are resolved quickly and inexpensively. The rules are simple and informal. The person who sues is called the plaintiff. The person who is sued is called the defendant. You are not allowed to have a lawyer represent you at the hearing in small claims court. But you can talk to a lawyer before or after court.

In small claims court you can sue someone, someone can sue you, you can have your case mediated, or you can actually go to court and appear before a judge.

A good idea is to observe an actual small claims court hearing. You'll learn a lot just by watching the process, seeing how people act, and learning what is asked of them.

Who can use small claims court?
You can sue in small claims court if you are at least 18 years old, or if you are an emancipated child. If you are not mentally competent, or you are under 18 years old (and not emancipated), a judge will appoint a "guardian ad litem" to represent you in small claims court. A guardian ad litem is an adult appointed by the court to represent you ONLY in this specific case.

If you decide to sue:
Think first, though, if this is the right path for you. If you sue and win in court, the court cannot collect the money for you. Is the person you are suing able to pay, and will you be able to pursue the collection? If you want to sue a neighbor because the neighbor behaves badly, will suing make the neighbor behave better, or will it worsen your living situation? Courts cannot force good behavior. Will the time and money it takes to go to court be worth the likely outcome?

Assuming you are prepared to sue, there are certain facts to gather, forms to fill out, and requests to make.

- **Correctly name the defendant:** You must name the defendant exactly. If they have used different names, list those names you know as well, using "aka." If you have more than one defendant, or if it involves a company, you must name all parties and companies involved.
- **You must (and should) ask for payment prior to going to court.** Write what's called a demand letter (your court or state may have an online resource to help you write this), and send it to the future defendant. In many cases this will resolve the situation, and you will get paid. If not, attach a copy of the demand letter to your court papers, and bring a copy with you to court.
- **Find out which specific small claims court is the correct court in which to file your claim.** If you file your claim in the wrong court, the court may dismiss your case and you will have to refile in the correct court. If the time to file your case (the statute of limitations) has run out, you may end up losing your case. In general, you can file your claim in the court where the defendant lives or does business. But there are some exceptions to this rule, so do your research on your court system's website, or consult the court's small claims advisor.
- **Fill out your court forms.** Again, research your court's website for guidance, or consult the court's small claims advisor (at least ask the advisor to review your forms—your case will be dismissed if you have not provided the correct forms).
- **File your claim, and pay your filing fee.** This fee can vary—depending on your state and county, and how much you are suing for. Take your forms and fee payment to the small claims clerk. They will review your paperwork, take your payment, and assign you a court date.
- **Keep track of your court date!** If you miss it, your case will be dismissed.
- **Who will serve the defendant with their copy of the court papers and notice of the court date?** Check with your small claims clerk, your court's website, or your small claims advisor about how this happens.
- **Go to your court date prepared.** Practice what you are going to say. Have all your court filing paperwork with you. Also bring any evidence you may need to present. Bring three copies of each document (check with your court). Bring any witnesses you have with you.
- **If you win, you will need to collect your judgment** (the money awarded to you). The court will provide papers supporting this, but it will be up to you to pursue it. If you lose, you will need to pay your judgment.

If you are sued:
You still have options available to you:

- You can settle your case before trial, coming to an agreement with the plaintiff.
- You can try to prove you were sued in the wrong court.
- You can go to trial and try to win.
- You can sue the person suing you.
- You can just agree that you owe the money and pay the plaintiff.
- If you do nothing and do not go to your trial, you will "default" and the judge will enter a default judgment against you. The plaintiff will probably get what he or she is asking for plus any filing fees or other court costs related to the small claims case. If this happens, the plaintiff can legally take your money, wages, and property to pay the judgment.

There is, of course, much more to know about taking a case, or defending yourself in small claims court. Consult your state's small claims court website for more detailed information.

How Much Does It Cost to Go to Jail?

You're right, it hardly seems fair that you have to pay for the privilege of having your freedom taken away, especially if you haven't even been convicted yet, charged with a crime yet, haven't had your case tried yet, or are simply waiting for transportation to where you *will* go to trial.

However, just like everything else, there are costs involved, costs that you will have to pay out-of-pocket.

These costs, of course, vary depending upon your situation, the crime of which you are accused, whether you are facing state or federal charges, and what state you live in (or what state your crime occurred in).

Let's just cover pre-sentencing for now. The situation changes dramatically if you are convicted and have to serve time.

Bail
Bail is for those who are arrested and taken into custody:

- If you are arrested in the process of committing a crime.
- If you have an outstanding warrant and are picked up by the police, FBI, DEA, or Marshals Service.
- If you are stopped for one thing (the infamous broken tail-light, for example) and the police find indications that you are committing or have committed a crime.
- If you have been accused of a crime and charges are now being filed against you.

For some, especially non-violent, cases, the judge may grant you the possibility of paying bail instead of cooling your heels in jail until your case is heard. Bail is literally your get out of jail card. But it's not free!

The money that you deposit with court is your guarantee that you will show up at your court date. If you don't appear, the court will keep the bail you have deposited, and issue an arrest warrant.

Bail can be paid with:

- Cash or check for the full amount of the bail set.
- Property worth the full amount of the bail.
- A bond that you secure from a bail bondsman—the bond costs 10% of your full bail amount, plus an administrative fee. Some bondsmen may also require collateral.

You may also be released on your own recognizance—no money or security required.

The judge is the person who sets the bail amount, not your attorney (if you have one), not the prosecutor, not the bail bondsman. However, if your crime is relatively common, many jails have standard bail schedules. You can get out of jail quickly by paying the bail amount on that schedule, instead of waiting one to several days to see a judge at your arraignment.

Remember that bail is granted with certain requirements that you must follow: terms of release. The terms are specific for each case, usually along the lines of obeying all laws, not leaving the city or state, etc. If you violate those requirements, or don't show up for your court date, you will forfeit all money or property you have deposited as bail.

Securing an Attorney

You may or may not require an attorney, depending on your case. Frankly, though, it's better to have someone on your side who understands the system.

Depending on your needs, an attorney can cost you $200 - $600 an hour or more. Fortunately, law firms frequently have clerks who bill at a lower rate. How to find an attorney who is qualified for your case? By personal referral, or lawyer referral services. Be sure to meet with the lawyer before hiring them, and understand what their qualifications are and what their specific experience is. That first meeting should be free. Do NOT hire an attorney who wants to charge for that first meeting.

If you cannot afford an attorney (and many of us cannot), the court can appoint one for you. There is no cost for a public defender. Although they are in fact "real" lawyers, public defenders tend to be drastically overworked and underpaid. They do their best, but they will not be able to devote as much attention to your case as you might wish. If the court appoints a public defender to you, you are stuck with them. You may not change to another attorney without a *very, very* good reason. On the plus side, besides the fact that they are free, public defenders are there to see that justice is done. They most likely know everyone in your court system. They have access to the resources of the public defenders' office, including investigators. Talk to your public defender immediately after they are assigned, and see what similar experience they have. How many cases have they handled? What will be their strategy for your case?

Other Expenses

You will be responsible for your own transportation and parking to and from the courthouse, your attorney's office, and any other court required services. If you are required to be under medical or psychiatric care, you are responsible for those costs. If you need to provide any kind of documentation, you are responsible for the costs involved in securing those documents (court, city, county, state, or federal fees) and postage as well.

And all this is BEFORE you even get to trial, or serve your sentence!

Manage Your Money in Jail or Prison

Frankly, once you are in either jail or prison the only money you'll be able to control is that which you either earn working certain jobs or that which is sent to you by your family.

But let's look at it step by step. The processes are a little different between federal prison and state prisons and jail.

There are even differences between prisons in different states. To be certain what to do, you'll need to look up the website for the prison to which you've been assigned.

Prepare, prepare, prepare

You'll want to prepare as much as you can, gather as much information as you can, and take care of as much as you can before you arrive at your facility. A day or so before you arrive, mail yourself any important information—you won't be able to bring anything with you in person. Addresses, a copy of your marriage certificate if it's recent, your prescriptions, etc. You could even order books from Amazon, or subscribe to magazines, set to arrive after you do. Make sure you or your family puts money in your commissary account. *Do* try to take your recently filled prescription medications in with you.

FEDERAL PRISON

Important:

If you don't already know what prison you'll be sent to, check frequently to see if your name and ID number come up on the list. If you are already incarcerated, have your family member check. When you have your assigned location and your ID number, you (or a family member) can wire money into your prison commissary account. In some circumstances it can be in your account in a matter of hours, so it can be sent the morning of your projected arrival.

Why is this important? This way, you'll have money available to you as soon as you get processed in (intake). At some prisons they let you shop the commissary the day you arrive if you have funds available; at least they will let you shop on the next available commissary day. You will want to purchase shampoo, soap and soap holder, toothbrush and toothbrush holder, toothpaste, aspirin, stamps, a pad of paper, and a laundry bag to hold your commissary items each week, and anything else you will need to get through the week. If it's winter, get a sweatshirt, sweatpants, and thermal undergarments. If you can afford it, also get a plain t-shirt. Don't depend on the prison providing these basics—if they do, you may not want to use them.

Some money transfer companies will only deposit money into your commissary account once you have physically arrived at your prison, and once you've been checked in.

Read the instructions carefully for any money transfer   company you want to use.

How to Get Money into Your Account
Your family must wire money or send it electronically into your account. *Do not* show up with cash or a check. *Do not* let your family send cash or a check. Neither will be accepted. *Do not* send money directly to the prison—all inmate funds are processed through a national lockbox in Washington D.C.

Currently there are a couple of companies you can use:

MoneyGram: ExpressPayment allows you to send money electronically.

- Funds are received and processed seven days per week, including holidays.
- Funds sent between 7:00 a.m. - 9:00 p.m. EST are posted within 2-4 hours.
- Funds sent after 9:00 p.m. EST are posted at 7:00 a.m. EST the following morning.
- Your family will need to read the instructions carefully, and be prepared with the information required (prisoner's ID number, name at time of conviction, location, at a minimum).
- Money can be sent either online or at a MoneyGram location.
- The fees will probably be around $12.00.

Western Union: Your family can send funds electronically using Western Union's Quick Collect Program.

Western Union's procedures are similar to MoneyGram's, above.

- Payment can also be made over the phone. Call 1-800-634-3422 and choose option 2.
- If payment is made with a credit card, extra processing fees will apply; no fees apply if payment is made with a debit card.
- Fees can range dramatically, from $5.00 to $15.00.
- To send money to an inmate being held at a privately managed facility, contact the facility or contract operator.

Now then, just what can you use the money in your account for? Three things: Commissary, email, and telephone calls.

Commissary
What is commissary? A prison commissary is a store within a correctional facility, from which inmates may purchase products such as hygiene items, snacks, vitamins, writing instruments, etc. Spices, including those packaged with instant ramen noodles, are a popular item due to the bland nature of prison food.

This is not a physical store that you shop with a basket. You'll fill out a preprinted list of items, and on your designated commissary day you'll submit your list and after a while, collect your items. If you don't have enough money in your commissary account, you won't get everything on your "shopping" list. Be careful about this, because it really annoys the commissary correctional officer to have to spend extra time on your order. Figure it out ahead of time. The exact items carried at a commissary vary a bit from location to location. Sample commissary lists are available on the Bureau of Prison's website, http://www.bop.gov.

Email
The Trust Fund Limited Inmate Computer System (TRULINCS) application enables electronic messages to be exchanged between an inmate, their family, and the general public in a secure manner.

Funding for the email program is provided entirely by the Inmate Trust Fund, which is maintained by profits from inmate purchases of commissary products, telephone services, and the fees you pay for using TRULINCS. Yes, you pay a fee to be able to use email, and if you don't have the money in your account, you won't be able to use the system.

You must be approved to use the system. People who you want to communicate with must give their permission to do so.

Inmates' access to TRULINCS is controlled, and inmates do not have access to the internet.

Telephone
Each telephone call costs money, which comes out of your commissary account. You also have a limited number of calling minutes available for you to use each month. If you run out of money or minutes, you won't be able to use the telephone system until you deposit more money in your commissary account, or until after the first of the next month when you are granted more telephone minutes.

Remember that all calls are recorded and monitored. You may have to submit a list of phone numbers you'll be calling, and wait for them to be approved. Some prisons may still require that you call a landline only, not a cell phone—but frankly, it's difficult for them to tell, and fairly impractical in today's world.

The usual practice is to simply place your call (during designated free time hours), the person you are calling will acknowledge they understand the call is coming from a prison, and you can talk as long as you want—as long as you have the minutes and money available. It's best, once you've grown acclimated a bit, to plan out how many minutes you can use each day, or how often you plan to call the outside world. There are usually lines of inmates waiting to use the telephone, so be prepared to wait and to know your place in the line.

A set dollar amount per minute is deducted from your account at the end of the phone call. The FCC has ruled to reduce the cost of calls originating from prisons; that may take place this year…or not. Calls can range from approximately $2.95 to $3.15 for a 15-minute call.

You can also place collect calls, but they are hideously expensive, and cannot be received on a cell phone. Jails typically only allow collect calls, and they are also used more in state prisons.

STATE PRISONS AND COUNTY JAILS

While many procedures are the same—a prison is a prison, after all—state prisons frequently have a big advantage over federal prisons: They allow your family to send care packages from a select list of items, through a dedicated third-party company. We'll go into more detail on that in our next article.

Again, let's look at California. Every California state prison has a commissary that provides inmates a bank-type account for inmate monies and for purchasing things not issued by the prison.

Friends, family, or other people can add money to an inmate's commissary account using Western Union or by mail. If sent by mail, the funds have to be in the form of a money order made out to the inmate's full committed name (your name at the time of your conviction) and complete eight-digit register ID number. Use a post office money order, since all non-postal money orders processed through the national lockbox will be subject to a 15-day hold period, during which time you will not be credited the funds. Inconvenient! The Bureau of Prisons will

184

return to the sender funds that do not have valid inmate information if the envelope has a return address. *Do not* send cash. *Do not* send personal checks.

Email
In order to send email to an inmate at a state prison your family must follow a specific process to make sure that the email letter gets to you. Check with your facility to see what procedures they have, and if they offer email.

Your family can also use an instant-letter service (for a fee, of course) like Email to Inmates or LetterQuick. It's basically an email that gets printed out in the prison mailroom (don't count on quick service, certainly not instant service), and delivered to the inmate, most likely with regular mail call. The fees are inexpensive, and be aware that there's a character limit for each letter.

Telephone
Telephone services are basically the same as in federal prisons.

- In some locations, calling cards may be allowed, though I suspect that would only be for inmates in solitary. Calling cards, like stamps, could (illegally) be used in lieu of cash and for barter.
- Collect calls are more the norm in state prisons, though that mostly likely varies from state to state.
- In California, your family can also set up a prepaid account, AdvancePay, and not have to use the more expense collect call system. There is a set-up fee of about $5.00, and your family can manage the funds online. They can also use AdvancePay to fund your commissary account.

For more answers to more questions
An extremely helpful website is http://www.PrisonTalk.com. Run by families of inmates, and former inmates, it covers all topics within state and federal prison systems. It's a good way to prepare for entry into prison, a good support system for families with questions, and a good resource for almost-real-time coverage of incidents at prisons (lock-downs, etc.).

FCC VICTORVILLE
ALL ITEMS HAVE BEEN APPROVED BY COMMISSARY COMMITTEE

LAST NAME, FIRST NAME (NOMBRE)(REQUIRED)   REGISTER NUMBER (NUMERO)(REQUIRED)   UNIT (UNIDA)

___ PHOTO TICKET (LIMIT 10) #_____ 1.00
___ COPY CARD (LIMIT 3 CARDS) 150 COPIES 6.50

STAMPS
STAMP PURCHASES LIMITED TO A TOTAL OF $9.20
(20 1ST CLASS STAMPS OR THE EQUIVALENT)

0.01 _____ EA. *   0.20 _____ EA. *

FOREVER 0.46 _____ EA*.   1.00 _____ EA. *

ELECTRONICS
___ RADIO-SANGEAN DT-110CL	50.65
___ RADIO-SONY	39.65
___ SANSA CLIP+ MP3 PLAYER	69.20
___ SILICON COVER – MP	32.60
___ HEAD PHONES – Skully Chops	22.50
___ HEADPHONES – Skully Ink's	22.50
___ HEADPHONES - KOSS R/10 40	34.45
___ COLBY CVE31 Earbuds	7.70
___ WATCH- Timex Atlantis	37.50
___ WATCH – Timex ironman	35.75
___ WATCH –(REPL) BAND Ironman	11.45
___ WATCH – (REPL)BAND G-Shock	9.10
___ BATTERIES AAA	2.20
___ BATTERIES AA	2.20
___ *WATCH BATTERIES	2.60
___ *ALARM CLOCK	10.50
___ BOOK LIGHT –Mighty Bright	12.95

FOOT WEAR

Check Commissary Lobby for current
styles of athletic footwear and prices.

___ SHOWER SHOES –L XL XXL XXXL	6.50
___ SHOE LACES – WHITE	1.10
___ SHOE LACES – BLACK	1.10
___ GEL INSOLES 6/7 8/9 10/11 12/13	9.95

PRE-ORDER WORK BOOTS BY COP-OUT

ICE CREAM
Limit of 1 Pint
___ BUTTER PECAN K	1.85
___ COOKIES &CREAM K	2.10
___ COCONUT CREAMBAR (2)	0.80
___ MANGO BAR (2)	0.80

PRODUCE
___ YELLOW CHILES K (3)	1.85
___ JALAPENO WHEELS K (3)	1.80
___ PICKLES K (5)	0.70

CHIPS
Limit 7 Total
___ PLAIN /RIPPLED CHIPS K	1.40
___ NACHO CHEESE TORTILLA CHIP K/H	1.50
___ TORTILLA CHIP	1.50
___ PORK SKINS HOT & SPICY	0.80

SOFT DRINKS
Limit 1 Case (12pk)
___ COLA	3.45
___ FIESTA PUNCH	3.45
___ D. TWIST	3.45
___ MOUNTAIN RUSH	3.45

JUICE / WATER
Limit 6 each
___ REAL LEMON JUICE	.50
___ WATER 16.9OZ	.40
___ V-8 JUICE K	1.05

CANDY
___ SNICKERS K (5)	0.85
___ REDVINES K	1.35
___ OBSESSION DARK CHOCOLATE (5)	1.30
___ KIT KAT K (5)	0.85
___ M&M PEANUT (5)	0.85
___ REESES K (3)	0.85
___ TWIX (5)	0.85
___ S/F BUTTER SCOTCH	1.45
___ S/F CINNIMON BUTTONS	1.45
___ S/F FRUIT BUTTONS	1.45
___ S/F GUMMIE BEARS	1.45

SEAFOOD/MEATS
Limit 12 Total
___ TUNA REGULAR POUCH K/H	1.55
___ ALBACORE TUNA K	1.80
___ MACKEREL K	1.00
___ SALMON K	2.80
___ CHICKEN BREAST POUCH	2.85
___ TURKEY BREAST POUCH	3.85

___ BEEF SUMMER SAUSAGE (HOT)	1.70
___ BEEF SUMMER SAUSAGE	1.70
___ TURKEY SUMMER SAUSAGE	1.90
___ CHINESE STYLE SAUSAGE	2.20
___ SPAM POUCH	1.30
___ RIP & READY ROAST BEEF	3.45
___ CRAB MEAT	1.15
___ SMOKED CLAMS	2.05

FOODS
Limit 14 Total
___ CHILI NO BEANS	1.30
___ CHILI W/BEANS	1.50
___ REFRIED BEANS W/SPICES K/H	1.60
___ REFRIED BEANS K/H	1.60
___ VEG. CHORIZO BEANS K	1.40
___ WHITE RICE K	0.80
___ BROWN RICE K	1.25
___ CHEESE RICE K	1.70
___ VELVEETA MAC & CHEESE K/H	1.05
___ CORN TORTILLAS	0.60
___ FLOUR TORTILLAS	1.25
___ SHARP CHEDDAR CHEESE BAR	1.55
___ MOZZARELLA CHEESE BAR	1.55

KOSHER ENTREES
Limit 14 Total
Max Line Item Quantity = 4
___ CHEESE RAVIOLI ENTRÉE K	4.15
___ EGG PLANT PARMESAN ENTREE K	4.15
___ STUFFED CHICKEN W/RICE ENTREE K	5.20
___ TURKEY SHWARMA ENTRÉE K	4.55

SOUPS
Limit 24 Total
___ CHILI RAMEN	0.25
___ BEEF RAMEN	0.25
___ CAJUN CHICKEN RAMEN	0.25
___ CHILE SHRIMP CUP-O-SOUP	0.50
___ CHILE LIME CUP-O-SOUP	0.50
___ CHEDDAR CHEESE CUP-O-SOUP	0.50
___ VEGETABLE CUP-O-SOUP	0.50
___ THAI NOODLES	0.60

CONDIMENTS
Limit 5 Total
___ PEANUT BUTTER-CREAMY K	2.25
___ PEANUT BUTTER-CRUNCHYK	2.25
___ STRAWBERRYJELLY	2.80
___ HONEY S/F K	3.25
___ OLIVE OIL K	2.45
___ BARBEQUE SAUCE	2.00
___ SOY SAUCE	1.50
___ MAYONNAISE K	1.85
___ MUSTARD	1.05
___ SWEET RELISH	1.70
___ TAPATIO HOT SAUCE	1.25
___ EL PATO SALSA	1.80
___ GARLIC CHILI SAUCE K	1.35
___ SRIRACHA HOT CHILI SAUCE K	3.00
___ SWEET & HOT ASIAN HOT SAUCE	1.95
___ LOUISIANA HOT SAUCE	0.85
___ JALAPENO SQZ CHEESE	2.75
___ SHARP CHEDDAR SQZ CHEESE	2.80
___ GRATED PARMESAN CHEESE K	1.60
___ CREAM CHEESE	0.45

COFFEE
Limit 2 Each
___ TASTERS CHOICE K	4.20
___ COLOMBIAN COFFEE K	2.90
___ COLOMBIAN COFFEE DECAF K	3.45
___ CAPPUCCINO K/H	1.70
___ SUGAR SUBSTITUTE K	1.20
___ COFFEE CREAMER-ORIGINAL K	1.00
___ COFFEE CREAMER-FLAVORED K	3.75
___ TEA BAGS (NESTEA) K	4.20
___ HERBAL TEA (BIGELOW) K	3.50

CRACKERS
Limit 4 Total
___ SNACK CRACKERS K	2.00
___ SALTINE CRACKERS K/H	1.85
___ CHEESE CRACKERS K	1.85
___ HONEY GRAHAMS K	2.25

SPICES
Limit 5 Total
___ SALT & PEPPER K	1.55
___ ADOBO SEASONING K	1.95
___ MRS. DASH SEASONING K	3.35
___ SAZON CON CULANTRO	1.70
___ NORI & BONITO	3.75
___ SEASONED SALT K	1.25
___ GARLIC POWDER K	1.25
___ MINCED GARLIC K	1.25
___ MINCED ONION K	1.25
___ VEGETABLE FLAKES K	1.30
___ CAJUN SEASONING K	

MISCELLANEOUS DRINKS MIX
Limit 10 Total
___ ICED TEA W/PEACH K	1.85
___ HAWAIIAN PUNCH BERRY BLUE	1.50
___ HAWAIIAN PUNCH FRUIT JUICY RED	1.50
___ HAWAIIAN PUNCH GREEN BERRY	1.50
___ HAWAIIAN PUNCH BERRY BONKERS	1.50
___ GATORADE	0.90
___ HOT CHOCOLATE K	1.30
___ DRY MILK K/H	2.60

BREAKFAST ITEMS
Limit 8 Total
Max Line Item Quantity = 3
___ OATMEAL ASSORTED K	3.25
___ ROLLED OATS K	1.65
___ RAISIN BRAN K	3.15
___ FROSTED SHREDDED WHEAT K	3.15
___ CEREAL FLAVOR	3.15
___ CEREAL FLAVOR	3.15

SNACKS/PASTRIES
Limit 5 Each
___ MARIA COOKIES	0.65
___ CHOCOLATE CHIP COOKIES K	0.65
___ VANILLA CREMES COOKIES	1.40
___ HONEY BUN K	0.60
___ DANISH, FLAVORED K	0.65
___ OATMEAL CAKES	1.65
___ CORN NUTS (FLAVORED)	0.75
___ POPCORN, CARAMEL	1.00
___ POPCORN, CHEESE	1.20
___ PEANUT BUTTER WAFERS	1.80
___ SWISS ROLLS	1.80
___ POPTARTS	1.85
___ STRAWBERRY WAFER K/H	0.65

HEALTHY SNACKS
___ PITTED PRUNES K	2.80
___ PITTED DATES K	2.85
___ GOODIE GOODIE TRAIL MIX	2.80
___ HEAVENLY TRAIL MIX	2.80
___ TROPICAL TRAIL MIX	1.00
___ ROASTED/SALTED PEANUTS	2.20
___ MIXED NUTS K	2.85
___ CASHEWS	1.70
___ PISTACHIOS	2.30
___ SUNFLOWER KERNELS	0.95
___ NUTS SWEET & SPICY	1.65
___ GRANOLA HONEY NUT W/ALMOND	2.95
___ GRANOLA LOW FAT W/RAISINS K	3.35
___ GRANOLA WILD BERRY	3.35
___ GRANOLA BARS VARIETY	3.25

VITAMINS
Limit 1 Each
___ MULTI VITAMINS-COMPLETE	1.90
___ MULTI VITAMINS-NO IRON	1.90
___ VITAMIN C 250 MG	1.95
___ CALCIUM-OYSTER	2.05
___ VITAMIN B COMPLEX	2.50
___ VITAMIN E 200 IU	2.55

SOAPS
Limit 2 Total
___ IVORY	1.95
___ LEVER 2000	1.05
___ IRISH SPRING 3PK	2.90
___ DIAL ANTI BACTERIAL	1.00
___ NEUTROGENA SOAP	3.50
___ AMBI COMPLEXION BAR	2.20
___ TONE	0.90
___ DOVE	1.95
___ NOXEMA (FACIAL)	1.65

HEALTHCARE
___ HALLS COUGH DROPS – S/F	2.50
___ PAIN RELIEVER – ACETAMINOPHEN	2.35
___ IBUPROFEN	2.50
___ NAPROXEN	4.15
___ ASPIRIN	1.40
___ TUMS	2.25
___ ANTACID TABLETS	3.50
___ LIQUID ANTACID - LIKE MYLANTA	3.35
___ MILK MAGNESIA	2.15
___ PINK BISMUTH (LARGE)	2.95
___ RANITIDINE (ZANTAC)	3.85
___ OMEPRAZOLE (PRILOSEC)	13.00
___ NATURAL FIBER - LIKE METAMUCIL	6.50
___ VAPOR RUB	1.95
___ HEMORRHOID OINTMENT	3.70
___ HYDROCORTISONE 1%	1.45
___ ARTIFICIAL TEARS	2.15
___ ALLERGY TABLETS	1.30
___ LORATADINE 10MG (CLARITON)	2.40
___ FOOT POWDER 1%	1.55
___ ANTI-FUNGAL CREAM - TOLNAFTATE	1.70
___ TRIPLE ANTIBIOTIC OINTMENT	4.90

___ ORAL PAIN RELIEVER BENZOCAINE 20

186

	1.40
SALINE NASAL SPRAY	1.80
COUGH MEDICINE – TUSSIN	2.35
MUSCLE RUB	2.35
EAR WAX REMOVAL	5.20

DENTAL HYGIENE

COLGATE TARTAR*	3.00
COLGATE MAX*	2.90
COLGATE SENSITIVE	4.30
FIX-O-DENT	4.15
DENTURE TOOTHBRUSH	1.80
CLOSE UP TOOTHPASTE*	2.55
DENTURE CUP	1.95
DENTURE CREAM	4.15
TOOTHBRUSH (SOFT) *	0.90
TOOTHBRUSH (MEDIUM) *	0.90
MOUTHWASH CLOSE UP	2.20
MOUTHWASH AIM	2.35
DENTAL FLOSSERS, MINT	1.30
DENTAL FLOSS, UNWAXED	1.60
TOOTHBRUSH HOLDER	0.40

SHAVING PRODUCTS

MACH 3 RAZOR	12.35
MACH 3 REFILL	18.50
DISPOSABLE RAZORS	2.10
PERSONAL CARE SHAVE GEL	1.70
MAGIC SHAVE	4.25
AFTER SHAVE GEL	1.30
AFTER SHAVE GILLETTE	3.90
BUMP STOPPER	3.90
TOILETRIES BAG	5.50

SKIN CARE

OIL OF OLAY	12.30
BABY POWDER	1.50
SUAVE LOTION	2.20
VASELINE INTENSIVE CARE	4.90
JERGENS LOTION	5.25
LUBRIDERM LOTION	10.35
COCOA BUTTER CREAM	2.55
NOXEMA CREAM	1.65
AMBI SKIN CREAM	5.90
COCOA BUTTER STICK	1.80
ACNE CREAM 10%	1.30
SUNSCREEN LOTION SP30	2.70
CARMEX LIP BALM	1.60
LIP EX	0.85
PETROLEUM JELLY	1.20

ANTIPERSPIRANT / DEODORANT

MENNEN SPEED ACTIVE FRESH	2.25
DEGREE EXTREME BLAST	2.80
DIAL ROLL-ON ANTI-PERSPIRANT	1.40
SPEEDSTICK	3.20

SHAMPOO / CONDITIONER

PANTENE SHAMPOO	6.05
PANTENE CONDITIONER	6.05
SUAVE DANDRUFF SHAMPOO	4.95
ELEMENTZ DANDRUFF SHAMPOO	1.50
T-GEL SHAMPOO	8.00
SULFER 8 MEDICATED SHAMPOO	3.90
SULFUR 8 MEDICATED CONDITIONER	3.95
V05 STRAWBERRY SHAMPOO	1.70
V05 STRAWBERRY CONDITIONER	1.80

HAIR CARE

MURRAY'S POMADE	2.30
AFRICAN GOLD SUPER	4.40
TWIST & BRAID BUTTER	3.65
PINK OIL LOTION	4.60
INSTANT MOISTURIZER	2.15
STYLING GEL	1.65
SOFTEE CURL	2.20
BLUE MAGIC	3.50
3 FLOWERS	2.40
HAIR FOOD	2.40
PRO-LINE TEXTURIZER	4.10
SHOWER CAP	1.50
RUBBER BANDS, BLK	0.75
HAIR TIES	1.20
AFRO PIK	0.45
MILITARY CLUB BRUSH	2.75
PALM BRUSH	0.45
WIDE TOOTH COMB	1.45
DU RAG	2.35
DU RAG WAVE CAP	4.40
PERM REGULAR SOFT N BEAUTIFUL	7.90

TOILETRIES

COTTON SWABS	0.95
FINGERNAIL CLIPPERS	0.85
TOENAIL CLIPPERS	1.10
TWEEZERS	1.10
MUSTACHE SCISSORS	6.35
MIRROR	2.20
SOAP DISH	0.50

SPORTS & CLOTHING
See Notice #12

T-SHIRT-GREY	
LG___ XL___	3.25
2X___	5.05
3X___	7.35
4X___ 5X___ 6X___	11.70

D UP CORE SHIRT-GREY	
LG___ XL___ 2X___	10.95
3X___ 4X___	12.70
5X___ 6X___	14.00

TANK TOP	
LG___ XL___ 2X___	7.35
3X___	10.35
4X___ 6X___	12.70

BOXER BRIEFS	
LG___ XL___ 2X___ (2PK)	7.45
3X___ 4X___ 5X___ (2PK)	8.75

SWEAT SHIRT	
LG___ XL___ 2X___	14.20
3X___ 4X___	14.65
5X___ 6X___	22.10

SWEAT PANTS	
LG___ XL___ 2X___	14.20
3X___ 4X___	14.65
5X___ 6X___	22.10

D UP CORESHORTS-GREY	
LG___ XL___ 2X___	16.90
3X___ 4X___	17.95
5X___ 6X___	18.95

THERMAL SHIRTS LG___ XL___	5.85
2X___ 3X___ 4X___	7.80
5X___	8.45
6X___	8.45

THERMAL PANTS	
LG___ XL___ 2X___ 3X___ 4X___	7.80
5X___	8.45
6X___	9.10

CREW SOCKS 3PK	3.60
SPORT ANKLE SOCKS (LIMIT 5)	1.25
INSOLES	2.15
ARCH SUPPORT SIZE_____	13.00
KNEE SUPPORT M – XL	10.80
ANKLE SUPPORT M – XL	10.80
ATHLETIC SUPPORTER M – XL	4.25
BASEBALL CAP FITTED S/M, L/XL	10.35
BEANIE CAP- WOOL	6.50
HEAD BAND	1.70
MOUTH GUARD-SINGLE	3.40
MOUTH GUARD-DOUBLE	3.95
RAIN PONCHO	1.60
GLOVES-KNIT #	3.75
SCARF-KNIT #	5.20
HANDKERCHIEF	0.80
COMBINATION LOCK *	5.60
RACQUET BALLS	5.40
HAND BALLS	8.15
DUFFLE BAG – MESH	9.10
SEWING KIT	1.95

STATIONARY

ENVELOPES	1.60
CLASP ENVELOPE	0.25
LEGAL ENVELOPE	0.30
ADDRESS BOOK	2.15
DOCUMENT FILE FOLDER	1.40
PHOTO ALBUM	2.70
PHOTO ALBUM REFILLS	5.85
WRITING PEN*	0.25
PENCIL*	0.15
COLORED PENCILS	2.65
ART PAD	9.85
LEGAL PAD (YELLOW)*	1.40
NOTE PAD (WHITE)*	1.50
TYPEWRITER RIBBON*	4.55
LIFT-OFF CORRECTION TAPE*	3.80
COPIER PAPER	1.95
SPANISH/ENGLISH DICTIONARY	1.60
ENGLISH DICTIONARY	1.60
GREETING CARD	0.65
BUBBLE MAILER, MP3 RETURN	0.85

LAUNDRY ITEMS

GAIN ULTRA DETERGENT	5.85
SIMLINE DETERGENT	1.80
BOUNCE FABRIC SOFTENER (25 CT)	2.65
AIR FRESHENER-VANILLA	1.10
AIR FRESHENER-CHERRY	1.15
CLOTHES HANGAR	0.20

MISCELLANEOUS
Limit 1 Each

PLASTIC BOWL 10.3 CUP	5.50
SERVING BOTTLE 2QRT	4.70
INSULATED MUG 64 OZ	6.45
INSULATED MUG 20 OZ	2.50
CLEAR CUP 16 OZ	0.80
FORK	0.40
SPOON	0.40
CHARMIN TOILET PAPER	4.00
DOMINOES	5.50
PINOCHLE CARDS	2.45
PLAYING CARDS	2.45
CHESS SET	14.30
BANDANA-AZTEC RED/BLK	1.65
SUNGLASSES COPPERHEAD	5.20
SUNGLASSES LOCS	7.60
CROAKIES	5.20
MESH BAG	9.10

READING GLASSES (CIRCLE)	1.50

1.25   1.50   1.75   2.00   2.25   2.50

SCENTED OILS	5.20 - 6.50
See Lobby for Available Fragrances	

YARN	3.80
See Lobby for Available Colors	

SPACE SAVERS
Limit 10 Each

PEANUT BUTTER PACKET	0.40
STRAWBERRY JAM PACKET	0.20
GRAPE JELLY PACKET	0.20
HONEY PACKET	0.25
LEMON JUICEPACKET	0.10
TAPATIO SINGLE PACKET	0.15
SOY SAUCE PACKET	0.05
KETCHUP PACKET	0.10
MAYONNAISE PACKET	0.25
MUSTARD PACKET	0.10
CHEESE PACKET	0.45
JALAPENO CHEESE PACKET	0.45
CREAM CHEESE PACKET	0.40
SKIN LOTION, CLEAR (1)	0.95
SHAMPOO, CLEAR (1)	1.25
DEODORANT, CLEAR (1)	0.85

NOTICE

1. PLEASE WRITE LEGIBLY AND ENSURE YOU MARKED THE CORRECT ITEMS.

2. ALL SALES FINAL AFTER DEPARTING SALES WINDOW.

3. CHECK COMMISSARY BULLETIN BOARD FOR PRICE / PRODUCT CHANGES.

4. K - DENOTES ITEM IS KOSHER

5. H - DENOTES ITEM IS HALAL

6. # - DENOTES LOCAL USE ONLY

7. ( ) - DENOTES LIMITS

8. NO CHANGES ALLOWED AT WINDOW.

9. NO ADD-ONS AT WINDOW.

10. ITEM LIMITS ARE SUBJECT TO CHANGE DUE TO AVAILABILITY.

11. SPECIAL SIZE CLOTHING, SHOE SIZES UNDER 7.5 AND EXTRA WIDE WIDTHS MUST BE ORDERED BY COP-OUT .

12. COMMISSARY RESTRICTION IS LIMITED TO $25.00 PER MONTH. HYGIENE ITEMS, OVER-THE- COUNTER MEDICATIONS, STAMPS, BATTERIES, AND STATIONARY MAY BE PURCHASED. LIMIT 1 ITEM EACH WITH THE EXCEPTION OF STAMPS.

_____
INMATE SIGNATURE (FIRMA) (REQUIRED)

Sending Mail to Prisons or Jails

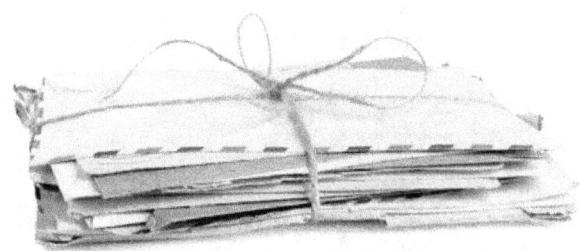

Regulations for receiving mail in and sending mail to prisons and jails differ a bit: Federal Bureau of Prisons has its own set, as do state prisons, county jails, and city jails. Usually, what you see on television and movies is not true. Packages and even regular mail are inspected and must meet certain requirements, going in AND going out.

Here's an overview of the three main incarceration systems, and their communication requirements and policies:

BOP (Federal Bureau of Prisons)
Probably the strictest.
All mail—letters and packages—is opened, often read, and always inspected for contraband.

What you *can send*:

- Letters
- Paperback books
- Magazines
- Magazine clippings
- Calendars

What you *can send* through a third party:

- Hardcover and paperback books, and calendars, shipped directly from Amazon, a bookstore, or the publisher
- Newspaper subscriptions sent directly from the newspaper
- Magazine subscriptions sent directly from the magazine

What you *cannot send*:
Basically, anything else, including:

- Newspaper clippings or sections of a newspaper
- Hardcover books
- Pornography
- Stickers
- Stamps or money
- CDs

Inmates are not allowed to receive mail from another currently incarcerated person, or one on supervised release. All phone calls are recorded and listened to by staff, and all mail checked and read. For more information on communication policies, check the Bureau of Prisons' website, http://www.bop.gov.

State Prisons
Check your own state's prison system for specific details. For this example, we'll look at the California Department of Corrections system. All mail—letters and packages—is opened, often read, and always inspected for contraband.

Packages:

- Less restrictive: You can send quarterly care packages from a variety of approved vendors on http://www.cdcr.ca.gov.
- You can send a wide variety of items: from cosmetics and clothing, to entertainment electronics—even televisions—and food.
- Packages have a weight limit of 30 pounds, and can only be sent once a quarter.
- Books, magazines subscriptions, newspaper subscriptions from the publishers or approved vendor
- Packages and mail may be inspected.
- Items available for purchase may vary depending on the security level and location of your inmate.

Mail:
Inmates are not allowed to receive mail from another currently incarcerated person, or one who has been released from prison during the previous year. Letters are restricted to fewer than 10 pages

What you *can send*:

- Photos may be sent, as long as you send fewer than 10 in one envelope, and sizes no larger than 8" x 10"
- Children's artwork
- Drawings
- Articles cut from newspapers and magazines

What you *cannot send*:

- Books, magazines, newspapers directly to an inmate
- Glitter or stickers (even stickers attached to the letter)
- Anything else

For more information on communication policies, check on http://www.cdcr.ca.gov.

County Jail
This example is from one of Los Angeles County's detention centers.

What you **can send**:

- Purchased care packages from approved vendors on http://www.accesscatalog.com
- Pre-paid calling cards

- Normal letter mail
- Maximum of five photographs (each photograph on a collage is included in this count and measured separately)
- Photographs or computer generated pictures that are a minimum of 3"x 5" and a maximum of 4" x 6"
- Paperback books from a bookstore or Amazon or the publisher; no more than 3 per week
- Magazine subscriptions sent from the magazine; no more than 3 magazines per week

What you *cannot send*:

- Hardcover books
- All envelopes and paper that have debris and/or any illegal substances, perfume/cologne, lip stick, or dried liquids.
- Food or cosmetic items
- Blank envelopes (with or without postage attached)
- Envelopes with metal clasps
- Postage stamps that were not used to mail package
- Envelopes with gang or suggestive drawings/artwork
- Copyright material (this includes printed song lyrics; book passages; articles)
- Cash, personal or second party checks, payroll checks, out of state checks
- Money order exceeding the $200 limit
- Blank money orders (money orders must be signed and made payable to the inmate)
- Out of state money orders (must be from a U.S. Postal Office)
- Greeting cards: that play music; plastic; blank; tri-fold; larger than 6"x 9"; pop up style; 3D style; include ribbons and/or bows; have been altered. Postcards larger than 6"x 9"
- Photographs or pictures that depict full or partial nudity; suggestive; depict gang tattoos or hand gestures
- Picture in picture photographs
- Photographs of headshots
- Identification cards or facsimiles
- Photographs that depict inmate for whom the mail is intended
- Paper clips, staples, pens, pencils, glitter, stickers, glued or gummed labels
- Rosary beads, balloons, string bracelets or jewelry items
- Lottery tickets or pre-paid telephone cards
- Any type of tape on letters
- Anything of a sexual nature

It goes without saying:
We will say it anyway because people *still* think they can get away with it: Unless you also want to land in prison *and* give your inmate additional time to serve, as well as a move to a more secure facility, **do not send** (or discuss on the phone or in an email):

- Escape plans
- Information or material that is a potential or current threat to another person
- Discussion of a future criminal act
- Plans to disrupt the security of the prison
- Coded messages
- Maps of the prison or surrounding area
- Gang-related information, comments, or photographs
- Fake IDs or photos of fake IDs

- Photos of nudity or sexual conduct
- Drugs

Addressing your mail:
When sending mail to an inmate in any system, be sure to do the following to ensure your letter gets delivered to your inmate:

- Write legibly, or print out your envelope
- Use your inmate's full name and ID number (in jails it may be a booking number)
- Include the name of their specific facility
- And the full address of the prison
- Remember to follow the prison's guidelines on the kinds of envelopes that may be used

Communication with the outside world, and with friends and family, is an essential part of your inmate's reintegration into society upon release, as well as keeping essential personal connections alive during incarceration. Don't be intimidated by the various procedures—they are all very easy to check off once you have the system down. In fact, make a checklist or calendar of what you need to do, if that would work best for you. Communication with loved ones and friends, and the outside world is one of the things that keep inmates going. Mail call is the highlight of the day! Keep at it!

Making a Will

What's the hardest part about writing a will? *Actually sitting down and writing it.* After all, it's usually not that pleasant to remind of one's mortality, and that life won't go on forever.

Nevertheless, it's a formality that must be done. Follow the steps below and your will should be finished before you know it!

Do you need a lawyer, or should you use online software? Unless you are upper-middle class, with complicated property and investment holdings, you should be fine using a legal online website to write your will. You may also be able to find discounted or free legal aid to help you with it.

Who will be your beneficiaries? Unless your family is complicated, and unless you have no family at all, it should be fairly easy to decide who will inherit what. There will be a place to identify beneficiaries on the will form.

Who will be the executor of your will? The executor's job is making sure the wishes in your will are carried out. You'll need to select someone responsible and willing to undertake the task. The best option is a neutral party, such as a bank or an attorney.

Will the executor receive compensation? If you choose a bank or lawyer as your executor, there will be a fee involved, which is usually between 2% and 4% of your estate's assets. If you want to choose a family member or friend, be clear about whether they'll be paid and, if so, whether it will be an hourly rate or a percentage of assets. Closing an estate can be a complicated job, and it's worth it to choose someone who knows what they are doing.

Who will be your children's guardian? You are not required to get permission from your friend or family member before appointing them guardian, but it's a good idea to ask them ahead of time. If they decline the responsibility when the time comes, a court will choose your children's guardian.

Be specific: If you want specific belongings to go to specific people, include that in your will. And if someone in your family isn't going to receive anything, make note of that, too—the implication could be that you forgot about them, and your heirs could be challenged in court.

What if you want to say more? Attach a personal letter to the will if you want to go into more detail, for example to your children or to their guardian.

Do you need witnesses? In a word, yes. As well, in many states, the witnesses can't be people who stand to inherit anything in the will. Your witnesses also need to be at least 18 years old. They should be people who will be able to testify in court if your will is challenged. You may need two or three witnesses, depending on the state you live in. It sounds easy enough, but remember that unless the will is signed absolutely correctly, it will be declared invalid, and at that point there will be nothing you personally can do about it.

Where should you keep your will? The best places are either a bank safety deposit box or a fireproof safe at home. Keep copies elsewhere, and make sure someone you trust knows where to find the original and any other important papers and passwords.

Should you update your will? It's a good idea to think about your will every few years and/or after any major life changes. It won't take long, and you'll know it will be executed exactly how you want it to be.

Why a Power of Attorney and Health Directive Are Important

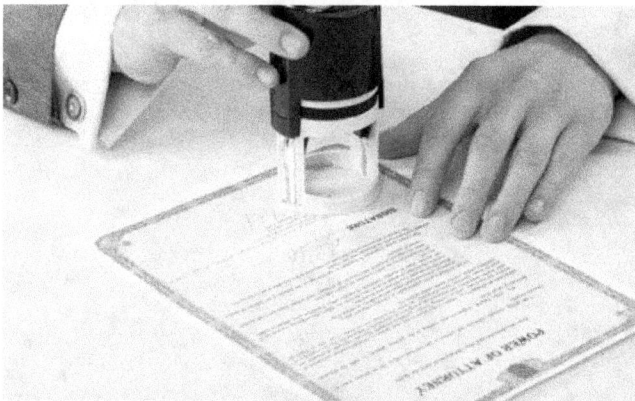

There are actually two types of Power of Attorney: one for financial matters, and one for health matters.

Let's see what the differences are, what they do, and why you should have both:

Durable Financial Power of Attorney

This is basically an easy way to legally have a person of your choice (your "agent") manage your finances if you are incapacitated and unable to make decisions. Without it, your family would have to go to court to petition for management of at least some of your affairs.

You have choices about when the Durable Financial Power of Attorney goes into effect, and you can specify those in the document:

- When you are traveling
- When you are incapacitated and cannot make decisions or physically manage your business matters
- When a doctor declares you incapacitated

Make sure you file a **Durable** Financial Power of Attorney, or else it will cease to be in effect once you actually are incapacitated. You can also have a simple Financial Power of Attorney if you just want someone else to manage your affairs while you are traveling, or ill but not incapacitated.

You also have choices about how much power and control your agent will have:

- Over all your finances
- Paying your bills
- Filing your taxes
- Handling your investments
- Collecting your Social Security and any other benefits
- Running your business, and/or handling your properties
- And more

Check on your own state's regulations, but in almost all states all you have to do is fill out the Durable Financial Power of Attorney form, and sign it in front of a Notary Public. If your agent is going to manage property that you own, file a copy with the local lands record office.

Some financial institutions have their own versions of Durable Financial Power of Attorney forms that they may want you to fill out as well. It's not legally necessary, but it will save your agent and family a lot of time and headache to do so. It's always a good idea to ask.

The Durable Financial Power of Attorney ends upon your death. If you have someone specific who you want to handle your estate and funeral details, you need to put that in your will. It will also end if: you revoke it; you get divorced; a court revokes it; your named agent is not available.

Durable Power of Attorney for Health Care
Similar to the Durable Financial Power of Attorney, the Health Care version allows you to assign an agent to handle your medical treatment and health care decisions. Without this, doctors, distant relatives, or even the court would make decisions about your care.

There are two kinds of documents in which you can specify an agent for your health care, and what care you wish to have, or not have. It's a good idea to have both.

- **Living Will**
    - A written statement detailing the type of care you want (or don't want) if you become incapacitated. It's not related to your regular will—it's actually not a will at all. It's simply a form in which you document your health care preferences.
- **Durable Power of Attorney for Health Care**
    - In this document, you appoint someone you trust to be your health care agent (sometimes called an attorney-in-fact for health care, health care proxy, or surrogate) to make any necessary health care decisions for you and to see that doctors and other health care providers give you the type of care you wish to receive.

You must be a legal adult and of sound mind in order to make a Durable Power of Attorney for Health Care or a Living Will.

You can purchase Power of Attorney forms from Nolo Press, http://www.nolo.com.

Personal Finance *for* Real People

Employment Topics

Filling Out a Job Application

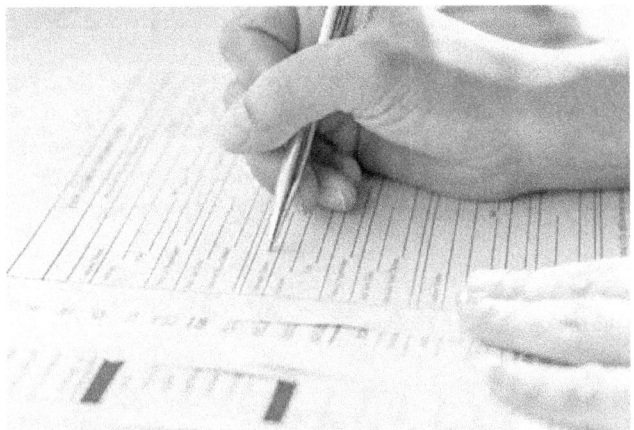

If you've never filled out an employment application before it can be daunting—all those questions! And even if you have, there can be pitfalls, as well as ways to make your application more effective.

Here are some suggestions to help you get that job:

Present yourself in a positive light. If you feel like you're not worth it, that impression will seep through into your application and interview. Smile, be polite, be positive, be respectful, and dress appropriately.

It's important to be sure that you are dressed neatly and have a professional appearance when you inquire about applications. You should dress up a bit more than would be expected in your target job.

Always be polite and show respect for any receptionist or clerk that you speak to. They may have the power to decide if you should be considered for any job openings, or if they should pass on your application. Smile warmly, look the person in the eye as you greet them, don't mumble, and be enthusiastic.

Plan out what you're going to say ahead of time when you ask for an application. If you are nervous about this, try practicing with another person. Prepare a short 10 - 15 second introduction requesting a job application, mention your interest in working with that employer, and be sincere. Don't flirt or joke around. Be prepared for a casual follow-up question like, "why do you want to work here?" or "do you have any similar experience?"

FILLING OUT THE APPLICATION

Practice filling out an application so you get familiar with the questions and information needed. You'll be more comfortable when the time comes to fill an application out for real. If you can, practice filling it out at home.

Neatness and legibility counts. After all, you want your prospective employer to be able to read your name and phone number in order to contact you! Have someone with nice handwriting fill out your applications with you if you have really terrible handwriting. Take it slow—if you try to rush, your writing will get sloppier.

Read through your application and check for spelling and grammar mistakes. Always have someone else review it—they will catch things you have missed.

Show your prospective employer that you can follow directions, and that you are detail oriented, by filling in all sections of the application form. If there's a question that is not relevant to you, just write N/A (not applicable). Review all the questions carefully to make sure you understand what is asked for.

Emphasize the job responsibilities of your past jobs or activities that are most relevant to the job for which you are applying. Do you have experience in customer service, even if it's in a different field? Do you have specific experience from school, from volunteering, or from your jobs in another country? They all count, so include them.

Include any awards or special recognitions you may have received, as well as any organizations you were active in or helped to found.

Make a copy of the application so it will be easier to fill out other applications.

Large retail employers like Target, Wal-Mart, and most supermarkets, may have hiring kiosks instead of paper applications. Sit down, log in, and fill out the application completely. Be sure you have all the necessary information with you.

GATHERING YOUR PERTINENT INFORMATION
Gather all the information you need to fill out the job application:

- **General Information:**
  - Name
  - Address, city, state, zip code
  - Phone number
  - Email Address
  - Social security number
  - Proof of eligibility to work in the United States
  - An employment certificate if you are under age eighteen
  - Have you been convicted of a felony within the last five years? *(Information about convictions varies based on state law)*
  - School(s) attended, degrees, graduation date
  - Certifications
  - Skills and qualifications
- **Employment History** *(for both current and prior positions)*
  - Employer
  - Address, phone, email
  - Supervisor
  - Job title and responsibilities
  - Salary
  - Starting and ending dates of employment
  - Reason for leaving
  - Permission to contact previous employer
- **References**: Have three references ready
  - Name
  - Job title
  - Company
  - Address, phone, email
  - How you know them
- **Availability**: When you could start the job and the days/hours you are available:
  - Days available
  - Hours available
  - Date you are available to start work

Certification

At the end of a job application there is usually a certification that you must sign and date:

I authorize the verification of the information listed above. I certify that the information contained in this employment application is accurate. I understand that false information may be grounds for not offering I authorize the verification of the information listed above. I certify that the information contained in this employment application is accurate. I understand that false information may be grounds for not offering employment or for termination of employment at any point in the future.

By signing the certification you are attesting to the truth of the information you have included on the job application. If the application is online, you will click a box to acknowledge that you are submitting complete and accurate information. That checked box counts as your signature.

OTHER ISSUES

Check your phone. You will need to list your phone number on the application, so be sure that the voice mail message on your cell is suitable for an employer to hear. Check messages regularly so you don't miss any calls from employers.

Check your social media. In this day and age, employers WILL check your social media activity. So make sure your posts are clean, not embarrassing, not in bad taste, and not offensive.

Follow up on your submitted application. When you have submitted a job application but haven't heard from the employer, follow up with them. Stopping back in, or telephoning, to check on the status of your application will show that you are really interested in the job. Even if you don't get the job you applied for, the employer will be more likely to keep you in mind for future jobs.

Tips to Ace That Job Interview

Interviewing successfully with a company is much more than just showing up. Factors like promptness, neatness, ability to speak clearly, and being able to answer questions on the fly, all contribute to the impression you give to your potential employer.

Research

The first tip starts even before you show up for your interview. Before you walk through the door, do your research on the company, the position for which you are applying, and even the hiring manager or whoever is interviewing you. Showing that you took the trouble to understand the company before the interview will make a very positive impression. You'll be able to make your responses to questions apply to the company and to the open position.

How to do this research? Review the company's website, Google the company for any news stories or articles, find out the company's competitors, products, and locations. Look up professional associations for the company's industry. And become familiar with the industry, if you are not already.

Resources:

- Hoovers
- Bloomberg
- *Forbes* America's Largest Private Companies List
- *Inc.*'s Fastest Growing Companies in America

To research the open position, peruse the jobs the company has listed, and access an organization chart if you can. If the job you are applying for is, say, IT Tech 3, you will know there are at least two levels above you.

To research your interviewer, again look for their name in the company research you do, look them up on LinkedIn, and even Google them.

Use your research to prepare a few knowledgeable questions about the company and its culture, management style, organization, and even growth plans or successful product launches.

Practice, Practice, Practice
Look up the most commonly asked interview questions (you can Google this as well), and practice answering them. If you can, don't just do it in your head, have someone help you by interviewing you.

The most difficult questions are the most open-ended: Where do you see yourself five years from now? What's your biggest fault? How would you define success? Develop answers to these, because you'll be sure to be hit with at least two or three in the interview.

Don't forget your accomplishments. If you performed well in your previous job, tell a specific story as an example. Keep it short, but make sure it shows how well you did, without simply bragging.

Dress Appropriately
Dress for success, and dress so that you fit in with the company. If you can, visit the company, or the parking lot as people leave at the end of the day. You want to dress like the people you see, but perhaps a little nicer.

It's always better to be overdressed than under. Make sure your clothes are clean and wrinkle-free; that they fit you; that they are not sexy; and keep jewelry and make-up to a minimum.

Don't eat prior to going in for the interview, and in fact, brush your teeth first.

Don't Be on Time: Be Early
Arrive about 15 minutes early for your interview. You may have to wait longer, but it gives you a chance to relax a bit, observe the company, be calm when you go in to the interview, and be available if the interviewer is ready early. A good first impression!

Be polite and greet each person you meet. When your interviewer arrives, stand, make eye contact, and have a firm, dry handshake.

Check Your Bad Habits
This is hard to see by yourself, so ask a friend to help you. Do you unconsciously interrupt the other person? Remember not to slouch, chew gum, fidget, hold your hand in front of your mouth, mumble, stare off into the distance, touch your face, or any other potentially annoying mannerism.

You want to make eye contact, sit up straight, nod, and show that you are paying attention, and that you are actively listening.

Thank Your Interviewer
As your interview closes, thank your interviewer for their time and interest, and get their business card if you can. If not, make sure you have their name and title. Also thank anyone else who participated in your interview.

After your interview, send a thank-you email, and mail a thank-you note to each person. Check your spelling, especially for their names and titles! Courtesy, thoughtfulness, and thoroughness will make you stand well above the crowd of applicants.

This may all seem like a lot of trouble, but that's exactly what the interviewer is looking for. They want to hire someone who will make a lot of effort at his or her job, be detail-oriented, self-starting, and not a human resources nightmare. The more effort you put in to the interview process and follow-up, the greater positive results you'll see.

Background and Credit Checks

Have you applied for a job lately, and had your potential employer do a criminal background check? You are not alone: According to a study by the Society for Human Resource Management, almost three-fourths of hiring companies run background checks for at least some job applicants.

Let's face it, personal data is more and more easily accessible. With that wealth of information, many new data providers have jumped into an eager market.

And not just for criminal or sex offender background checks; credit checks are increasingly being requested for job applicants and for rental applicants.

What can you do about it?

First be aware:
Not all data providers are reliable or accountable. Many of these companies have started, and conduct themselves, with no government oversight. They buy data, from a wide variety of sources, without being concerned if the collection is legal, accurate, or even for the correct person.

Sometimes the information itself may be flawed. Names can be confused—a person with a similar name and a criminal record can leave you without that job offer. A misplaced digit in your Social Security Number can lead to incorrect information. A settled dispute regarding a debt may not have been cleared off your credit history. Past minor offences can suddenly show up categorized as major crimes, or sealed records suddenly are unsealed. Arrests that did not result in convictions may also show up on criminal background checks.

Know your rights:
Make sure you know what is legal. More and more cities and states are looking at regulating this issue. In San Francisco, for example, employers may no longer use the results of background and credit checks as the sole reason for not hiring an applicant.

And in Hawaii and Oregon, employers may ask about and consider criminal convictions less than ten years old that are rationally related to the duties and responsibilities of the job (banking, for example). Employers must first make a conditional offer of employment before running the background check. The conditional job offer may be withdrawn if the applicant has a conviction record rationally related to the job.

You must give written permission to allow another person, even a potential employer, to request your credit report. If you are denied employment as a direct result of your credit report, the potential employer must give you a copy of the report and let you know you have the right to challenge it. For more information from the Small Business Administration visit http://www.sba.gov.

If you have declared bankruptcy, it will show up on your credit report. However, Federal law prohibits employers from using that as a reason for not hiring.

Take action:
Review your credit report at least annually (it's free!), especially if you are about to need it for a job or rental application. Take action to correct any mistakes.

If you are denied employment or housing, ask to see the supporting information collected about you. Check for errors, and make sure your potential employer or landlord knows the truth.

Remember that errors are common, and more and more companies are requesting background checks of one kind or another. It's up to you to protect your rights, and make sure information reported about you is correct.

How to Decide on Your Tax Withholdings

```
                                    M /02
nings Information      Current
                       4,389.30
nal Gross                  0.00
uctions                    0.00
itions                     0.00    Year to Date
rtime
     EARNINGS TOTAL     4,389.30       5,277.30
                         351.14         418.18
-Taxable Gross         3,971.12       4,859.12
able Gross
```

```
atutory & Other Deductions  Current  Year to Date
                             311.17        311.17
eral Withholding               0.00      *****
litional Federal Withholding 135.96        135.96
ite Withholding                0.00      *****
litional State Withholding     0.00         55.06
3DI                           62.67         75.55
iicare                         0.00          0.00
iicare Buyout                  0.00          0.00
ate Disability Insurance     351.14        351.14
RS                             0.00          0.00
RS                             0.00
     Retirement               67.04          0.00
```

When you earn income, you owe taxes: true for most of us. How much you pay in taxes is determined by how you fill out your W-4 form (you've filled one out for each job you've had). Your employer will deduct taxes based on the number of allowances you claim on your W-4.

This is fine if you're a standard taxpayer who files as a single person, has one job, and claims a standard deduction. But if you don't fit into the standard category—and many of us don't—it's likely that you are having too much or too little tax withheld.

The trick is finding the spot where you don't owe taxes at tax time, *or* get a big tax refund. Yes, it's nice to get that big check in the spring, but when you have too much money withheld from your paycheck (resulting in your refund) you end up giving the government an interest-free loan. Wouldn't you like to take home more money in each paycheck instead? And you certainly don't want to be penalized by the IRS for owing *too* much tax at the end of the year (yes, they can do that!).

How do you know how many allowances to claim?
Worksheets come with the W-4, and they are kind of helpful. You can also get detailed and complicated instructions in the IRS's publication 505. There's also an IRS online withholding calculator—it might take some time to go through the questions, but it depends on which way is easiest for you to understand the information. The more allowances you claim, the less tax is withheld. Your easiest allowance is 1, for yourself. You also have the option of simply putting the total dollar amount you want deducted on Line 6/Additional Withholdings on your W-4.

Pay attention to your W-4 through the year
The solution is to pay attention to your W-4 both when you start your job, but also whenever you have a life change. Several common life changes and events can change your tax liability. You'll want to adjust your withholdings when any of these occur:

- You get a second job
- You get married
- You get divorced
- Your spouse gets a job
- You and/or your spouse have a significant change in income (up or down)
- You are unemployed part of the year
- You have or adopt a baby or other dependent

It's easy to make adjustments to your withholding allowances
Calculate your new allowances by using one or more of the methods detailed above.

- Tell your employer you need to change your withholding allowances, and ask for a new W-4.
- Fill it in with your new allowances. You can claim as many as are warranted by your specific situation.
- Turn it in to your employer.

You can adjust your W-1 any time you want during the year. Remember though, that adjustments made toward the end of the year will have less impact on your taxes for that year.

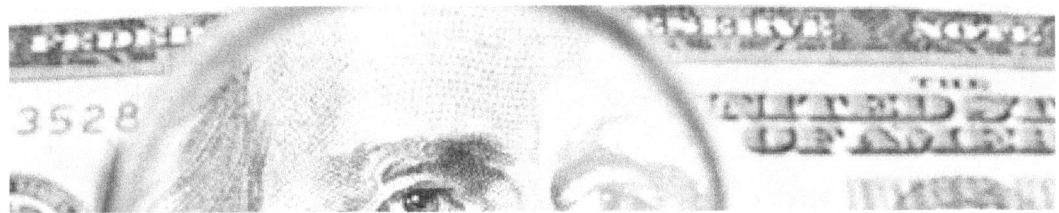

Your New Job

Congratulations! You just got a new job! There were other applicants, and they picked *you*—now how do you keep that positive momentum going?

For your first few months on a new job, you are basically, and perhaps legally, on probation. Your boss and co-workers are waiting to see if you are a positive addition to the company, if they can count on you, if you are responsible, and if you can work with the rest of the employees. They are also waiting to see if you can learn quickly, if you are curious and interested, and if you respect the company, the managers, and your coworkers.

Sounds like a tall order? Not really. Remember, they hired *you* for a reason. You just need to remember the basics:

Minimum: Show up to work on time.
Better: Get there at least a little early. Ask a co-worker to show you where something is, to explain a part of a job, to tell you about the company's customers, and just get to know your co-worker and the company. *This does not include gossip!*
Worse: Arriving late more than once. And that once should have a very good reason.

Minimum: Don't leave before your co-workers do. Spend your first few days observing the company's work patterns, and when your co-workers arrive and depart.
Better: Don't leave until your boss does. If that seems undoable (and maybe creepy in some situations), just check in with your manager before you leave, and see if there's anything else that needs taking care of that day. If there is, handle it.
Worse: Leaving early. Also, leaving before checking that everything you were supposed to do that day has been done; and not cleaning up your workspace.

Minimum: Ask questions about the details of your job.
Better: Ask questions with a broader scope. How does your manager prefer you to communicate with her? What are the priorities of the company? Who are the key people you should meet, and why? What are the priorities of your job? Are there any ways your manager would like you to expand your job responsibilities?
Worse: Only asking questions about yourself, when you can leave, vacation time, overtime, or when you can expect a raise. If you have questions about these issues, go to human resources, or consult the employee handbook. Ask for clarification about certain topics from your co-workers or human resources.

Minimum: Get to know your co-workers by name and what areas they work in.
Better: Join co-workers for lunch, or happy hours at least a few times, and participate in company events.
Worse: Over-sharing: Keep political and religious views to yourself; only talking about yourself; making off-color, racist, and demeaning jokes about men or women.

Minimum: Cheerfully do any job or task that is asked of you.
Better: Checking to make sure that task is completed and done to your manager's satisfaction.
Even better: Volunteer for projects, especially those no one else wants to do.
Worse: Reluctantly doing a task and complaining.

Minimum: Make sure you are well groomed, clean, and dressed appropriately for each workday.
Better: Dress to be promotable: How do the managers or the upper management dress? Dress for the job you want. You are also showing that you are capable and responsible enough to meet with clients or customers, and to participate in upper level meetings.
Worse: Dress like it's your day off; like you just rolled out of bed; or like you are going on a date.

Minimum: Keep your social media neutral and in good taste.
Better: Post thoughtful and interesting articles about your industry, and occasionally comment positively on your company or a company event.
Worse: Over-sharing: posting photos from that party where you drank too much; ranting about politics, religion, or genders; posting cartoons in bad taste or just plain offensive.

If, after a few months, you find that your new job just isn't right for you, or that you really don't like the company, make sure you leave on good terms. Give extra notice, start looking for a new job *in your free time away from work,* and still do excellent work while you are there. You don't want to burn any bridges, and you don't want to get fired.

When Your Wages Are Garnished

Your wages can be garnished for a number of reasons, and not all of them are in your control. Wages can be garnished for past debts you owe, for unpaid medical bills, or alimony or child support, or if you have an unsettled tax dispute with either your state or the federal government.

Last year, over 7% of workers across the country had their wages garnished. More than 40% of those were for child support; 20% were for back taxes; and the rest for outstanding consumer debt.

Wage garnishment is not a creditor's first tactic—they'd much rather come to an agreement with the person who (they believe) owes them money. In order to garnish wages, the creditor must first sue the debtor, and then get a court order. There are some exceptions to this, however:

- Unpaid income taxes
- Court ordered child support (up to 60% of your disposable income can be garnished to pay child support, PLUS another 5% for payments that are more than 12 weeks late)
- Past due child support
- Defaulted student loans (up to 15% of your disposable income)

Federal law limits wage garnishment to no more than 25% of disposable income. Disposable income in this case means that amount of income left after deductions (tax withholdings, Social Security, etc.) are taken out of your paycheck.

State policies that apply in addition to federal law vary from state to state. For example, in Hawaii, creditors can garnish:

- 5% of your first $100 of disposable earnings per month
- 10% of your second $100 of disposable earnings per month
- 20% of your disposable earnings over $200 per month

Generally, across the states, Social Security, welfare, workers comp, and unemployment are exempt from garnishment. But check with the proper authorities to make sure it applies to you.

Employers are not happy about have to deal with wage garnishment orders—it's extra work for them. They might want to fire you to avoid dealing with it, but luckily, federal law prohibits termination for one garnishment order. Most state laws declare that employers cannot fire, suspend or discriminate against you because of wage garnishment.

What can you do?
The first thing you can do is to try to avoid getting in this situation in the first place. If you are falling behind on payments, contact your creditor and see if you can work out a payment plan.

Review your debts. How much are you paying in interest? Getting a loan with 5% to 10% interest makes more sense than paying down a credit card debt directly, if the credit card carries a 36% (or more) interest rate.

Did you receive a judgment? Now what?
Did you move? Unless you fall into one of the above categories, you should have received notice of the lawsuit, and then the notice of the court order. If you did not, perhaps the company used an old address. You can use that as grounds to request cancellation of the garnishment. (But you'll still have to come to an agreement to repay the debt.)

Review the judgment and make sure everything is correct. If it's not all correct, your next step is to contact a lawyer. The National Association of Consumer Advocates has a directory of attorneys specializing in garnishment issues (as well as other issues).

Make sure that you are not being garnished more than allowed by federal or state law (see above, and consult an attorney), and see if you can challenge the judgment.

As mentioned above, think about getting a low-interest loan. Calculate the math, and make sure it works for you and your income situation.

Last resort: Declare bankruptcy. There are certain specific debts that can't be discharged through bankruptcy, but you can eliminate most consumer and medical debt. Talk to a bankruptcy attorney to review your situation and your options (the first visit should be free). The National Association of Consumer Bankruptcy Attorneys will help you look for a lawyer in your area.

What to Do When You've Been Laid Off

It's happened to everyone, for reasons ranging from a company downsizing or going out of business, to personal conflicts, to job responsibilities and departments being "reassigned" or eliminated.

But how you handle your departure from a small or large company will affect how and whether you find your next job. It will also affect your income in the short term, and your mental health.

First of all, don't say or do anything you'll regret later. Even if you are angry, you are the only one who will suffer from your actions and words. Your dismissal may be grossly unfair, it may put you in a financial bind, and it may be hurtful and a mental shock. Still, keep yourself together. Don't get angry. Don't unload on your social media accounts. Don't sabotage your work or workplace. Take a deep breath, and try to be as pleasant as you are able. Accept whatever assistance your employer may be offering, and depart on responsible and cordial terms.

Why? You will want, at the very least, a good reference and a good reputation. You will also want any assistance the company may offer to a departing employee. You'll also want to be able to reach out to your co-workers for the scoop on available jobs in your field, and references.

If you work for a large company, they may offer some kind of assistance including severance and outplacement help. What are they, and why are they important?

Severance:
This is money in addition to regular salary that a company will offer to an employee who is being laid off, whose job has been eliminated, or sometimes when they and the company have parted ways for other reasons. Severance is not a legal requirement. It can be as little as one or two week's pay, or it could be a formula based on the employee's time with the company. If you are offered severance *take it!* Even if it doesn't seem like much, it will most likely see you through the month, or maybe longer.

Outplacement help:
The company will pay for an outplacement employment service company to help a laid-off employee prepare to find a new job, handle the transition and departure from their now-previous company, reorient them to the current job market, and help with tasks like putting together a resume. It may not seem like much, but at least it's a place to start.

File for unemployment as soon as you can. See our companion article, *Collecting Unemployment* for more helpful information.

Compose your exit story:

What you **_don't_** want to say to people, and prospective employers, is that you got laid off because the company was mean to you, unfair, picking on you, persecuting you, or that it was because you got into a fight with your boss or supervisor. That is _exactly_ the way **NOT** to get hired again.

Instead, during the meeting in which you are laid off, ask your employer to portray your layoff as a voluntary departure, even while telling Uncle Sam they've let you go (which is true) so you can collect unemployment.

After the shock wears off, start crafting your story in a positive light:

- You are now able to do something more fulfilling.
- You'll be able to work better hours.
- You'll be able to work closer to home, or in a better neighborhood.
- You are looking forward to working with more (creative, hands-on, innovative, etc.) people.

If you have a specific, different, area you want to get a job in, add that to your story. Update your status in Facebook and LinkedIn, and use it as a place to let people know you are looking for work. Remember to present yourself positively.

You may be feeling depressed and panic-stricken. That's okay—everyone does! Do a few exercises to bolster your confidence, and also prepare yourself for a job interview:

- List your top 10 accomplishments. Ask your family and friends if you can't think of that many. Then narrow those down to your top 5. Think about which one you enjoyed the most. That will not only come in handy in an interview, but it will possibly point you in an employment direction just right for you.
- List where you want to be, and what you want to be doing, in five, ten, and twenty years. This also will be good in an interview, and help you hone in on what is important to you.
- List your best and worst qualities, and attach an example to each. Again, a standard interview question, but it also helps you view your talents and where you might need additional coaching or education.
- List your talents. What are you good at? Include everything from working with customers to drawing to making free throws to cooking. Ask your friends and family to add to the list. This will help build your self-esteem, and also give you some direction on what work you should be doing.

Don't immediately start answering every online job ad. Online ads are the least effective way to find a job. When the time comes, reach out to your former coworkers and industry contacts. Plus, you are not really ready for an interview yet.

Give yourself at least a little time to mentally recover, get yourself together, get your family together, and prepare yourself for your next opportunity!

Filing for Unemployment

If you have become unemployed through no fault of your own—you were fired, laid-off, or even laid-off for a specific amount of time only—you should be eligible to collect unemployment benefits. Unemployment in no way replaces your previous hourly pay or salary—it's much less—but it will help you in your transition time. Any money coming in right now is a good thing!

For this example we'll look at the unemployment eligibility rules and other matters in California. Your own state may have different regulations, but it should be similar over all.

To collect unemployment benefits (money), you must meet three eligibility requirements:

- Your past earnings must meet certain minimum thresholds.
- You must be unemployed through no fault of your own, as defined by California law.
- You must be able, available, and actively seeking work.

Let's look at these one at a time:

Past earnings:
States will look at your prior year earnings to determine how much unemployment compensation (money) you are eligible for. Most states will use as your "base period" the earliest four of the five previous calendar quarters before you filed for unemployment. They don't count the most recent quarter because you were most likely not collecting pay for some of that time. So, if you filed your unemployment claim in October, your base period would be from June of the previous year through May of the current year.

In California, you must have earned at least $1,300 (gross) in your highest-paid quarter ($1,300 in a three-month period), OR you must have earned at least $900 (gross) in your highest-paid quarter of the base period *and* at least 1.25 times your earnings in the highest-paid quarter during the entire base period. Yes, it's confusing!

Reasons for being unemployed:
You are eligible for unemployment if:

- You are out of work through no fault of your own.
- You are laid off, get downsized for economic reasons, or your job is eliminated.
- If you are fired because you lacked the skills to perform the job.
- If you are fired because you simply weren't a good fit.

You are *not* eligible for unemployment if:

- You are fired for misconduct. In California, misconduct makes you ineligible for unemployment benefits *only* if all four of these statements are true:
    - You owed a material duty to your employer: a duty that is properly part of the job (showing up for work and performing your job duties, for example).
    - You didn't perform the duty. A minor or one-time transgression isn't enough to disqualify you from receiving benefits.
    - Your non-performance of the duty showed a wanton or willful disregard for that duty—you weren't just careless or thoughtless but showed a reckless disregard for the consequences. Inefficiency, inability to perform the job, or good faith errors in judgment do not meet this standard and won't make you ineligible.
    - Your non-performance of the duty must harm the employer's business interests.
- You quit your job. You won't be eligible for unemployment benefits *unless* you had a good reason for quitting:
    - A reasonable person who truly wanted a job would have left under the same circumstances.
    - Illegal discrimination, harassment, unsafe working conditions, or fraud by your employer.
    - You must have taken reasonable steps to resolve the situation before quitting.
    - If you left the job for compelling family or health reasons—domestic violence, need to relocate to follow your spouse, or need to care for a seriously ill family member, etc.

Availability to work:
To keep your eligibility for unemployment benefits active, you must be able to work, available to accept a job, and be looking for work.

- You must make a reasonable search for work, and certify (on your unemployment claim that you file) that you have done so.
- You should keep records of the employers you contacted, the dates you made contact (filled out an application, sent a resume, had an interview), and the outcome (you did not hear back, you were turned down, etc.). You may be asked to provide this information.

Now, just how much will you be able to collect?
In California, your weekly benefit amount is determined by dividing your earnings for the highest paid quarter of the base period by 26, up to a maximum of $450 per week. Benefits are available for up to 26 weeks.

How to file your unemployment claim:
You can file your claim for unemployment benefits in California online, by phone, by fax, or by mail. You can find online filing information and contact information at http://www.edd.ca.gov.

Once your application is processed, you'll receive some documents, including a Notice of Unemployment Insurance Award indicating how much you will receive if you are found eligible for benefits (despite the title of this notice, it does not mean you have qualified yet).

If you were fired or quit your job, you may be required to have a telephone interview to determine your eligibility. If you are found eligible, you'll start receiving your benefits checks and claim forms every two weeks. You'll need to return your filled-out claim form every two weeks.

How Does Workers' Comp Work?

First of all, just what exactly IS workers' compensation?
Workers' compensation is a kind of insurance, paid for by an employer, which provides a level of wage replacement and coverage for medical expenses to employees who are injured on the job.

Each state has its own workers comp laws, so the details and regulations vary a bit state by state. We'll cover the basics in this chapter.

In exchange for getting payouts from workers' comp, the employee gives up their right to sue their employer for negligence. Exceptions to this can happen if the employer intentionally causes harm or injury to an employee.

Specialized private insurance companies provide workers' comp insurance coverage to employers. In some states (California is one), there are state insurance programs available for businesses that can't afford the private insurance.

What is covered?
Medical care:

- Injuries that require medical care—injuries that happen while you are performing your job duties.
- Injuries that happen while you are on your way to or from work are *not* covered, unless travel is part of your job or is involved in tasks assigned to you (running errands, for example).
- Typical injuries include:
    - Repetitive motion and overuse injuries (RSIs), which can include carpal tunnel syndrome from keyboarding, to tendonitis, and back pain.

214

- Hearing loss, most frequently as a result from noise at manufacturing plants or construction sites.
- Stress related injuries: These are very much harder—though not impossible—to prove, and difficult for which to get workers comp benefits.
- Stress resulting from workplace physical injuries, including sleep disorders, anxiety, and depression resulting as a direct result of a workplace injury.
- Occupational illnesses: Illness that result from on-the-job exposure like black lung, asbestosis, or AIDs/HIV.

Temporary disability payments:

- Partial wage replacement if an injury prevents you from doing your normal job. This amount is usually 2/3 of your usual weekly salary or hours.

Permanent disability:

- If you are permanently or totally disabled as a result of your work-related injury or occupational disease, you will likely be entitled to a lifetime pension under your state's workers' compensation system. Each state's workers' comp laws are different, but each state has some kind of regulations to award a lifetime pension.

Death benefits:

- Eligible dependents are usually entitled to workers' comp death benefits when an employee dies as a result of work injuries or illness.
- Eligible dependents include spouse, children, and/or other family members who lived with the employee.

Filing a workers' comp claim
It's very important to follow the correct procedures from the moment of your injury or illness in order to receive medical coverage and wage compensation.

Get medical treatment:

- If you are hurt, get immediate treatment at a doctor's office or hospital. If you have an illness, get seen by a doctor.
- If you do *not* see a doctor or receive treatment for some time after an accident, the workers' comp adjuster will assume that you have no lasting damage or ill effects.
- Get documents from the doctor or hospital, and make your own notes about everything that happened. Include everything about your injury or illness, how it happened, the financial impact, and how it is affecting your daily life. Keep track of, and take notes on, every conversation you have about your injury or illness. If you are able to take photos, do, or get photos from others.

Can you see your own doctor?

- It depends on which state you live in. In some states you can see your own doctor, and in others you must request permission in writing, before the injury.
- Most of the time you must initially go to a doctor or medical treatment group that your employer designates. If you must see a doctor who is paid by your employers, keep in mind that their business relationship may motivate the doctor to downplay the seriousness of your injury, or to report it as a preexisting condition.

- Keep notes, and you may be able to change doctors if you are unhappy.
- Talk to your human resources department, or to whoever handles your company's worker's comp claims.

File a work injury accident report immediately after receiving medical treatment for your injury or illness.

- If you have a long-developing illness or injury, file a report as soon as you realize it was caused by your job.
- If you do *not* file an injury accident report within 30 days (check your state regulations), you run the risk of losing your compensation and coverage.
- Your employer may have their own claim forms that need to be filled out, and if not, you should be able to get forms from your state's workers' compensation board.
- Make a copy of your completed form to keep before you turn in your filled-out form.
- Give your completed form to your employer. They will now fill out their part of the form, and file it with the workers' compensation claims administrator and state workers' comp board office.

What needs to be included in the injury report:

- What the injury is, including all parts of the body that are affected.
- How the accident, injury, or illness occurred.
- What other employees (or other people) were involved.
- The date, time, and location of the accident, injury, or illness.
- Medical treatment you have received.

Do you need a lawyer?
If you have a serious injury, are out of work for a few days to a week and more, if you have broken bones, a long-term illness, or are facing medical bills of more than $2,000, you may want to consult with a personal injury lawyer.

The lawyer will evaluate your claim, and can help you navigate within the workers' comp world, or take your case to court to receive compensation.

Can you get in trouble for filing a Workers Comp insurance claim?
Although it is illegal in all but two states to fire someone for filing a workplace injury claim, sadly, it can still happen. It's not always easy to prove this kind of discrimination. If this happens to you, you might want to consider seeing a personal injury lawyer.

Do your research
Don't forget to speak to your company's human resources department, or to whoever in your company handles workers' comp claims, so you are fully informed on what procedures to follow and who to contact.

For more information on workers' comp, check with your state workers' compensation officials. https://www.dol.gov/owcp/dfec/regs/compliance/wc.htm will direct you to the contacts in your own state.

What Is OSHA and How Does it Help You?

You may have seen those OSHA posters in the back room of a place you worked, or in the staff break room. Have you ever wondered if there was more to OSHA than the posters?

OSHA was created as both an act of Congress and a national public health agency in 1970. Its mandate is to ensure that no worker should have to choose between their life and their job, and that the right to a safe workplace is a basic human right.

By 1970, an estimated 14,000 workers were killed on the job each year. Since OSHA's creation, workplace injuries, illnesses and deaths have fallen by more than 65 percent. Nevertheless, far too many preventable injuries and fatalities continue to occur. OSHA standards and regulations, and enforcement of those continue to save lives.

Employers are legally responsible for providing a safe and healthful workplace for their workers. OSHA regulations and enforcement assure safe and healthful conditions for working people by setting standards and providing training, outreach, education, and compliance assistance. Both federal and state governments administer OSHA.

Who is covered by OSHA?
OSHA covers most private and some public employers and their workers in all 50 states.

What do employers have to do?

- Follow all OSHA safety and health standards.
- Provide a workplace that does not have serious hazards.
- Find and correct safety and health problems.

- Try to eliminate or reduce hazards by making possible changes in working conditions rather than relying on personal protective equipment such as masks, gloves, or earplugs.
- Prominently display the official *OSHA Job Safety and Health—It's the Law* poster that describes rights and responsibilities under the OSH Act.
- Inform workers about chemical hazards through training, labels, alarms, color-coded systems, chemical information sheets, and other methods.
- Provide safety training to workers in a language and vocabulary they can understand.
- Keep accurate records of work-related injuries and illnesses.
- Perform tests in the workplace, such as air sampling, required by some OSHA standards.
- Provide required personal protective equipment at no cost to workers.
- Provide hearing exams or other medical tests required by some OSHA standards.
- Notify OSHA within 8 hours of a workplace fatality or within 24 hours of any work-related inpatient hospitalization, amputation, or loss of an eye.
- Not retaliate against workers for using their rights under the law, including their right to report a work-related injury or illness.
- Post OSHA citations and injury and illness data where workers can see them.

OSHA standards are rules that describe the methods employers are legally required to follow to protect their workers from hazards. Before OSHA can issue a standard, it must go through a very extensive and lengthy process that includes substantial public engagement, notice and comment. The agency must show that a significant risk to workers exists and that there are feasible measures employers can take to protect their workers.

What rights do workers have? Workers are entitled to:

- Working conditions that do not pose a risk of serious harm.
- File a confidential complaint.
- Have their workplace inspected.
- Receive information and training about hazards, methods to prevent harm, and the OSHA standards that apply to their workplace.
- Have training done in a language and vocabulary they can understand.
- Receive copies of records of work-related injuries and illnesses that occur in their workplace.
- Receive copies of the results from tests and monitoring done to find and measure hazards in their workplace.
- Receive copies of their workplace medical records.
- Participate in an OSHA inspection and speak in private with the inspector.
- File a complaint with OSHA if they have been retaliated against by their employer as the result of requesting an inspection or using any of their other rights under the OSH Act.
- File a complaint if punished or retaliated against for acting as a "whistleblower" under the 21 additional federal laws for which OSHA has jurisdiction.

What to do if you've been injured on the job

- Report the injury to your supervisor immediately.
- Seek medical care as soon as possible. Check with your supervisor to see if you need to go to a company-approved doctor, or if you can see your own.
- If it's an emergency, obviously get to a hospital emergency room!
- As soon as you can, notify your supervisor in writing about your injury, and get a Workers' Comp claim form. Until this claim form is completed, the employer has no obligation to provide benefits. If you cannot

get a claim form from your company, your doctor or hospital may have a copy. If not, contact your state Workers' Compensation Office.

- Keep a copy of the claim, and a copy of any communication to your supervisor.
- Return the filled-out claim (fill out the Employee section only) to your employer.
- Make sure to file as quickly as you can—there are time limits for reporting an injury and filing a claim.
- Get documentation from the doctor you see.
- Keep in mind that a doctor paid for by your employer's insurance company is not your friend. They may be motivated to minimize the seriousness of your injury or to identify it as a pre-existing condition.
- If the doctor asks if your injury is related to a pre-existing condition, just say "no" unless you have suffered a significant previous injury or chronic condition that is related to your injury.
- The Workers' Comp insurance company has 14 days to mail you a status letter about your claim. If you don't receive this letter, you should call the insurance company.

For more information, visit OSHA's Workers' Rights page at http://www.osha.gov/workers.

Learn about filing a workplace safety complaint here: https://www.osha.gov/workers/file_complaint.html

Find information for employers here: https://www.osha.gov/employers/index.html

Find your state's OSHA office here: https://www.osha.gov/html/RAmap.html

Personal Finance *for* Real People

Housing Issues

Renting Basics

Renting can be cheaper, and certainly a faster process, than buying a home. It's more flexible, too: You can pack up and leave for a job in a different area, or to move in with family, or just to travel and live in another area for awhile.

Some areas of the country, though, are a landlord's market: There are not enough apartments or rental units to satisfy demand. This means that the landlord or management company can be as picky about choosing a renter as they want to be. Whichever category your area falls into, it's best to be prepared and choose your next home carefully.

STARTING THE SEARCH

- **Will you need a rental agent to find an apartment?** This depends largely on where you live. In Los Angeles, for example, various fee-charging services will send you lists of available apartments in the neighborhood you want. In New York, you'll *have* to work with an agent in order to view and sign an apartment. Agents will charge you a fee for their service, which can often be a month's rent or more.
- **Check out the neighborhood.** It should be comfortable, clean, and safe, plus convenient. Visit the area, and your potential rental, at different times of the day, evenings, weekends, and rush hour. Do you feel safe as you drive or walk around?
- **How convenient is transportation?** How close is the freeway? Is there public transportation nearby? How long will it take you to get to work?
- **Is this property in a good school district?** (If that's a consideration for you.)
- **What are the businesses nearby?** How close is fast food? Gas stations? Where is the closest market? Is there a bar in the neighborhood close to your apartment, or a pawn shop, or a homeless hangout?
- **Take a close look at the rental property.** Is the trash area neat? Is the building kept up? Is the landscaping tidy? Are there any broken windows? You want a rental that the owner has invested time and money in. If that's so, odds are that your apartment will be kept up, too.
- **Is there parking?** Are you going to have to fight for a spot on the street?
- **Try your cell phone.** How much cell phone reception do you receive on the property?

THE RENTAL APPLICATION

- **Don't delay!** Fill out a rental application as soon as possible after finding your desired apartment, since landlords will continue showing it until someone has officially been approved.
- **Be prepared with your information.** On the application you should expect to include all of your personal information, including either a social security or driver's license number, along with employment information and references.

- **Be ready for application fees.** If you are seriously in the running, the property manager will most likely ask you to pay an application fee, a credit fee, and a background check fee. Expect to pay as much as $100 or more per person just to apply for an apartment in some areas.
- **Income verification:** Most landlords include an area on the application for your monthly income, and they will almost always require you to provide proof, so bring along copies of recent pay stubs, or possibly your last W-2. They will most likely also call your employer for proof of employment, and ask to verify your salary. Many companies don't answer those questions for legal reasons, though they can verify your employment.
- **Credit check:** The landlord will ask for your permission to check your credit. The credit check is important for landlords—it gives them an idea of how financially responsible you are. If you don't have credit or have new credit, it's harder for them to check your dependability. Talk to them about it at the time of application—you may need to provide a co-signer. Order your credit report before applying for a rental. This will show you any potential problems, and give you a chance to fix any errors on the report. Credit score requirements vary by landlord—680 or higher is considered to be a good credit score. Fixing credit problems, such as improving your payment habits and paying off defaulted accounts, improves your odds of getting a rental. But if you can't fix bad credit, explain it on your rental application, as some apartment managers may show leniency after a job loss, divorce, or illness.
- **If you need a co-signer:** Co-signers are people who sign the lease with you, saying they take legal responsibility for covering your rent if you can't. If you don't have a rental history, the property manager won't be able to check on your dependability, or verify that you've never caused damage. If you have poor credit, or no credit history, you may need a co-signer.
- **Background check**: The landlord will also ask your permission to run a criminal background check, again to get an idea of your personality and dependability. In some states you may not have to disclose convictions after a certain number of years. Check to see what your state's requirements are.
- **References:** Many property managers will do a check on your rental history by speaking to your past landlords. If you can, before you leave your current apartment, try to get a reference from your landlord. At least get their contact information. You can also provide references from employers.

YOU'VE FOUND A PLACE

- Ask for a showing of the apartment and the property.
- Are parking spots reserved or first come? Can you pay extra for additional reserved spots or a garage? Is there guest parking?
- Will you receive lots of natural lighting or will your apartment feel like a cave?
- Are utilities included? How much do they generally cost?
- Is there enough storage space in the apartment? What about additional available storage on the property?
- Have a quick look at the residents' cars parked. Are there a lot of beat-up dirty old cars? Are there "noisy" cars (turbo, big trucks, motorcycles)? Just like the property itself, you want your fellow renters to be interested in keeping up their apartments and their property. And, you have to decide on what noise level you're comfortable with, especially if your apartment is by the parking area.
- Take a look, if you can, at the other residents. Are there children? Elderly? Young professionals? Is this a group in which you would fit and be comfortable?
- If you have pets, find out if the landlord accepts pets (don't try to sneak in your cat). Is there an additional monthly rental fee, or an additional pet deposit?
- Is there a pet area or park where you can walk your dog?
- Do other residents pick up after their dogs?
- Does the building have quiet hours, or fees for using communal spaces, such as a gym?
- Are there laundry facilities? Or can you have a washer and dryer in your apartment?

- Is there Wi-Fi?
- How does the property manager handle a maintenance problem in the apartment? How do you report that, and how quickly do they respond?

- Make notes of anything that is in disrepair. Realistically, the apartment may have some signs of wear and tear, such as scratches on floors or countertops. Take photos and either ask the landlord to repair it if it's necessary, or at least document that it existed prior to your rental.
- Check that everything works: faucets, hot water, lights, outlets, toilets, shower, stove, refrigerator, locks, windows, doors, etc.
- Look around for any signs of leaks—leaks can lead to black mold.
- Check for any signs of insects and rodents—look for droppings, and dead insects.
- Secure rental property insurance. The landlord may require it, but it's also a good idea to have, just in case.

Read your lease. Leases, like any legal document, are long and boring, and it can take time to read the entire thing. But that's just the point: it is a legal document, and once you sign, you are committed. Make sure that you agree with all the terms, and ask questions. Sign the document only if you're comfortable with the terms of the agreement.

Questions to ask:

- What are your upfront costs?
  - Security deposit
  - Pet deposit
  - First and last month's rent
  - Application fee and credit/background check fees
- Is your rent prorated on half months?
- What's the policy around subletting?
- When can the landlord terminate your lease, and under what circumstances?
- What are the laws regarding rent increases? This is something you should research, as well as ask the property manager. Laws regarding renters are different in each state. In any case, be prepared for at least one rent increase further down the road.
- If you have a co-signer or joint applicant (roommate), can they be removed from the lease later, if circumstances change?
- Ask if you need the property manager's permission before painting. Putting up wallpaper, driving nails into the walls, hanging artwork—all of that might need to be pre-approved and/or reversed when you move out, or you risk losing your security deposit.
- Under what circumstances are allowed to break your lease: job transfer, illness, etc.?
- Is there a fee if you have to break your lease?

- Keep the apartment clean.
- Put out garbage in proper containers.
- Use electrical and plumbing fixtures properly.
- Follow local housing, health and safety rules.

- Do not damage the landlord's property.
- Do not disturb neighbors.
- Make sure guests do not destroy the landlord's property or disturb other residents.
- Use appliances with care, and only for what they are intended.
- Notify the landlord when repairs are needed.
- Control any insect or rodent infestations, or notify the landlord.
- Do not use a grill inside or on a balcony, or possibly even on your patio—check with the landlord beforehand.
- Pay your rent and utilities on time and in full.
- Use only your own parking space.
- Clean up after your pets.

LANDLORD RESPONSIBILITIES

- Obey all health and safety laws and regulations.
- Make all repairs needed to maintain the property in good condition.
- Keep all common areas safe, clean and in good repair.
- Maintain all electrical, plumbing, heating and air conditioning fixtures and applications that the landlord provides or is required to provide.
- Provide and maintain garbage cans and provide for trash removal where there are four or more units in the building.
- Supply running water and enough hot water and heat at all times, unless there are separate heating or hot water units for each dwelling unit and the utility fees for the heating and hot water are paid directly by the tenant to a public utility company.
- Give at least 24 hours notice to a tenant before trying to enter his or her apartment and enter only at reasonable times unless there is an emergency.
- Cannot shut off utilities.
- Cannot take anything that belongs to you.
- Cannot change the locks or otherwise lock you out of your apartment to force you to pay rent or leave the apartment.
- Cannot raise the rent or threaten to evict you in retaliation for taking legal action against the property management company, building manager, landlord, or owner.
- Cannot abuse the right to enter the apartment—the landlord is not allowed to harass you with repeated visits.
- Refund your security deposit within 30 days of the end of the rental agreement.
- May deduct from your deposit the cost of any repairs that need to be made other than maintenance from normal wear and tear. Charges deducted must be listed separately and sent with the remainder of the deposit. If you disagree with the deductions or you do not receive the security deposit, you may sue your landlord.

EVICTION

Hopefully your rental experience will not include an eviction. But if you don't pay your rent, don't live up to your end of the lease agreement, or refuse to leave at the end of the lease, your landlord may evict you.

Check your state law for eviction procedures—they do differ from state to state. The landlord must serve you a written eviction notice. After a certain length of time, the landlord can file that eviction notice in court. If the landlord wins his suit for eviction, and you still don't vacate, after a certain length of time the landlord can ask a local law enforcement officer to remove you from the apartment.

You can also be evicted for reasons having nothing to do with you—the owner is selling the building, etc.—and it will not go on your credit report or be held against you.

RENTING MAY HELP YOUR CREDIT SCORE

If you want to qualify for a mortgage loan in the relatively near future, and want to improve your credit score, there's good and bad news regarding rent payments helping your FICO credit score. The many landlords do not report to the credit bureaus, but there are new credit bureaus that have started tracking payments like rent and utilities.

When You Move

There are really only two main commands when it comes to moving:

Reserve your movers, even if they are just two guys you know, as soon as you've figured out your moving date.

Purge, purge, purge, and toss, toss, toss!

Somehow, your belongings will get to their destination, for better or worse.

To save your sanity, your money, and your time, follow as many of these moving tips as you can. It only seems like more work up front—and it will save you much frustration and time when you get to your new residence.

Purging:

- Sort through everything—and we mean everything—and be brutal. Almost empty bottle of something? Toss it! Clothes you haven't worn? Donate them. Books you are never going to read, or are duplicates? Donate them! Start when you know you will be moving so you aren't faced with it on moving day.
- If you own items that you want to get rid of but are too valuable to just give away, start selling on eBay, Etsy, or Craigslist at least six weeks before moving. You can use the extra money to help pay for your move.
- If you have furniture that hasn't sold on the above sites, call a charitable organization to pick it all up. Remember to schedule this as far ahead of time as you can—they do get booked up.
- If you have children—especially young children—start gradually and quietly sorting through their toys, clothes, and belongings well before moving. The time to start is when you know you'll be moving sometime, but don't have a date yet.

Pre-clean your new house:

- Either clean your new house before the move-in, or hire housecleaners to do so.
- Have the carpets steam-cleaned a few days before your furniture arrives.

Your emergency kit:

- Set aside those things you know you absolutely have to have upon arrival or the next day.
- Pack an overnight bag containing all the essentials. Chances are, you'll be too tired to unpack your things. You'll need a change of clothes as well as all your toiletries and medications.
- Pack your laptop and accessories in a backpack—it could run the risk of getting stolen during a move.
- Assemble a bag of snacks and drinks for moving day. Get extra water and coffees for your movers.
- Pack the household items you will need access to first in a clear plastic bin, and keep it in your car. This includes things like a box cutter, paper towels, trash bags, eating utensils, select cookware, power strips,

phone chargers, toilet paper, tools, etc. The clear bin allows you to see inside; it also separates itself from the pile of cardboard boxes.
- Get extra cash before moving day.
- Tip the movers upon the successful delivery of your belongings.

Packing:

- Try not to use liquor store, supermarket, or used boxes. They might not be strong enough any more, and you may also be bringing uninvited guests to your new home. And certainly don't use boxes with no tops!
- Seal your boxes—don't just tuck in the flaps.
- Use packing tape to seal your boxes, not duct or masking tape.
- Start packing items you won't need immediately ahead of time.
- Wrap your breakables (dishes, glasses, etc.) in clothing to save on bubble wrap.
- For extra padding, pack your glasses and stemware in clean socks.
- Pack plates vertically, like records. They'll be less likely to break.
- If you have a lot of fragile valuables, hire professional movers, or move those items yourself.
- Pack important and sentimental documents separately to be easily accessible including: children's health records, passports, family records, insurance information and photo albums. It's probably best to move these yourself, if you can, so they don't get lost.
- Cover the openings of your toiletries with plastic wrap, and then put the tops back on—no leaks!
- Use a roll of stretch wrap, and wrap around your furniture. Drawers won't come out, and surfaces will be protected.
- Use sandwich bags for holding any small parts of things you have to take apart, like curtain rods, shelf holders, or mounted flat-screen TVs. Masking tape the sandwich bags to the back of the item they came from.
- Take a photo of how everything connects to your computer, and your TV, in case you don't remember how everything fits back together.
- Use larger plastic zip bags for the cords for your electronics, and masking tape them to the unit.
- Use all of your baskets, laundry bins, hampers, and suitcases as packing boxes.
- If you can, make a detailed list of what's in each box by number. This makes it easier to ensure you won't forget any boxes. Personally, I've never been able to do this!
- If you have something valuable in a box, don't label it with that information.
- Check the owner's manuals for large appliances to see if there are special instructions for moving.
- Avoid mixing items from different rooms in the same box.
- Use only small boxes for books. They get very heavy, very fast.
- Vacuum-seal your out-of-season clothing: They'll take up less space, and can go directly into storage in your new home.
- Use wardrobe boxes to make closets easier to pack. Clothes in drawers can be placed in suitcases.

Labeling:

- Pick a color code for each room and use duct tape in that color to label that room's boxes. Label the door of each room in the new house with the same duct tape so that movers know where to place the boxes.
- Label what's in your boxes, add what room they'll be going to.
- Label the sides of the boxes, not the tops—you'll be able to identify them even if they're stacked.

Unpacking:

- When you arrive at your new home, unpack by room. The unpacking process will be much more manageable.

More tips:

- If you're renting, take photos of your cleaned-out old home and your new home before moving in. This will help you get your deposit back.
- Change your address at least two weeks prior to moving. You can change your address with the post office online.
- Call all your utilities; give them the date of your move, and your new address.
- If you are going to be ordering anything immediately, don't forget to change your address with that retailer or service.
- After you've arrived, take about a week to continue changing your address the rest of your services, retailers, your bank, magazines, and, of course, your family and friends.
- Do not give your address out on social media.
- Make your last grocery trip two weeks prior to moving. Use up what's in your freezer, fridge, and pantry.
- Think of whatever other services you need to cancel—gardener, newspaper—and let them know at least a week prior.

Clean your old house or apartment:

- Clean and defrost (if necessary) your refrigerator at least a day before moving.
- Clean the stove and oven also at least a day before moving.
- Clean the baseboards and window tracks once all the furniture is out.
- Before you leave, check each and every cupboard, closet, and drawer.
- Leave enough cleaning products and tools behind so you can finish cleaning your old house once everything is out. Then you can take that to the new house, and finish up whatever cleaning needs to be done.

***Not* purging:**

- Make the move easier to take for your children by offering them a chance to redecorate their rooms. They can think of what colors or themes they want (if any), and take a trip to Target or IKEA, and thrift stores, once you've moved in.
- Make it fun for yourself, too. Get new dishtowels that color-coordinate with your new kitchen, change up your bathroom colors with new towels and shower curtains.

Where to Find Housing Assistance

Find housing and rent assistance from your state

Tough financial times can make it difficult for low-income families to meet the cost of housing. As a result, the U.S. Department of Housing and Urban Development (HUD) and Public Housing Authority (PHA) in each state provide two housing options to low-income state residents. Section-8 and Low-Rent programs provide affordable housing based on available funds and the family's household size and income. To apply for emergency low-income housing, you must go through the PHA for your county.

How to apply:

- If your family cannot afford to pay the rent, contact your local PHA.
- Locate and click the link to your county's PHA website from the list on the HUD California Housing Authorities website.
- Verify the county's procedure for applying for low-income housing. Not all counties allow you to apply online. Certain counties have wait lists and, if the wait lists are closed, the county is not accepting applications at that time.
- Gather documents that contain your personal information and income. Personal information that is required to complete an application includes your Social Security number, date of birth, and California driver's license or state I.D. number. Provide information on all income sources on your application, such as wages, tips, child support, unemployment, Social Security and self-employment.
- Fill out the application online, if available. If an online application is not available, certain agencies offer a printable application, which you can fill out and mail. If neither option is available, you must contact the PHA and complete an application with an agent in person.
- If your family is homeless, contact your local PHA immediately. Certain counties have emergency funds available, even though applications for housing are closed.

In addition to the federal rental assistance, homeownership and home buying assistance programs, there may be programs that are sponsored by your state or local government or other organizations that can help you. Check http://www.hud.gov to search your state.

Federal Rental Assistance

Federal rental assistance helps over 5 million low-income households to afford modest homes. Applicants can earn no more than the income limit.

Three major programs assist about 90% of these households:

- Section 8 Housing Choice Vouchers

- Privately owned subsidized housing/low rent apartments
- Public Housing

Income Limit Guidelines

- **Very low-income:** 50% of the MFI (Median Family Income) for that specific area, subject to specified adjustments for areas with unusually high or low incomes relative to housing costs.
- **Low-income**: 80% of the MFI for that specific area, subject to adjustments for areas with unusually high or low incomes or housing costs.
- **Extremely low-income**: 60% of the four-person family very low-income limit, adjusted for family size, but not allowed to fall below the poverty line.
- Income limits are adjusted for family size so that larger families have higher income limits.

Federal programs

- **Housing Choice Voucher Program (Section 8)**
  - Find your own place and use the voucher to pay for all or part of the rent. The Section 8 program allows private landlords to rent apartments and homes at fair market rates to qualified low income tenants, with a rental subsidy administered by Home Forward. "Section 8" is a common name for the Housing Choice Voucher Program, funded by the U.S. Department of Housing and Urban Development.
  - How to get on Section 8: Check whether your local PHAs are accepting applications.
- **Privately owned subsidized housing**
  - The government gives funds directly to apartment owners, who lower the rents they charge low-income tenants. You can find low-rent apartments for senior citizens and people with disabilities, as well as for families and individuals.
- **Public Housing**
  - Affordable apartments for low-income families, the elderly and persons with disabilities. Public housing was established to provide decent and safe rental housing for eligible low-income families, the elderly, and persons with disabilities. Public housing comes in all sizes and types, from scattered single-family houses to high-rise apartments for elderly families. There are approximately 1.2 million households living in public housing units, managed by some 3,300 HAs.
  - Who is eligible? Public housing is limited to low-income families and individuals.
  - An HA determines your eligibility based on:
    - Annual gross income
    - Whether you qualify as elderly, a person with a disability, or as a family
    - U.S. citizenship or eligible immigration status.
- If you are eligible, the HA will check your references to make sure you and your family will be good tenants. HAs will deny admission to any applicant whose habits and practices may be expected to have a detrimental effect on other tenants or on the project's environment.

Other programs

HUD's Office of Native American Programs (ONAP)
ONAP administers housing and community development programs that benefit American Indian and Alaska Native tribal governments, tribal members, the Department of Hawaiian Home Lands, Native Hawaiians, and other Native American organizations.

Indian Housing Block Grant (IHBG) program

The Indian Housing Block Grant Program (IHBG) is a grant that provides a range of affordable housing activities on Indian reservations and Indian areas.

- Eligible IHBG recipients are federally recognized Indian tribes or their tribally designated housing entity (TDHE), and a limited number of state-recognized tribes.
- An eligible tribe must submit to HUD an Indian Housing Plan (IHP) each year to receive funding. At the end of each year, recipients must submit to HUD an Annual Performance Report (APR) reporting on their progress in meeting the goals and objectives included in their IHPs.
- Eligible activities include housing development, assistance to housing developed under the Indian Housing Program, housing services to eligible families and individuals, crime prevention and safety, and model activities that provide creative approaches to solving affordable housing problems.

The Native Hawaiian Housing Block Grant (NHHBG) program

The use of NHHBG funds is limited to eligible affordable housing activities for low-income (not exceeding 80% of the median income for the area) native Hawaiians eligible to reside on Hawaiian Home Lands.

- Eligible activities include new construction, rehabilitation, acquisition, infrastructure, and various support services. Housing can be either rental or homeownership.
- NHHBG funds can also be used for certain types of community facilities if the facilities serve eligible residents of affordable housing.
- In order to qualify for an annual grant, the Department of Hawaiian Home Lands is required to submit proposed activities in an annual Native Hawaiian Housing Plan to HUD for review. Grant funds are then made available to the DHHL.

Home Purchase Basics

The home buying process certainly looks daunting and confusing. And, it can be. The idea of committing yourself to this much debt, plus the responsibility of a house *and* the investment is a little scary. But is accomplishable if you are prepared, are ready to buy, and if you have a good team working with you.

FINDING YOUR HOME

One adage still matters, and it matters a lot: location, location, location. You can change the house, but you can't change the location! You won't be happy if you choose the wrong location, and the wrong location will affect your ability to resell at a good price. Research where you want to live.

Drive around areas that you like. If you are moving a distance away, take a weekend to get to know the town, the neighborhoods, the traffic and the amenities. Visit restaurants and stores in each area, and talk to neighbors if you can. Go to open houses. Look at listings posted in realtors' windows, look at listings online, look at listings in brochures. Look, look, look. Think about each home's style, size, price and how long they stay on the market.

WHAT YOU NEED TO DO

- Find your real estate agent while you're still looking around. You'll want to get an agent in the area where you want to live--a neighborhood expert often can find you the best house at the best price, and will know the good and bad parts of the neighborhood. Your real estate agent's job goes far beyond finding the house. Her assistance will be a necessary part of the purchase process, and can make a purchase go smoothly or very, very badly. Your agent will structure and present your purchase offer, and then will (or should) troubleshoot issues that come up between contract (when you make your formal offer for the house) and closing (when you are the new owner). A good agent can also help you craft an offer that will be accepted. He'll know if you are buying into a buyer's market (more available houses than buyers) or if it's a seller's market (few houses, and plenty of buyers). You need an agent who will advise you honestly on preparing your offer, and who will include things that wouldn't normally occur to you. She should also be able to fix you up with a great mortgage professional, a title company, repair people, and anyone else you need in the process.
- **Make sure you're really ready to buy:** Are you ready to stay in this house for at least several years? Do you have cash for a down payment? Are your finances and income steady? Is a house really what you want? If the answer to any of those questions is no, it's better to wait.
- **Be realistic about what you can afford:** Your real estate agent should be able to recommend a mortgage broker or banker at the start of your search to find out how much house you can afford and how much cash you'll need to close. Do the math. Just because a bank says you can borrow $200,000 doesn't mean you should. If you have credit issues, outstanding loans, lawsuits, owe back taxes, are in a complicated family inheritance, realize that this part could take several months.

- **Calculate all the expenses you'll have once you are a homeowner:** The purchase price and the mortgage payment are just the beginning. There may be home association or condo fees, homeowners insurance, mortgage insurance, and real estate taxes. Don't forget to budget for utilities, repairs and maintenance. Sometimes you can get copies of utility bills from the current owner; you should at least be able to get ballpark figures.
- **Don't leave yourself without resources:** Don't spend all your cash by emptying your bank account for your down payment and closing costs. You still have to move, possibly put down utility deposits, and make some new purchases like paint or a lawnmower. There will always be unexpected repairs.
- **Don't get distracted by surface issues when viewing possible houses.** The owner's gold frocked wallpaper, paint colors, dirty carpet, window covering from the 1950s, and old kitchen appliances are easy to change before you move in, or later. You can't easily add another bedroom or bathroom, beautiful large trees, a better location, a view, or a more functional floor plan. You also can't subtract things like freeway noise, school noise and traffic, or bad neighbors with their outdoor barking dogs.
- **Visit your favorite neighborhoods frequently and at different times.** Are the evenings quiet? Will you be able to exit your street during rush hour?
- **Don't expect a perfect house.** Know which contingencies you're willing to waive. In the ideal scenario, a purchase offer is contingent on a satisfactory home inspection, approval of your mortgage, and an appraisal that equals the purchase price. In most parts of the country, those contingencies are in the contract. But in a competitive market, you may be competing against buyers who have agreed to waive contingencies.
- **Get ready to move quickly once you find THE house.** Good homes that are well-priced, in good shape, and in desirable areas always sell quickly. You should take some time to think before you make your offer, but don't wait weeks. Your house will be sold by then. Your agent should be able to advise you on other offers, other potential offers, the current owner's attitude, and the market situation.
- **Get your priorities set.** No house will be absolutely perfect. Where will you be willing to compromise? Would you buy a smaller house so you could get into a specific school district? If you want a view, would you be happy with a condo? Are you willing to accept a longer commute to get a larger house? Are you willing to take a fixer-upper and create your own dream home?

THE MORTGAGE

- **Preapproval:** If you have good credit, an income that will support your mortgage and other expenses, and money in the bank, you'll be able to secure mortgage preapproval quickly and proceed straight to the home buying process. But if you have less-than-stellar credit, are self-employed, or only have a little cash to bring to the table, you'll want to start the preapproval process before you even start looking at houses. Give yourself plenty of time to get through this step.
- **Review your credit report:** Your annual free credit report helps you identify problems, but won't show you the same credit score your mortgage officer will see. Take steps to correct any mistakes on your credit report before meeting with a mortgage broker.
- **Pay off as much debt as you can:** This will keep your debt-to-income ratio down. Lenders look at your income and all your debts—student loans, car payments, credit-card debt—to determine how much you can afford to borrow. If your total debt, with the new house payment, would be more than 35 - 43% of your income, you're less likely to get the loan.
- **You should have good credit habits long before you plan to buy:** Missing payments loans, or paying your bills late will lower your credit score. This will, in turn, make borrowing for a home almost impossible, especially in a competitive market. Once a bill goes into collections, it can take months or years for your credit to recover.
- **Have a solid work history:** You'll have a hard time getting a mortgage until you've had a job, or worked for the same company, for at least two years.
- **Get your documents in order and available:** Be prepared to produce documents, and lots of them, starting with several years of tax returns and many months of bank statements. Lenders will want proof

of your income, paycheck stubs, to know about all your debts, and the source of any big deposits. If your parents gave you money for a down payment, they will need to write a letter documenting that. The lender will also verify your employment and income, once at the beginning of the process and again a day or two before closing.

- **Have available cash:** Besides documents, you'll need money. Money to put down with your offer, for your down payment, closing costs and more than a year's worth of taxes and insurance payments, for a start. Lenders will also want to see that you have enough in reserve in case you lose your job, or the furnace breaks down.
- **Don't buy anything on credit or apply for any credit while your loan is pending:** You may be tempted to buy new furniture for your new home and put it on a credit card. Or, perhaps you realize you'll have enough cash left for a down payment on a new car. Don't put anything on credit cards, and don't apply for any credit—you may jeopardize the deal.
- **If you're self-employed, be prepared to jump through more hoops:** People who own small businesses often can't qualify for a mortgage until they've been in business two years, though exceptions are likely for professionals, such as doctors, who leave a staff position and become self-employed in the same field. Most self-employed professionals write off enough expenses on their taxes to make their adjusted gross income much lower than their actual income. The lender will consider that lower number your income. You may have to go to more than one mortgage broker or bank for funding.
- **Talk to several lenders or mortgage brokers:** Not all lenders can offer the same loans. You can choose whether you'd like to pay more upfront, in the form of "points," to get a lower interest rate, or pay a quarter percent higher on your loan to avoid that upfront expense. If a lender offers you a "no closing costs" loan, find out where you're being charged extra to compensate for that.
- **The house itself will also have to qualify:** The house has to be insurable, and the appraisal must be equal to or higher than your purchase price. There must also be no liens on the house, pending lawsuits, permit issues, or property line issues.
- **How much your down payment should be:**
  - You can buy a house with as little as 3.5% down with a Federal Housing Administration mortgage, 5% with a conventional mortgage, or nothing down with a VA loan available to military veterans. However, the less you pay down, the bigger your monthly payment will be.
  - If your down payment is less than 20% of the purchase price, you'll have to pay private mortgage insurance (PMI) or the FHA equivalent, known as mortgage insurance premium. This can add another $100 or more onto your monthly payment.
  - You should also get a lower interest rate with a higher down payment. As well, with 20% down or more, the scrutiny on your income eases up a bit.
- Purchasing a home can take a long time, be fraught with tension and emotions, cost an arm and a leg, and be a temporary inconvenience. But the rewards: The satisfactions of owning your own home, of having an investment that will hopefully increase in value, make it all worthwhile. Just be prepared!

When Foreclosure Happens

Foreclosure happens when you fall behind on your house payments and your lender uses procedures to be granted the ability to sell your house. Foreclosure works differently in different states: In some, the lender has to file a lawsuit to foreclose (judicial foreclosure), while in others, it can foreclose without going to court (non-judicial foreclosure).

Understand the process
If you are in foreclosure, facing foreclosure, or just falling behind on mortgage payments, it's crucial that you understand the foreclosure process—its procedures and consequences.

If you stop making your mortgage payments, you will most likely lose your home to foreclosure. Foreclosure is the legal process that allows the owner of your home loan to sell your home to satisfy the debt that you owe.

With both types of foreclosures—judicial and non-judicial—the foreclosing party (your lender) must mail you a notice telling you that foreclosure proceedings will start if you don't get caught up in payments. The notice generally provides 30 days for you to pay the past-due amounts; otherwise the foreclosure will begin. In addition, some states offer homeowner pre-foreclosure mediation or other ways to help the homeowner avoid foreclosure.

Judicial Foreclosures
In a judicial foreclosure, your lender, the foreclosing party, starts the foreclosure by filing a lawsuit in state court as a plaintiff. You'll receive a copy of the complaint (sometimes called a petition) to foreclose and get a certain number of days to respond to the lawsuit. If you don't respond to the lawsuit, the court will grant a judgment of foreclosure in favor of the plaintiff and set a sale date for your home.

The foreclosing party must publish notice of the foreclosure sale in a local newspaper for a certain number of weeks before the sale, and provide you with a copy of the notice. The foreclosure sale is a public auction where the public (and the foreclosing party) may bid on the property. The highest bidder (if there is one—not all properties sell in a foreclosure sale) becomes the new owner.

Non-judicial Foreclosures
In a non-judicial foreclosure, the foreclosing party must take one or more of the following steps (depending on the state requirements):

- Mail you a notice of default that tells you how much time you have to get caught up on payments.
- Record the notice of default in the local land records office.
- Mail you (or post it on your property) a notice of sale that tells you the date the property will be (or try to be) sold.

Each of the notices have time limits and specific content requirements regarding the property and the loan. Your property is then sold at an auction where the public (and the foreclosing party) may bid on the property.

Right to Redeem

In some states, you get a certain amount of time to regain title to the property after a foreclosure sale by paying the foreclosure purchaser the sale price plus accrued interest and other expenses. This is called the right of redemption.

What Happens After the Foreclosure Sale

You own your home, and may stay there, up until the foreclosure sale. In some states, you can stay in the home until the redemption period expires or until the sale closes. If you don't leave your home at this point, the purchaser at the foreclosure sale—the new owner—will take steps to evict you.

Eviction regulations differ in each state. It's better to leave the house voluntarily, and before eviction procedures that could cost you money, inconvenience, and even more emotional stress.

Defenses to Foreclosure

Depending on the circumstances in your situation, you may have a defense to a foreclosure. Some common defenses to foreclosure include:

- The foreclosing party (your lender) can't prove it owns the debt.
- You are on active duty in the military and entitled to protection from foreclosure under the SCRA.
- The foreclosing party didn't follow state foreclosure procedures.
- The foreclosure servicer made a serious mistake.

At this point, if you decide to raise a defense, you should seek legal counsel. You'll have to either file your own lawsuit, or prepare a formal answer to the foreclosure complaint from your lender.

Personal Finance *for* Real People

Education

What is FAFSA? Federal Student Aid

The Free Application for Federal Student Aid (FAFSA) is the first step in the financial aid process. You use the FAFSA to apply for federal student aid, such as grants, work-study, and loans. In addition, most states and colleges use information from the FAFSA to award nonfederal aid.

Federal Student Aid, a part of the U.S. Department of Education, is the largest provider of student financial aid in the nation. At the office of Federal Student Aid, 1,200 employees help make college education possible for everyone by providing more than $150 billion in federal grants, loans, and work-study funds each year to more than 13 million students paying for college or career school.

Federal Student Aid ensures that students and their families can benefit from these programs by:

- Informing students and families about the availability of the federal student aid programs and the process for applying for and receiving aid from those programs
- Developing the *Free Application for Federal Student Aid* (*FAFSA®*) and processing approximately 22 million FAFSA submissions each year
- Accurately disbursing, reconciling, and accounting for all federal student aid funds that are delivered to students each year through more than 6,200 colleges and career schools
- Managing the outstanding federal student loan portfolio and securing repayment from federal student loan borrowers
- Offering free assistance to students, parents, and borrowers throughout the entire financial aid process
- Providing oversight and monitoring of all program participants—schools, financial entities, and students—to ensure compliance with the laws, regulations, and policies governing the federal student aid programs.

Deadlines:

- You should complete and submit your FAFSA as soon as possible on or after October 1.
- Online applications must be submitted by midnight Central Time, June 30 of the following year.
- Any corrections or updates must be submitted by midnight Central Time, September 15 of the following year.
- Be aware that each state has a different deadline.
- Each college may also have a different deadline. Check with the college(s) you are interested in attending. You may also want to ask your college about its definition of an application deadline—whether it is the date the college receives your FAFSA, or the date your FAFSA is processed.
- Your college must have your correct, complete information by your last day of enrollment for the next school year.
- Find more detailed information on deadlines on http://www.fafsa.edu.gov.

Providing tax information:

- The easiest way to complete or correct your FAFSA with accurate tax information is by using the IRS Data Retrieval Tool. Most students and parents who filed a prior year tax return can view and transfer their tax return information directly into their FAFSA.
- If you (or your parents) have missed the prior year tax filing deadline of April 15, and still need to file a prior year income tax return with the Internal Revenue Service, you should submit your FAFSA using estimated tax information, and then you must correct that information after you file your return.
- Both parents or both the student and spouse may need to report income information on the FAFSA if they did not file a joint tax return for the prior year.
- If you or your family experienced significant changes to your financial situation (such as loss of employment), or other unusual circumstances (such as high unreimbursed medical or dental expenses), complete this form to the extent you can and submit it as instructed.

Using the information on your FAFSA and your EFC (Expected Family Contribution), the financial aid office at your college will determine the amount of aid you will receive. The college will use your EFC to prepare a financial aid package to help you meet your financial need. Financial need is the difference between the cost of attendance (which can include living expenses), as determined by your college, and your EFC. If you are eligible for a Federal Pell Grant, you may receive it from only one college for the same period of enrollment. If you or your family has unusual circumstances that should be taken into account, contact your college's financial aid office. Some examples of unusual circumstances are: unusual medical or dental expenses or a large change in income from the prior year to this year.

Any financial aid you are eligible to receive will be paid to you through your college. Typically, your college will first use the aid to pay tuition, fees and room and board (if provided by the college). Any remaining aid is paid to you for your other educational expenses.

If you are completing a paper FAFSA, you can only list four colleges in the school code step. You may add more colleges by doing one of the following:

- After your FAFSA has been processed, go to the FAFSA website. Click the **Login** button on the home page to login to FAFSA, and then click **Make FAFSA Corrections**.
- Use the Student Aid Report (SAR), which you will receive after your FAFSA is processed. Your Data Release Number (DRN) verifies your identity and will be listed on the first page of your SAR. You can call 1-800-433-3243 and provide your DRN to a customer service representative, who will add more school codes for you.
- Provide your DRN to the financial aid administrator at the college you want added, and he or she can add their school code to your FAFSA.
- Your FAFSA record can only list up to ten school codes. If there are ten school codes on your record, each new code will need to replace one of the school codes listed.

Remember that there's only so much money in the FAFSA pot—once applications open and the clock starts ticking, you need to get your application in as soon as possible. Delay could mean that FAFSA funds have all been granted, and you will be out of luck!

Free Money for College

There's no bad time to think about the costs of school—especially college.

If you have a student attending—or considering attending—college this year or next, now is a good time to start planning and researching your options for grants and scholarships. With college tuition dramatically rising every year, it's more important than ever to maximize these sources of free money for college.

The trick is finding the grants and scholarships available and then filling out the applications to meet the deadlines.

Your first stop should be the school's financial aid office. They can help you with deadlines, information required, and available programs.

Grants
Grants make educational funds, from small to large amounts, available to in-need students. Grant funding can be sourced from Federal and state governments, from the colleges and universities themselves, and from public and private organizations.

Grants fall into four categories:

- Student-specific grants
- Subject-specific grants
- Degree-level grants
- Minority grants

The Pell Grant is perhaps the most popular and widely known grant. The amount granted is a calculation based on the family's income and whether the student will be full or part-time. Check http://www.fafsa.ed.gov for more information and to apply. You must apply by the end of June, for the fall school semester. However, don't wait until then! There's a limited amount of grant money available, so apply as soon as you can after January 1.

The FAFSA application is necessary for most grant programs, including Pell Grants.

Native Americans are eligible for specific Federal grants for college. For more information, go to the Federal grants website, https://www.grants.gov. You *may* need the birthdates and birth locations of your native ancestors.

Your state may also offers a grant for underprivileged students who reside in and who will attend college in your state.

Those are just a few examples. Grants are available for students majoring in certain courses of study (math, teaching, nursing, foreign language, science, technology, etc.); for minorities (African-American, Asian, Hispanic, Native American, and women); for specific athletic sports (track and field, tennis, bowling, and many more); for students with disabilities, both physical and mental; for help with housing, living expenses, and supplies.

Scholarships
Just like grants, scholarships are available for students in the same above categories and, *unlike* grants, are not necessarily need-based. Once again, filing a FAFSA is necessary. The more applications for scholarships you send in, the more likely you'll receive one. Don't limit yourself to large scholarships—you may be more eligible, and have a greater chance at success, with multiple small scholarships.

For more information on grants and scholarships, explore these websites:
http://www.collegescholarships.org/
http://www.fafsaonline.com/college-grants/
http://www.studentscholarshipsearch.com
http://studentaid.ed.gov/redirects/students-gov

Grants for College and Higher Education

Unlike student loans, college grants do not require repayment. College grants are just like scholarships with one exception: Scholarships may be need-based or merit based, whereas most grants are typically need-based.

College grants are primarily awards of free money, not requiring any repayment on the part of the student. They can be directed toward specific educational expenses, specific types of students, or general purpose. Unlike scholarships, which are typically awarded on the basis of academic achievement or athletic, artistic or extracurricular performance, grants are awarded according to financial need. Academic merit will still be a factor, but financial need is given greater weight in the final decision-making process.

Grants for college-bound students are offered by a variety of different sources, including:

- Federal and State Governments
- Colleges and Universities
- Public and Private Organizations
- Professional Associations

Regardless of the source of the grants, the purpose remains the same: To make a college education more accessible to all students by supplying the necessary supplemental funds to help them meet their total college costs.

Federal Grants

Federal grant programs for college-bound students form the foundation of all financial aid. These programs should be the first stop for you if you're looking for financial assistance to help pay for college. Federal education grants are funded by the government, and administered through the U.S. Department of Education. Federal education grants help thousands of students pay for college every year. Without these grants, many students would not be able to realize their higher educational goals.

The following federal grant programs are offered:

- *The Federal Pell Grant*: Since 1972 the Federal Pell Grant has been helping students fund their college educations. More students rely on Pell grants for financial assistance than any other grant program in America.
- *The Federal Supplemental Educational Opportunity Grant*: This grant is designed to give financial aid to undergraduate students with extreme financial need. The FSEOG program is funded by the federal government, and administered through the financial aid offices of participating colleges and universities. Students must apply through their college of choice, and grants are awarded on a first come, first served basis.

242

- *The Federal TEACH Grant*: The TEACH Grant is an example of an award-for-service program. The grant provides federal funding to students who agree to take up a teaching position in a high-need field, or critical shortage facility, following graduation. Student recipients must sign a contract agreeing to a predetermined time of service. Students who fail to fulfill their teaching obligations will have their grant revert to a student loan, and will be responsible for the full repayment, plus interest, of that loan.
- Students must fill out a FASFA to check their eligibility for federal grant programs.

State Grants
Every state has a Department of Higher Education that monitors, and regulates, the colleges and universities within that state. Most states offer their resident students some degree of college financial aid, either through their Department of Higher Education or through a dedicated Student Assistance Commission. Scholarship and grant programs are common at the state level, and are typically supported by state and local taxes, and/or state lottery funds.

State-funded college grants typically address financial needs of low-income students, as well as women and minority students. States also often offer career-specific grants-for-service to those pursuing degrees and careers in high demand fields such as teaching and nursing.

Grant programs will vary widely from state to state, and you should refer to http://www.CollegeScholarships.org for more information on state-funded financial aid programs, and for links to information on financial aid programs specific to your state.

Non-Government Grants
Once you've exhausted the available federal and state-supported grants, you should look to other sources for financial assistance. Many grants for college-bound students can be found in the private sector. Corporations and professional associations often offer grants for deserving students who are pursuing degrees in fields closely allied to that business or organization. College grants can also be found through religious organizations, as well as clubs and associations dedicated to community service. These grant programs may have very specific eligibility requirements, but they do offer substantial financial assistance to those students who meet the necessary criteria.

Colleges and universities can also be prime sources for grants. Often, colleges will be given private endowments from individuals and businesses for the purpose of providing financial aid to deserving students. Again, privately endowed grants and scholarships tend to have highly specific eligibility requirements, and may target certain portions of the population such as women or minorities. They may also be dedicated to students pursuing degrees in specific fields or disciplines.

Your search for non-government funded college grants should begin by combining your status as a student (undergraduate or graduate), your field of interest, and your personal background (minority status, gender, etc). Many grant programs can be found through a focused search of the internet, or through the financial aid offices of colleges and universities. This can be time consuming, but the rewards can be substantial.

Grant Categories
Some college grant programs are open to all students regardless of background or field of study. These are considered General Grants, and typically are decided according to financial need and academic performance. A great number of college grants, however, are designed to target specific portions of the population or students pursuing particular degrees or career paths. These can be broken down into the following categories:

- Student Specific
- Subject Specific
- Degree-Level Specific
- Minority Specific

As with all college grants, funding may be provided by a variety of sources, including state governments, professional associations, corporations, colleges and universities.

Popular Student-Specific Grants
The width and breadth of the student population continues to grow and change as more and more students head to college to improve their education and professional opportunities. The collegiate population is made up of a diverse array of students of all types and backgrounds. Grants for college-bound students are often designed to benefit specific types of students, and to address their particular financial needs. The most common student-specific grant programs fall into the following categories:

- Non-traditional
- Low-income and culturally disadvantaged
- Military and their dependents

Women and minorities make up a large section of the national student body, and there are a large number of grant programs that target both groups.

Low-Income and Disadvantaged Students
Most college grants are designed to address the needs of students who are facing a financial shortfall in their college funding. However, there is a wide range of grant programs that are dedicated to providing financial aid to students in more extreme circumstances. Grants for low-income students are specifically designed to address the financial needs of students from economic or socially disadvantaged backgrounds. Typically, state and federal governments, advocacy groups and charitable foundations sponsor these programs.

In addition to grants dedicated to the economically disadvantaged, there many grant programs designed to target the needs of students with both physical and mental disabilities. Grants for students with disabilities help to increase college accessibility to students facing a wide range of personal challenges, including blindness, hearing impairment, autism, and decreased mobility due to physical impairment. Disabled students looking for grants to help them pay for college should begin their search by focusing on advocacy groups and charitable foundations dedicated to the needs of people with their particular disability.

Subject-Specific Grants
Many grant programs are dedicated to the needs of students pursuing specific degrees, and with specific career goals. Typically, these programs are designed to encourage and support those students who are pursuing professional careers in high need fields. These subject-specific grants are sponsored by a variety of sources, including federal and state governments, corporations and professional associations. Popular fields include STEM subjects (science, technology, engineering, and math), healthcare (nurses, nurse practitioners, and primary-care physicians), and teachers.

Degree Level Specific Grants

- *Undergraduate Grants*: Grants for undergraduate students are a large part of available financial aid. These programs may provide general grant funding for students pursuing any number of degrees, or they may be specific to undergraduates enrolled in science, mathematics or engineering courses. Grants for undergraduate students are available from federal and state governments, colleges and universities, corporations and professional associations.
- *Graduate And Doctoral Students*: Grants for doctoral candidates and graduate students are highly competitive, and focus on the financial needs of students engaged in research to complete their high level degrees. These grants are often referred to as fellowships, and are typically sponsored by colleges and universities as a way of bringing the best and brightest graduate students to their campuses. Unlike the more traditional undergraduate grants, these programs place a great amount of weight on academic achievement. Financial need is a secondary consideration. Grants for graduate and doctoral students are typically high dollar awards, and will include funds for research related travel and stipends for living expenses.

Minority-Specific Grants

Many grant programs exist to serve the needs of minority groups who have a history of being under-represented in the higher education system. While great strides have been made over the last few decades, more work needs to be done to expand and diversify. Grants for minorities, and for women, are sponsored by a variety of sources, including state and federal governments, professional associations, corporations, colleges, universities, charitable foundations and advocacy groups.

- *Grants For African American Students*: African American students can find a wide range of grants designed to help them pursue their college education. African Americans have been under-represented in higher education. But with the help of publicly and privately funded grant programs, they are beginning to take their place on college campuses across the country. Dedicated grant programs for African-American students are helping more and more students of color pursue higher education degrees.
- *Hispanic Students*: Hispanics are now the fastest growing minority population in the United States. The rise in population numbers is not reflected in the number of college-bound Hispanic students. This is beginning to change and the availability of dedicated college grants for Hispanic students is increasing. Grants for Hispanic students are supported by charitable foundations and advocacy groups, as well as by corporations and professional associations dedicated to diversifying the workforce. Hispanic students can find a large number of grants designed to encourage them to pursue specific career paths, with an emphasis on science, mathematics and technology.
- *Native American Students*: Grants for Native American students may be less prevalent than those for other minorities, but they are increasing. State governments, advocacy groups and private endowments support a growing number of grants dedicated to helping Native Americans pursue a college education. Many of these programs target members of specific Native American tribes, and students will be required to present documentary evidence of their American Indian heritage. A large number of grants for Native-American students are career-specific, with an emphasis on healthcare, education, science and technology.
- *Asian American Students*: Asian Americans are one of the fastest growing ethnic populations in the United States. While Asian immigrants have been part of the workforce for more than a hundred years, they have been historically under-represented in mainstream colleges and universities. Now, more Asian American students are headed to college than ever before. Grants for Asian American students are supported by a variety of charitable foundations, corporations and private endowments. Like many grants dedicated to the financial needs of minority students, many grants for Asian Americans place a particular emphasis on specific career paths, including science, technology, education and journalism.
- *Grants For Women*: Women make up 51% of the population, yet are still considered a minority. While the numbers may prove that women are a majority of the populace, they remain under-represented on most mainstream college campuses across the country. Private women's colleges have a long history of providing

solid educations with an emphasis on career self-sufficiency. But the need for greater diversity at mainstream colleges and universities still remains, as does the need to diversify the workforce. Many organizations, professional associations and advocacy groups have developed a wide range of grants designed to help women pursue higher education. Grant programs for women are designed to encourage female students to pursue degrees, and careers, in a wide range of fields in which they have been historically under-represented. Education grants for women typically focus on disciplines in need of greater diversity, such as science, mathematics, technology and business.

Grants provide much needed financial support for students of all types, and from a variety of diverse backgrounds. For many students, education grants mean the difference between achieving their college dreams and having those dreams deferred. Students should make the search for college grants a priority when preparing for college. Before considering any high cost college loans, students should investigate the many and varied grant opportunities that may be available to them.

For more detailed information on available grants: http://www.CollegeScholarships.org

Finding Scholarships

Many scholarships—literally thousands—are available for students, and, unlike grants, are not necessarily need-based. Scholarships, like grants, provide you with free money for college that does not have to be paid back.

The more applications for scholarships you send in, the more likely you'll receive one or more. Don't limit yourself to large scholarships—you may be more eligible, and have a greater chance at success, with multiple small scholarships.

Scholarships and grants are the first places you should look when planning out how to finance your education. And don't feel that you are limited by age or any other personal consideration. There are scholarships for every person and field of study. In the most recent college year, more than 34% of student college costs were covered by scholarships and grants. It's definitely worth making the effort!

Choosing a scholarship:
Search for scholarships that are most relevant to your background, field of study, sport, skill, interest, achievement, or other attribute. Whether you're in grad school, were just accepted into college, or partway through college, there are sure to be scholarships for which you qualify and for which you should apply.

Finding a scholarship:
Find what scholarships are available: Contact the financial aid office at the school you plan to attend; research at the public library; do your research online.

Places to look:

- University, college, or career school financial aid office
- High school or TRIO counselor
- U.S. Department of Labor scholarship search
- Federal agencies Student Aid website
- Your state's grant agency
- Local public library reference desk
- Organizations related to your area of interest and study: foundations, religious or community organizations, local businesses, civic groups
- Your employer or your parents' employers

When you are looking for a scholarship, certainly apply for the general-interest ones, but don't forget to look at those scholarships that apply to a certain set of people,   or specific subjects, or by education-degree level:

- **Demographic groups**: Women, African Americans, Native Americans, Hispanic Americans, Asian Americans, other minorities or ethnicities
- **Family-specific:** First in family, adult students, foster children, non-traditional students, low-income
- **Subjects:** Teaching, medicine, psychology, science, math, technology, religion, criminal justice, social work, and just about any interest you can think of
- **Fortune 500 scholarships:** Companies like Target, McDonald's, Ford, Apple, Pepsi, and more have scholarship programs
- **Military:** Veterans, spouses and children of veterans or currently serving military
- **Athletic:** Available for most sports
- **Medical condition:** Scholarships for student with specific medical conditions such as cancer, diabetes, epilepsy, ADHD, and disabilities
- There are many more targeted scholarships available

Applying for a scholarship:
Before you start your applications for scholarships, you will need to fill out a FAFSA (free application for federal student aid). Once that has gone through, then get the application from the scholarship's website. Make sure you read applications carefully, fill them out completely, and meet the application deadlines. Each scholarship will have its own requirements.

When to apply:
Each scholarship has its own schedule and deadline for application: Some are not that far in advance, but others may need to be submitted a year or so before your college starts.

Other things to know:

- Your scholarship money may go directly to your college, or may be sent directly to you. Be sure to ask about this, if the information isn't supplied.
- All your student aid added together cannot be more that the cost of your attendance. Make sure you understand just what your scholarship can apply to—does it cover textbooks or just tuition? Does it cover costs of living—rent, food, or transportation? If you are confused, talk to your college's financial aid office.
- *Beware of scams!* You do *not* need to pay to find scholarship or grant information. Make sure the offers you receive are legitimate. You do *not* need to pay a fee to apply for FAFSA. Do not share your FAFSA ID with anyone. Don't give personal or financial information over the phone, through email, or on the internet unless you initiated the contact. You *don't* have to pay for financial aid advice. Keep track of what you've applied for, and what you've received. Keep receipts and documents and when you no longer need them, shred them.

Start your research early, know and meet the deadlines, and you will be on your way to one or more scholarships. A scholarship might cover all the cost of your tuition and housing, or the cost of your textbooks, or just a general award of a few hundred dollars. But in any case it will reduce the cost of your education!

About Student Debt

For the first time in history, total student loan debt has now equaled total credit card debt, according to the Federal Reserve Bank of New York, and the U.S. Department of Education. Some speculate that total outstanding student loan debt could rise to as much as $1 trillion, with up to $1 billion borrowed this year alone.

Those are enormous numbers, and are resulting in a big impact on the economy, and a big impact on the lives of students and parents. Students now start their lives immediately deep in debt, forced to indefinitely delay purchases, including buying a car or home. They are even delaying marriage, and starting families. More adult children are living with their parents for a much longer time. The burden is on parents, too, who may have cosigned a student loan, or who are still supporting their adult children.

And it's not affecting only those students in college for the first time. Workers trying to get retraining, or professionals looking to add a degree to make themselves more employable are also borrowing for their education and additional training. For-profit schools utilize the most student loans, and have the highest loan default rate.

Why has student debt risen so dramatically?

Students are borrowing more, 63% more, than only a decade ago. The percentage of student loan borrowers more than nine months behind on payments continues to increase each year.

College tuition costs have risen faster than the rate of inflation—between 25% and 37% or even more for some institutions. Tuition has increased because federal and state subsidies to colleges have been greatly reduced; and administration, property maintenance, technology, and security costs have increased.

Student loan debt is structured differently than consumer debt, and cannot be discharged during bankruptcy. In 1998 federal students loans were restricted from inclusion in bankruptcy discharges, and in 2005 private student loans were also restricted. Unlike all other debt, for student loans, once it's borrowed, it's owed for life.

The increasing burden of student debt, combined with other debt, impairment of income, dissolution of savings, and unstable and difficult job market, combines like a perfect storm to keep the economy from recovering.

Start Teaching Your Children About Money

Is there a "best time" to teach your children about money and finance? Some would say that you can't start too early, and we agree. Obviously kids need to be old enough to count first, but once they are, it's time to start.

Early Steps
Currency is an excellent way to teach counting and money concepts. Making pretend purchases, giving change, and delving into the components of money equivalents (10 dimes make a dollar, etc.) are all a great basis to learn math *and* understand how money works.

Start early with an allowance, even a very minimal one. Have discussions about how much your child can buy with their allowance, and the value of their purchase. Now is a good time to begin working on the concept of saving, and also allocating or budgeting. Let's say your child has one dollar—he can break it up into various saving and spending categories. For example: Ten cents for church collection or donating to charity; twenty cents to save for a special purchase; ten cents to contribute to mom's present for Mother's Day; and the rest on whatever he wants.

Set an Example
The more your children are used to seeing you working on a budget, or carefully considering each purchase, the more likely they will use your example later in life (eventually!). Conversely, if they see you impulsively blowing your budget, and the family's finances going wildly up and down, odds are they won't know how to (or want to) set up their own responsible finances when they are adults.

Start explaining your purchase decisions, especially while grocery shopping, while your children are young. They'll begin to understand about priorities and budgeting. Work through your reasoning with them (this can of beans is exactly the same as the other can of beans, but less expensive because it's not a big brand, etc.).

How Much Should You Share?
Giving your children an awareness of the family's financial state is good, but be careful how you do it. You want them to understand that they play a part in the family's well-being, and how their wants and needs fit into everyone else's. You want them to understand *why* they sometimes can't have that special something they want so urgently. This can help make your family stronger, and start your kids off on the right path.

On the other hand, you do *not* want your child to feel the weight of adult responsibility. It's not up to her to ensure your family's financial welfare. You do want her to remain a child, and not have adult worries.

You also do not necessarily want to share too much information about the family's financial matters. Exactly how much you earn is not really your children's business—it's private, and keeping it that way is a good lesson in privacy. And you do not want your children starting to do their own theoretical family budgets (using savings to buy a child a new car is not a decision they should make or suggest, for example).

As Your Children Get Older
As your child grows up, you can start teaching him more complex issues about money, and how he can handle it—especially if he is making his own money.

Help your child open a savings account, and eventually a checking account. Discuss how credit cards work, and even (if you are comfortable) sharing your own credit card statements, charges, and payments. You can do a credit card test-run by giving your child a reloadable prepaid debit card and help her manage it. A prepaid debit card is also good for older children to use if they purchase items online—music or books, etc.

And when she is old enough, start the discussion on choosing and paying for college.

Here are some good websites for more information about teaching your children about money:

- https://www.cnn.com/business
- https://www.forbes.com/personal-finance
- https://www.parents.com/
- https://www.usa.gov/education?source=kids

Teaching Teenagers the Facts About Money

Teenagers today seem to be woefully uneducated about money: where it comes from, how to handle it, how to manage it, and how to respect it. Why is that? Is it that the education system has cut back classes and curriculum to only bare essentials? Parents are too busy? Teens just aren't paying attention? In fact, many teenagers are cynical about the banking and investment institutions, and more willing to look at alternative money management solutions—but they are also not fully educated on the pluses and minuses of each.

As parents, it's really our responsibility to make sure our children get at least the basic understanding of money and how to handle it. Don't think that some generous outside person or institution will take care of that for you.

It sounds a bit overwhelming, but not if you break it down into specific areas. Sometimes you may not even have to go into much detail—just giving them the basic knowledge or experience is enough.

Basic Money Life Lessons: Topic Suggestions

Income

- How do you apply for a job? What personal information should you bring to a job interview and to fill out the application?
- What benefits, if any, come with the job? Do they provide additional financial benefit (free meals, health insurance, discount on products)?
- What does direct deposit mean?
- What are the deductions that are taken out of a paycheck?

Money management and banking

- How do you write a check, get and/or send a money order, get a prepaid debit card?
- What kinds of bank accounts are available? What are the fees and account minimums to look out for?
- What happens if you bounce a check, or overdraw funds?
- How and when do you use an ATM?
- How do you make a budget? How do you know what expenses to include? (check our other chapters on budgeting expenses, and budgeting income).
- How do you save for a goal?
- How do loans work?

Taxes

- When do teenagers have to start paying taxes?
- How do you file a tax return? How many tax returns do you have to file?
- What happens if you don't have money to pay your taxes?

Education expenses

- See our other sections about grants, scholarships, and loans for students.

Credit cards

- At college, students are bombarded with credit card offers. When should you accept one, and how should you select one?
- What happens if you miss a payment?
- What are interest rates?
- What fees are involved?
- What happens if you can't pay off your credit card?

How to rent a place to live

- What information is needed for a rental application?
- What happens if you miss the rent payment?
- What do you need to consider when getting roommates?
- How do you sign up for utilities?
- What happens when you miss a utility payment?
- What is a security deposit, and how can you make sure you get it back?

Keeping your finances secure

- What scams should everyone watch out for?
- How do you keep confidential information secure?
- What passwords are most secure?
- How can you be careful at the ATM, and at stores and restaurants?
- How do you shop carefully online?
- What information should you share (and not share) in social media?
- What is identity theft?
- How do you keep your postal mail secure?

Investments

- What are the different kinds of interest rates, and in which situations are they used?
- What are realistic rates of return on investments?
- How do you set out a good investment plan for your young adult years?
- What is inflation?
- How does the stock market work, and why is it   important?

253

It seems like a lot of information, and we're just scratching the surface. But if you tackle each topic one at a time, even one a week, you'll get through them in no time.

Don't hesitate to draw in authorities on each subject if you can. Take your teen with you to the bank or to a local financial services center and go over the options available. Know someone who is a manager? Ask them to talk to your teen about hiring practices. You get the idea!

And of course, if financial classes are offered at school, make sure your teenager takes advantage of them. Some high schools do offer classes on basic finance, and there may be adult education classes available.

Other resources:
http://www.ItAllAddsUp.org/, a website about personal finance for teenagers
JumpStart, https://www.jstart.org/ another personal finance website for students
https://www.bankrate.com/ offers quite a few handy financial calculators

There are also quite a few books on personal finance for teens and kids, and some may be available at your library, or available for purchase.

Use Summer Break to Make Learning About Money Fun

Teaching your children about money is an important job for parents, but not always necessarily a fun one. However, this is a lesson that will last for your children's lifetimes, and even affect your children's children, so it's important to get started.

But, it's summer! There are plenty of ways to make learning financial lessons fun and entertaining.

Use your library for good stories that include a financial lesson.

- Read them aloud to your children, or let them explore the books individually.
- Most public library systems have a very fun summer reading programs. Encouraging the love of reading and literacy is a big part of learning to be financially knowledgeable and responsible.
- U.S. News & World Report also has a good list of children's books that contain financial lessons on http://www.money.usnews.com
- Ask for suggestions in the children's library section.

Draw on familiar characters from television and games:

- Nickelodeon's Nick Jr. has a fun list of money games to play with your kids on http://www.nickjr.com.
- Savings Spree is a game app that also teaches lessons about money decisions.
- Other iPad, iPhone, or iPod games and apps include:
  - *Kid's Money*, a savings calculator.
  - *Roosterbank* tracks spending and pocket money with games and more.
  - *Celebrity Calamity* helps players learn about debit and credit cards by managing a budget for a clueless celebrity.
  - *Star Banks*, from T. Rowe Price, helps kids learn smart saving and spending habits.

Don't forget board games:
Board games are enjoying a resurgence in popularity; don't be afraid your kids will think you are hopelessly old-fashioned!

- Pull out old favorites like: *Monopoly, Life, Payday*.
- Newer games include: *The Allowance Game, Millionaire Maker, Puerto Rico, The Farming Game, Wise Money*, and *Awesome Island*.

Go online for inspiration, activities, and more games:

- *Financial Peace Junior*, https://www.daveramsey.com/store/product/financial-peace-junior from Dave Ramsey, is an entire kit that teaches your children that money comes from work, and about the importance of giving, saving, and spending.
- *Money Smart for Young People*, https://www.fdic.gov/consumers/consumer/moneysmart/young.html put together by the FDIC, includes programs for all age groups.

Put it into practice:

- Start your child on an allowance: Have discussions about how much your child can buy with their allowance, and the value of their purchase. Now is a good time to begin working on the concept of saving, and also allocating or budgeting. Try establishing an allowance just for the summer, or for the family vacation. Your children can be in charge of their own money for a short, experimental period of time, and you'll have more of chance to help them with their decisions.
- Have your child be in charge of checking the change you receive back from purchases.
- Explain some of your purchase decisions, and what your financial priorities are—as an individual, and for the family.
- If your child is older, go with them to the bank and help them open a savings account, and then show them how to make deposits into it.
- A prepaid debit card is another way to get your children used to handling their own money. Give your child a prepaid card for a modest amount, and give them a time limit for which that money has to last (for the month, for the summer, for vacation, or through the rest of the year). This is a good tool for learning how to budget and make purchasing decisions. Review your child's progress and help them through any rough spots. You can get a prepaid debit card for any amount at your local financial services center.

As your child grows up, you can start teaching him more complex issues about money, and how he can handle it—especially if he is making his own money. Make a good start this summer!

Protect Yourself

Identity Theft

Identity theft is a growing problem—don't make it easy for someone to steal your identity and credit information!

Here are some steps everyone should follow:

Guard your personal information:

• Don't share your Social Security number unless you have a very good reason to do so, and don't carry your card in your wallet.

• Don't share your birth date, your home phone number, or mother's maiden name.

• Put as little information on your checks as possible—definitely **not** your Social Security number or Driver's License number, and not your home phone number.

Shred, shred, shred, shred!
Thieves search through trash to find statements you've thrown away, credit card offers, and other information they can use to recreate your identity. Don't ever discard something with your personal information, passwords, account numbers, or enrollment forms. **Shred!**

In your wallet:
Sign your credit cards and bank cards—you can even write "Check Photo ID" in that space as well, if you want to be extra careful.

• Make a copy of all your identification (everything in your wallet), with notification phone numbers, and keep in a safe place. Be sure to keep this updated.

Out in public:

• Be aware of your surroundings when entering your pin number in public places—don't let someone look over your shoulder.

• Try to pay cash in coffee shops with a lot of laptop users—they can lift your card information.

• Don't shop online, do mobile banking, or enter secure information on a public Wi-Fi system.

• Have your mail collected by a neighbor or put on hold if you will be away.

• Don't leave bills or other revealing mail in your home mailbox for pick up—mail at the Post Office or at a Post Office box.

Online:

- Create a strong password system, and don't use the same password on all sites you frequent. Don't use easily accessible information for your password: your pet's name, your birthday, etc.; and mix up your password with numbers and capital letters.

- Don't include your personal data (full name, birth date, phone number, address) on Facebook or other social networks.

- Don't expose your location/time/place in real time online (Facebook, FourSquare).

- Keep on top of your online privacy settings.

- Keep your antivirus settings up to date.

- If you make purchases online, buy only on a secure encrypted website—look for the small padlock at the bottom or top of the screen.

- Monitor your account activities online—this makes it easy to see if there's any unauthorized activity. Check over your statements each month.

And finally…

- Review your credit reports at least once a year. You'll be able to check for mistakes, and to see if a thief has taken credit out in your name.
- You are entitled by law to a yearly free copy of your credit report from each of the major agencies—do it!
    - Equifax: 1-800-525-6285
      Experian (formerly TRW): 1-888-397-3742
      Trans Union: 1-800-680-7289
      Social Security Administration (fraud line): 1-800-027-1369

What to Do When Your Identity has Been Stolen

In spite of your careful monitoring, the worst has happened: Your identity has been stolen. It's not your fault; these things do happen in spite of your best efforts. But what do you do now?

Don't panic, but do act quickly!

There are some basic steps you need to take in all situations, and additional steps that depend on your exact situation.

FIRST

- **Notify companies** where actual fraud has occurred, and tell them your identity has been stolen. Perhaps you noticed a bogus charge on your credit card statement, received a bill from a utility that you don't use, or were notified that the company was hacked, or had your wallet stolen.
- **Call** the company
- **Close,** freeze, or change your account
- **Change your login,** your password, and your pin number
- **Contact just one of the major credit bureaus** and place a fraud alert. That one company is required to notify the other two credit bureaus. Placing a fraud alert is free, and will make it a lot harder for someone to open more accounts in your name—the credit bureaus will be keeping watch.

    - http://www.Equifax.com, Credit Report Assistance, 1-888-766-0008
    - http://www.Experian.com, Fraud Alert, 1-888-397-3742
    - http://www.TransUnion.com, Fraud, 1-800-680-7289

- **Get a copy of your** free credit report, and review it—report any transactions or accounts you don't recognize. 1-877-322-8228
- **Report your identity theft to the Federal Trade Commission.** Once you complete their complaint form, you'll receive an Identity Theft Affidavit. This will come in handy during this process. Print out your Affidavit immediately, and save it—once you leave that page on the website, you won't be able to access it again. FTC Complaint Form 1-877-438-4338

- **Report your identity theft to your police department.** Ask for a copy of the police report—you'll need it later. The combination of your Identity Theft Affidavit and the police report (both equal your Identity Theft Report) proves to businesses that you have had your identity stolen, and guarantees you certain rights. Take these with you to the police station:
- A copy of your Identity Theft Affidavit
- Your government-issued photo ID
- Proof of your address: rental agreement, or utility bill
- Any proof you have of the theft

NEXT

- **If accounts were opened in your name,** call each company and close those accounts. Ask the company to send you a letter confirming that the fraudulent account is not yours, that you are not liable for it, and that it is (or will be) removed from your credit report. Keep this letter, and write down whom you talked to, and when you talked to them.
- **Perhaps instead of fraudulent accounts, you simply have fraudulent purchases or charges.** Follow the same procedure: Contact each company, have them remove the charges, ask them to send you the same letter, and keep track of who you talked to. Keep this letter, as well.
- **Clean up your credit report.** Write to each credit bureau, explain that your identity has been stolen, attach your Identity Theft Report (the Affidavit and your police report), and proof of your identity (name, address, Social Security Number).
- Tell the credit bureau what information on your report is fraudulent and from identity theft. Ask them to block this information. Once the information is blocked, it won't show up on your credit report, and those companies can't try to collect the debt from you. You must have your Identity Theft Report, though.
- Add an extended fraud alert to your credit report—this will keep the credit bureau on watch for any possible fraudulent activity, and keep you informed.
- Think about adding a credit freeze—this stops all access to your credit report unless you lift it or remove it.

SPECIAL ISSUES

Depending on the situation of your identity theft, and what information was stolen, you may have to also take one or more of these additional steps:

If you have a tax-related identity theft:

- Respond to any IRS notices
- Did you get an IRS notice saying an employer paid you, but you don't recognize them? Send a letter to the employer stating that someone stole your identity.
- Complete the IRS Form 14039, Identity Theft Affidavit and mail or fax it in.
- Keep notes about whom you talk to and when, and keep copies of all correspondence.

If your Social Security card was lost or stolen:

- Contact your local Social Security office, or apply online for a replacement card.
- Replace your Social Security card.

If your Driver's License was lost or stolen:

- Contact your local DMV branch to report it and get it replaced.

If your passport was lost or stolen:

- Call the State Department to report it: 1-877-487-2778
- Submit the replacement form at a Passport Application Acceptance Facility.
- If you need it replaced very quickly, apply in person at a Passport Agency.

If your name or personal information was used by someone who was arrested:

- Contact the specific law enforcement agency (police or sheriff's department, etc.) that made the arrest.
- File a report about the impersonation.
- Provide your fingerprints, a photo of yourself, and copies of any identifying documents.
- Ask the law enforcement agency that made the arrest to:
- Compare your information to the imposter's.
- Change all records from your name to the imposter's real name.
- Give you a clearance letter/certificate of release, to declare your innocence.
- Keep this clearance letter with you at all times. It may take a while for the corrections to make their way through the system, and you certainly don't want to be detained for just a traffic stop!
- Keep notes about to whom you talked and when.

If a court prosecutes someone who is using your name:

- Contact the court where the arrest or conviction took place.
- Contact the appropriate district or U.S. attorney for records to help clear your name in court records.
- Provide proof of your identity.
- Ask the court for a certificate of clearance, to declare your innocence.
- Keep this clearance letter with you at all times.
- Contact your state Attorney General's office, and see if your state has an Identity Theft Passport, which you can use to resolve financial issues resulting from your identity theft. Ask if they have any other help for identity theft victims.
- Ask any and all law enforcement agencies, courts, attorneys, that you contact what information brokers buy their records, and where else your information will appear. Write to the brokers and ask them to remove the errors from your file. Keep notes about who you contacted and when.

If someone is writing bad checks against your checking account:

- Contact your bank, and stop payment on stolen blank checks plus any fraudulent checks.
- Close your checking account.
- Ask the bank to report the theft to the check verification system—they will then tell businesses to refuse the stolen checks. If this is taking a while, you can also contact the check verification companies yourself:
    - Telecheck: 1-800-710-9898
    - Certegy: 1-800-437-5120
- Contact any businesses that accepted the bad checks, and explain what has happened. Don't hesitate— you don't want them to start collection proceedings, or for fees to start accumulating.

- You can find more detailed instructions, sample letters, an overview of your rights as an identity theft victim, and warning signs of identity theft at the FTC's Identity Theft website, https://www.ftc.gov/faq/consumer-protection/report-identity-theft.

Shop Safe Online

Just as you use caution when you are making a purchase, or when you are handling your money out in the "real" world, the same is true when you're shopping online.

E-commerce is mostly safe, and with a little caution and a few extra steps you can make it much safer. Here are some things to think about:

Check to make sure the website is secured with encryption technology. Don't worry—it's easy to do! Once the website asks you to start entering your information, look for one or more of these things:

- The website address should now start with https://. The "s" means that this is a secure page. There may also be an image of a locked padlock next to the URL.
- A bit more rarely nowadays, at the bottom of the screen there may be an image of a closed padlock or an unbroken key.
- If you are still concerned, read the merchant's privacy and security policies.

Do a quick check to make sure you are at the legitimate website address. Look at the URL at the top of your screen to make sure that if you wanted amazon.com, it says amazon.com. Still unsure? Get the URL you want to go to (say, www.amazon.com), and start typing it into the URL address box. Press Enter, and you should be directed either back to the page you were on, or to the real website page.

Think through your purchase: Is it something you might need to return or exchange? Check the merchant's policy BEFORE you make your purchase.

How much is shipping? Remember that if you are shipping outside the continental U.S., you will need to make sure that the merchant is able to do so, and that they can ship the specific item you want. Be aware that even if the merchant claims "free shipping," it still might not apply to shipments going to Hawaii, Alaska, U.S. territories, or other countries. And always check the shipping costs—it can cost much more to ship to those places, so you'll want to figure that into your purchase budget. If you're confused, a good plan is to call the merchant and talk to a live person at customer service.

And don't forget to include sales tax into your final purchase cost.

Double check your purchase before clicking the Purchase button: Is the size/color/quantity you wanted selected?

If this is a website you haven't visited before, or a merchant you are not familiar with, take a minute to do a little research. You can check with the Better Business Bureau, do a Google search to see what turns up, or call the merchant to ask some questions. Look to see that they post a physical address (not just a P.O. Box) and a phone number on their website.

Try to shop with merchants who are located in the United States—you are more protected by consumer laws.

Use a credit card or a prepaid debit card to make your online purchase. With a credit card, you'll be protected under the federal Fair Credit Billing Act, in which you have the right to challenge charges on your credit card, to dispute charges, and to withhold payment while your claim is being investigated. If your credit card was used without your authorization, you are only responsible for the first $50 in charges (though a prompt reporting of an unauthorized use will usually result in not paying even that charge). Don't use a debit or ATM card—they link directly to your bank account. By using a prepaid debit card, you can make your online purchase while controlling the amount of your risk, and you do not make your bank account vulnerable to thieves. Another good idea is to purchase a retailer-specific gift card to use for online purchases.

Do not use a money transfer to pay for your online purchase.

Be sure to always check your bank account and your credit card statements for any unauthorized purchases.

Do not give out your social security number. A merchant has no reason to ask for it.

Do not give out unnecessary personal information. The more information about your life that you share, the more likely you are to receive spam email, telephone solicitations, and even to risk identity theft. The merchant will usually mark with an asterisk (*) the questions that absolutely need to be answered to place your order. If you are still asked questions you don't want to answer (age, birth date, etc.), just leave and do your shopping elsewhere.

Don't respond to "phishing" emails. If you receive an email from a merchant or business that looks legitimate asking you to update your information, send in new or more information, to download a form or file, or to click on a link to do any of those…STOP RIGHT THERE. Just delete the email. A legitimate business will not ask you for such information via email. If you have any doubts, close the email, open your internet browser, enter the website's URL (the real one, not one copied from the email), and go there to check your account.

Use a secure password that's specific for this website only. Don't use easily findable information (driver's license number, social security number, mother's maiden name, birth date, etc.). Do create a password with at least eight characters: one that includes numbers, letters, and characters, if possible.

Print or save a copy of your order, and keep any correspondence from the merchant about your order.

And, of course, use your brain! If something sounds too good to be true, or if something makes you uncomfortable or feels not quite right, you are probably correct.

Don't be afraid—just be reasonably careful!

A good resource about e-commerce: The Federal Trade Commission guides for online shopping.

Beware of the Most Common Frauds

Scam
Alert!

Western Union offers a great overview of the most common types of frauds, along with excellent advice. We probably all know someone who has fallen victim to one of these—the fraudsters are very clever!

Fraud prevention is everyone's responsibility. Your best defense is to be aware, educate yourself and use good judgment.

Don't be a victim: Learn how to spot the warning signs of a scam or scammer before it's too late.

From Western Union:

Fraudsters Gain Your Trust, and then Steal Your Money
They use any means to contact victims—telephone, snail mail, email, and the Internet. They gain your trust and when they have you hooked, they ask you for money; then they take it and run. The scenarios they use to lure you in change, constantly. But you can protect yourself and your friends and family by arming yourself with knowledge of the most common types of fraud.

Types of Scams

- **Advanced fees and Prepayment:** Scammers pose as representatives from phony loan companies and use authentic-looking documents, emails, and websites to appear legitimate. They charge "fees" in advance of making loans. Consumers pay, but the loans never come through. Scammers are long gone and they sometimes regularly change the name of their "businesses" to avoid law enforcement.

  - This is one variation of a scam called the "advance fee" or "prepayment" scam. Scammers can also lure victims in with promises of investments or inheritance gifts in exchange for a fee. But it all comes down to the same theme: Victims pay money to someone in anticipation of receiving something of greater value and then receive little or nothing in return.

- **Mystery Shopping:** Mystery shopping scams are popular with criminals who target employment websites. The ploy is simple: Scammers send victims a check and tell them to use the funds to "evaluate" Western Union's money transfer service (or another company's service). Victims wire the money only to find out later that the checks bounce and they're responsible for paying the bank back.

- **Overpayment:** With overpayment scams, fraudsters play the role of buyer and target consumers selling a service or product. The "buyer" sends the seller a legitimate-looking check, usually drawn on a well-known bank, for an amount higher than the agreed-upon price. They contact an explanation for this overpayment and instruct the seller to deposit the check and wire back the excess funds. Weeks later, the victim learns the check is fake, but is still on the hook to pay the bank back for any money withdrawn.

- **Employment:** Employment scams generally start with a too-good-to-be-true offer—work from home and earn thousands of dollars a month, no experience needed—and end with consumers out of a "job" and out of money. They generally follow one of three patterns:

    - Scammers pose as a new "employer" and send victims a check to cover up-front expenses, like supplies. Victims deposit the check, buy the necessary supplies and wire any remaining funds back to the scammer. Weeks later, they find out the checks are fake and they're on the hook for the entire amount.
    - Scammers pose as "recruiters" pitching offers of guaranteed employment or as "employers" extending job offers on the condition that victims pay up front for things like credit checks or application or recruitment fees. Victims pay, but job offers never materialize.
    - Scammers pose as "company" representatives and seek sensitive personal and/or financial information from victims under the guise of doing credit or background checks. They then target victims later on for identity theft.

- **Lottery or Prizes:** Lottery or prize scams follow two similar patterns:

    - A victim gets an unsolicited phone call, email, letter or fax from someone claiming to work for a government agency or representing a well-known organization or celebrity, notifying them that they've won a lot of money or a prize. The scammer gains their trust and explains that, in order to collect the winnings, they first have to send a small sum of money to pay for processing fees or taxes. Following these instructions, victims immediately wire the money, but never get their "winnings." And they're out the money they paid for "fees and taxes."
    - Victims get an unsolicited check or money order and directions to deposit the money, and immediately wire a portion of it back to cover processing fees or taxes. Weeks later, victims learn that the checks are counterfeit, but have already wired the money to cover the "taxes" and can't get it back. And they're on the hook to pay their banks back for any money they withdrew.

- **Rental Property:** Sophisticated scammers use the Internet, and particularly free classified websites, to prey on unsuspecting real estate victims. Rental property scams generally happen in one of two ways:

    - Renters are looking for a house or an apartment to lease and get scammed by an "owner." Victims come across a place in a great area, at a great price. The advertisement looks legitimate so they start communicating with the "owner," generally by email. The owner says the place is theirs if they wire money to cover an application fee, security deposit, etc. They wire the money, and then never hear from the "owner" again.
    - Owners are renting out their house or apartment and get scammed by a "renter." The "renters" contact victims, generally by email, and express interest in renting the house or apartment. Scammers send a check for the deposit but then cancel the deal. Victims wire the money back only to find out the check was a fake.

- **Emergency and Grandparent:** Emergency scams play off peoples' emotions and strong desire to help others in need. Scammers impersonate their victims and make up an urgent situation—"I've been arrested," "I've been mugged," "I'm in the hospital"—and target friends and family with urgent pleas for help, and money.

    - Emergency scams also come in all shapes and sizes. There's the Grandparent Scam where con artists contact the elderly claiming to be their grandchild, urgently asking for money. And the

Social Networking Scam where con artists hack into social networking accounts and then target friends with frantic requests for money, claiming injury, arrest, etc.; they do the same by hacking email accounts. They use the information in these accounts to supply enough personal detail to make their requests appear legitimate.

- **Internet Purchase:** In the internet purchase scam, criminals prey on victims who bid on items using an online auction website or service. It generally plays out in one of two ways:

  - Victims win the bid, which is likely a sham or set up, and are told the seller only accepts money transfers for payment. The seller tells the buyer to put the transaction in a fictitious name, or the name of a loved one. Scammers convince victims this protects their money until the goods or services are received. The seller then creates a false ID in the fictitious name and retrieves the funds. The merchandise never arrives.
  - The other variation is when the original auction is legitimate but the victims don't win the bid. They're contacted later on by another party offering to sell them the same item under similar terms and instructed to wire the money as payment. The money is sent but the buyer never receives the goods.

- **Relationship:** The relationship scam starts simply: A man and woman meet on the internet. The relationship progresses: They email, talk on the phone, and trade pictures. And, finally, they make plans to meet, and even to get married. As the relationship gets stronger, things start to change. The man asks the woman to wire him money; he needs bus fare to visit a sick uncle. The first wire transfer is small but the requests keep coming and growing—his daughter needs emergency surgery, he needs airfare to come for a visit, etc. The payback promises are empty; the money's gone, and so is he.

- **Fake Check:** Fake checks play a starring role in lots of different scams: advance fee or prepayment scams; mystery shopping scams; lottery prize scams, and more. Victims get an unsolicited check or money order and directions to deposit the money and immediately wire a portion of it back to cover various expenses, like processing fees or taxes. Weeks later, victims learn that the checks are counterfeit, but they've already wired the money and can't get it back. And they're on the hook to pay their banks back for any money they withdrew.

Transfer Money Safely

Western Union offers a great overview of the most common types of frauds, along with excellent advice. We probably all know someone who has fallen victim to one of these—the fraudsters are very clever!

Fraud prevention is everyone's responsibility. Your best defense is to be aware, educate yourself and use good judgment. Don't be a victim: Learn how to spot the warning signs of a scam or scammer before it's too late.

From Western Union:

Here's some important information to remember about making a money transfer.

Lower your chances of falling victim to fraud by checking out these eight things you should never do when using a money transfer service.

- Never send money to people you haven't met in person.
- Never send money to pay for taxes or fees on lottery or prize winnings.
- Never use a test question as an additional security measure to protect your transaction.
- Never provide your banking information to people or businesses you don't know.
- Never send money in advance to obtain a loan or credit card.
- Never send money for an emergency situation without verifying that it's a real emergency.
- Never send funds from a check in your account until it officially clears—which can take weeks.
- Never send a money transfer for online purchases.

Fight Fraud: Warning Signs

Western Union offers a great overview of the most common types of frauds, along with excellent advice. We probably all know someone who has fallen victim to one of these—the fraudsters are very clever!

Fraud prevention is everyone's responsibility. Your best defense is to be aware, educate yourself and use good judgment. Don't be a victim: Learn how to spot the warning signs of a scam or scammer before it's too late.

From Western Union:

General Warning Signs

- Scammers have many excuses why they can't meet you in person. They list numerous reasons why they need money and always seem to be in trouble.
- Scammers claim they have been in an accident, are in the hospital and their medical bills have to be paid in full before they can leave.
- Scammers will tell you to send the money in the name of a friend or family member to verify you have funds or to act as an escrow until you receive the purchased goods or services.
- Scammers need money because they were mugged and their money, passport, and ID were stolen while traveling.
- Scammers continue to ask for money for a plane ticket to see you, or to "float" them until payday.
- Scammers claim they've been in an accident or have a sudden family tragedy right before boarding a plane to meet you, or are held up in Customs and needs money for their release.

Protect Your Finances While You're Away

"What?" you're saying. "Can't I even relax on vacation, or while I'm visiting family?"

Of course you can, and that's what a few simple precautions will let you do, even if something goes wrong.

Protecting your finances at home while you're away

If you have a bank account, sign up to be notified via email or text about deductions made to your account. You'll know what's going on, and know what your current balance is.

While you're at it, arrange for your bank and credit card statements to be delivered electronically. Then your banking information won't be sitting in your mailbox, at a neighbor's house, or languishing at the post office.

Pay any current bills and any bills you can expect to receive. You can pay online with your bank, with the service provider, or at your financial services location. If you don't have your bill yet, pay in advance what you estimate the bill will be.

Make copies of important documents and stash them in a safe, secure place. Think protection not just from theft, but also from fire or floods. You can hide them in your house in a fireproof safe, at a relative's house, or maybe even at work. You could also get a safe deposit box. At the same time, make TWO SETS of copies of any documents and ID you are taking with you—an extra set for your suitcase, and a set to leave at home. If your wallet or travel documents get stolen, you'll have back-ups.

Tell your reliable and trustworthy neighbors that you will be away. They don't have to do anything, but they can keep an eye out for suspicious activity—be sure to give them your phone number!

Put your mail delivery on hold at the post office.

Plug in some inexpensive timers to turn your lights and TV or radio on and off.

On the road

Bring your copied set of IDs and travel documents. Stash them in a somewhat hidden place in your luggage or your car.

Slip some extra cash in your phone—tuck it between the phone and its case. In some phones you can even put it inside the phone, just inside the battery door (make sure it doesn't overheat the phone, though!).

If you are traveling by car, hide a pay-as-you-go phone, a prepaid calling card, a prepaid debit card, important phone numbers, and some cash in a secure place in the car (hint—NOT the glove compartment). If you are renting a car, don't forget to remove it when you turn the car in!

Take prepaid debit cards in fixed amounts with you. You can then budget what you want to spend on food, gifts, souvenirs, etc., by assigning a debit card for each activity.

If you are taking your own car, double-check your insurance to make sure you are covered both for where you are traveling and for any activities you might be participating in.

It's not a long list, and you'll be able to relax that much more knowing that you've done all you can to both travel safely and to make sure you come back to a secure home.

Personal Finance *for* Real People

Shopping Strategies

10 Ways to Keep Away Those Post-Holiday Financial Blues

We've all been there: The shock of opening up the first credit card bill after the holidays. How did those expenses pile up so quickly and get so high?

The good news is you still have plenty of time to get control of your holiday spending and make sure your January is just as happy as your December.

First establish your total budget for holiday spending. Estimate how much you can afford to spend, and set that figure as your TOTAL expense goal.

- Make a list and check it twice. Do you really need to buy gifts for everyone on your list? Distant relatives would be happy with a card and a personal note, and coworkers with a potluck.

- Make your holiday and gift list and stick to it. Establish a dollar budget for each person, and remember to include the cost of wrapping and shipping. Don't forget to include any charitable donations, holiday meals, entertaining, gasoline, travel, and postage. And don't go over your budget!

- Resist those impulse buys. Stick to your plan!

- Shop smart. See our *Shop Smart* chapter for ideas on how to make your holiday shopping dollars go further.

- Use a specially designated debit card just for holiday shopping. Load up your debit card with the amount you want to spend this season. Use it for all your purchases—that way you won't overspend.

- Don't sign up for special financing plans or new credit cards. Additional store credit cards will only make overspending easier, as will 0% down and payment plans.

- Keep track of your spending. A simple list, or a notebook you can carry with you, will make it easier to keep notes on what you're spending through the season.

- Use your free time and recreation wisely—don't hang out in the mall, or go shopping "just to look."

- Start thinking about next year. Set aside a small planned amount each month either into a Christmas Club account, a savings account, or start loading a specially designated debit card. Starting in January, save for the holidays in other ways: Put all your change into a jar (kids can do this, too).

Shop Smart: Stretch Your Holiday Dollars

Before you head out the door to holiday shopping, read our list of ways to make your hard-earned holiday dollars go further:

•   You have a plan. Now, wait and watch prices rather than try to power through your shopping in one day.

•   Check sales flyers, sign up for store emails, and check online comparison-shopping websites for the best pricing (http://www.PriceGrabber.com is one).

•   Don't buy something just because it's on sale—buy it because it is planned and fits in your budget.

• Check out discount stores when shopping for holiday meals, and gifts: dollar stores, closeout stores, warehouse clubs, craft shows, and swap meets.

• Use store coupons and promo codes. Frequently these are offered when you sign up for emails, or agree to do a survey. Search online for "coupon" or "promo code" and the name of the store you want. Try a coupon exchange with your family and friends.

• Use your discounts. Are you a senior or a student, military, or member of an insurance group like AAA? Ask what discounts you qualify for.

• Use your points. Do you have airline, hotel, or points credit cards? Now is the time to use those accumulated points! Check online and see what you can redeem them for: gifts, gift cards, even gift vacations.

• Save time and money by buying ingredients in bulk for holiday cooking, and think about food as a gift idea—cake or cookies in a decorative box, jam or spiced nuts in a decorated jar are all welcome gifts.

• Don't wait till the last minute to ship your gifts. Expedited shipping will add a lot to your holiday expenses. Be sure to add enough time to allow for shipping and mailing.

• Try to make some purchases after Christmas. Won't see your best friend till after the holidays? Buy their present afterward and on sale! Use after-Christmas sales to stock up for next year: wrapping paper, ribbon, cards, decorations, and gifts will all be marked down.

• Pass up extended warranty plans. They aren't worth the money, and the repair you might (or might not) need is likely to be cheaper than the warranty.

• Don't let the salesperson "up-sell" you into adding more items or services to your purchase.

• Keep your receipts. If you have to return, exchange or contest the price of a gift, you WILL need these.

Most important: Remember the real reason for the season, and enjoy and appreciate your friends, family, and life.

Have a wonderful holiday season!

Take Charge of Holiday Spending

Christmas Shoppinglist.
- christmas tree
  decoration
- champagne
- Wishcards + stamps
- candles
- present mam

From *America Saves*:

The holiday season can be a financially challenging time. In addition to the cost of gifts for friends and family, many people have extra expenses for travel, entertainment, food, decorations, tipping, charitable gifting, and utilities. The holidays don't need to cause financial stress.

This year, while there is still time, take these 10 steps to reduce your stress, expenses, and regrets:

Create a Holiday Spending Plan: Include gifts, of course, but also hidden costs of gifts such as wrapping and shipping. Also factor in other expenses noted above. http://www.Bankrate.com has a great online Holiday Spending Worksheet.

Match Expenses to Income: Determine how many paydays are left from early November through mid-January. Then match holiday spending to your income, including any year-end bonuses, so expenses are paid with current income. For example, if you have $900 of holiday expenses and six paychecks, you'll need to set aside $150 per paycheck.

Play the Float: Time charges on credit cards so bills can be paid in full when they arrive. For example, if your statement ending date in the 3rd of the month and you buy things on the 5th, you may have six or seven weeks before payment is due.

Use Credit Cards Wisely: Don't charge more than you can repay. A bargain isn't a bargain when interest is added to a purchase! Check your account statements to make sure all charges are correct and avoid unnecessary expenses such as late, over-the-limit, and cash advance fees and penalty APRs.

Make a Gift List: List the names of people/families receiving gifts and determine a monetary value for each gift so the cost of all gifts stays within your overall holiday. Then stick to the list.

Look for Bargains: Specific strategies include deeply discounted online deals with free shipping, online and print coupons, "door buster" sales at certain hours, and high-end thrift shops.

Set Realistic Expectations: If your budget is tight, have a conversation with family and friends about ways to cut back. For example, consider replacing individual gift giving with drawing names and buy one nice gift rather than many gifts.

Make a Gift: Homemade gifts show thought, effort, and love. Consider baked goods, fancy pillowcases, photos, artwork, and embroidered, personalized items. Homemade "gift certificates" for car washes, pet-sitting, house-cleaning, or baking are also appreciated and White Elephant exchanges are fun.

PowerPay Your Debt: If you run up an outstanding balance, use the free online Powerpay program, https://powerpay.org/, to pay it off quickly. Powerpay generates a debt repayment calendar. As soon as you pay off a debt, you apply its monthly payment to another, generally starting with the highest-interest rate first.

Save Now for Next Year: Open a "Holiday Club" or similar savings plan with a financial institution or through an employer-related credit union. Then make regular deposits throughout the year. Come fall, you'll have the money you need without the stress of having to cut spending or use credit for purchases.

Now is the time to take charge of your finances to get the most out of the upcoming holiday season without financial stress.

From America Saves, www.americasaves.com, and written by Barbara O'Neill, Ph.D., CFP®, Extension Specialist in Financial Resource Management, Rutgers Cooperative Extension

Last Minute Gift Ideas

What do you do when there's less than two weeks until Christmas, and you still have shopping to do? Don't panic! We've all been in that situation—including shopping on Christmas Eve. Even if you still have a full week of work ahead, you can shop for some easy and great last minute gifts.

Our favorite suggestions:

From your local financial services center:

- **Preloaded debit card:** Load one up with a special, significant number: $40 for 4.0 grade-point average, $128 for an anniversary (January 28).
- **Money order:** The easiest way to send the gift of money.
- **Phone and phone service:** Help your kids or parents stay in touch!

Give the gift of travel:

- **Museum membership:** Your local museums and cultural organizations offer memberships, often with added benefits and discounts.
- **Bed and Breakfast getaway:** Order a gift card at http://www.bedandbreakfast.com with free shipping or email delivery, and you can upload your own photo.

From the supermarket:

- **Flowers**, of course!
- Flowering or lush green **plant**
- **Candy**: Put fun and colorful candy in a basket, mug, or bowl with a ribbon.
- **Fruit basket**: Get one ready-made, or put one together yourself.
- **Gift cards**: Available at many retail locations, there's sure to be one that's a perfect fit.
- **Wine**: A nice selection and usually gift bags are located nearby.
- **Candles**: Several attractive candles with a high-end lighter or fun matches.
- **Balloons**
- **Magazine subscription**: Pick a favorite magazine, fill out the subscription card (and mail, or enter the information and payment online), and package the copy of the magazine with a card.
- **Phone minute** cards
- **Stuffed animals**
- Local interest **t-shirts** and **tote bags**
- **Games**

From your local coffee shop:

- Coffee travel **tumbler** and **coffee**
- **Teas**: Choose a variety; wrap with a mug and tea strainer, and some cute cookies
- Branded **t-shirt** or **tote bag**--package up a selection of coffee and put in a tote bag.

From the convenience store:

- **Candy**: Another great place to put together a fun candy selection.
- **Snack-**pack basket
- **Phone minute** cards
- **T-shirts**
- **Magazine subscription** (see above)
- Wacky **souvenirs**

From the comfort of your desk:

- Netflix**,** Hulu, Acorn, or Britbox **streaming subscriptions**
- **Ebooks**
- **Website** domain name: Choose something entertaining, or a name to go with a project they've been thinking of.
- *The New York Times* or other media digital subscription.
- **Amazon.com** gift cards: This online retailer provides many instant gift card delivery systems, including printing it yourself, free one-day mail delivery, email, and via Facebook; upload your own photo to customize your card.
- **Downloadable art** on Etsy.com—then all you need is a frame!
- **Donate** to a favorite charity in your recipient's name.

Have a wonderful holiday season!

Smart Quinceanera Shopping

You've read about really deluxe quinceaneras in magazines, and seen them on YouTube. Maybe you even know a family who had a big bash for their daughter.

The reality is, most people can't afford a party that costs thousands, or tens of thousands of dollars. It's possible to have a wonderful Quince without breaking the bank. We'll show how you can manage it!

The important thing to remember is the purpose of the party: It's to celebrate your move from a child to a young adult, and that you are now ready to accept responsibilities and blossom into adulthood. That is what a quinceanera is all about, not about how much it costs or how big it is.

Ready? Let's get started!

First, make a plan:
You need a realistic budget, a schedule, and a list of everything you need to spend money on.

- **Your budget:** Of course, the earliest you can start saving for this the better. If you can't quite swing it, consider asking family members and close friends to help support your party as madrinas and padrinos. Your budget will equal the cost of your list of necessary items for the quinceanera.
- **Your list:** Go through the party in your head, and list everything that you need, those things that you have to spend money on, and those that you don't. Assign a dollar amount budget for each item that you have to buy. Do your research, and explore alternatives. We'll go into more detail later.
- **Your schedule:** Allow yourself enough time to accomplish all your goals, and to do your selecting and shopping thoughtfully. Work out a schedule for each week, and what you have to do that week, from addressing invitations to buying stamps to picking music. The best option is to allow a year for this process—that gives you plenty of time to make the event be exactly what you want, and it gives you time to find the best deals.

Here are some ideas on how to limit your expenses and still have a great day:

- **Venue:** Yes, a ballroom at a four-star hotel would be great, but you can still have a wonderful time at someplace much less expensive. Think about the possibilities of your own home; the house of a family member or friend; the beach; a park; a campground; by the river or lake; at a historical building or site; or at other recreation halls such as at your church, at the VFW, etc. You'll want to make your reservation as early as you can, to avoid any price increases, and to give you time to plan the seating and decorations.
- **Guest list:** Limit your list, and you limit your expenses. Try to match up the size of the venue with the size of your guest list. You don't have to invite every single person you know—family and close friends are the most important guests. If you keep the list to 50 or under, you'll be able to have manageable expenses and still feel like you're having a large party.

- **The dress:** Plan on spending between $150 and $300, depending on how formal you want to be. If you select a dress that can be adapted, or even used as is, you can also wear that dress to the prom—and you just cut your costs in half!
- **Accessories:** You can buy a small tiara for under $20, wear family earrings and jewelry, buy something vintage at a thrift shop, or find cute fashion-forward jewelry and purse at inexpensive stores like Target, or accessory shops at the mall. You can find your high heels for the "Changing of the Shoes" ceremony at upscale discount stores like DWS or Marshalls, or at Target.
- **Hair and makeup:** Do your hair, facial, and makeup yourself. That way you can also afford an upgrade in a makeup brand!
- **Photography:** Rather than paying a professional photography, you can buy disposable cameras to have at every table, or just ask your friends and family to take lots of photos and send them to you afterward. You can then pick out a few of the best and have them printed at a larger size. Share the photos on Instagram, and create a #hashtag for your event.
- **Ceremony fees:** These won't be negotiable, so be sure to factor them in to your budget.
- **Music:** Create your own playlist on your iPod, and rent or borrow speakers.
- **Invitations:** Buy preprinted cards, or order inexpensive ones to be printed online—don't forget to check for discounts! Or you can print them yourself at home: get blank cards at Michaels, PaperSource, or Hallmark.com. Have your guests RSVP via email, and you won't have to worry about response cards.
- **Decorations:** There are so many cute, inexpensive options available now, it almost seems like a crime to spend a lot of money on decorating! You can get helium balloons at the Dollar Store: use them as background, or on the tables instead of centerpieces or flowers. Speaking of the Dollar Store, put together your centerpieces with glass bowls and containers filled with sand, rocks, or shells and water, and float tea lights and flowers. Also look at all the possibilities in a Michaels store. Craft your candles with plain candles in glass containers, wrapped with decorative paper and ribbons or flowers. If you do use fresh flowers, remember to select flowers that are in season—much less expensive! Look for plates at discount stores, or more interesting ones at places like HomeGoods, also a good source for tablecloths. And consider sourcing some things at thrift shops: a selection of mismatched plates that are color-coordinated is a great look, and the plates can be used later. Have a family party where you all make favors for the party guests. You can also hand-make traditional items like your kneeling pillow and guestbook.
- **Food:** Even if you don't have padrinos, there may be family or friends who are willing to help with cooking food. Have a variety of appetizers instead of a sit-down dinner. Serve homemade, traditional food, with some family specialties.
- **The cake:** Have one smaller, decorated bakery cake, and then have homemade cupcakes decorated similarly to the bakery cake. Display them on cake stands. Or have several different types of coordinating homemade cakes.
- **Event dates:** Have your quinceanera around a holiday, like Christmas, or a family reunion. Out-of-state relatives are more likely to be around then. This can save them money on transportation, making it easier for them to support your party as madrinas and padrinos.
- **Establish a registry:** Ask padrinos and madrinas to sponsor certain things for your quinceanera. Be sure to write appreciative personal notes requesting their support.

Popular quinceanera themes:

- Galaxy
- Mardi Gras
- Black and white
- Candyland
- 1950s
- Enchanted forest
- Under the sea

- Popular culture

A suggested planning list:

- **One year ahead:**
  - Determine your budget
  - Set your date
  - Select potential godparents (contributing sponsors)
  - Plan on number of guests
  - Collect magazines and catalogs for ideas
  - Start a Pinterest board for ideas
  - Make a planning notebook
  - Choose theme and colors
  - Contact church priest (determine parish requirements, book date)
  - Research possible event sites for availability and the security measures they offer
- **Eleven months ahead:**
  - Discuss budget plans with potential godparents
  - Visit event sites
  - Select style of invitation
  - Start thinking about your dress—color, style—and start looking online and in stores. Start a Pinterest board for dress ideas.
- **Ten months ahead:**
  - Select your Quince court (the number in the court is your decision, 7 couples are recommended)
  - Reserve event hall
  - Verify that church is available on event date and reserve
  - Order your invitations if you are not doing them yourself
  - Choose your colors
- **Six months ahead:**
  - Meet with your Quince court to discuss their physical attire (after selecting yours)
  - Select accessories and shoes
  - Select, purchase, or create party favors
  - Select and purchase "Last Doll," if you are celebrating that particular custom
  - Select and purchase the Bible
  - Reserve hotel rooms for guests
  - Reserve limousine, if necessary
  - Start practicing the quinceanera waltz if you are going dance during the reception
- **Two months ahead:**
  - Send out invitations
  - Verify details with your service providers
  - Remind guests who have not responded (in order to avoid unnecessary expenses)
- **One month ahead:**
  - Have a formal quinceanera picture taken with your quinceanera dress
  - Create seating chart and place cards
  - Write a speech or speeches (you may choose a poem for the church and a speech for the reception or vice-versa, or you may choose a song)
  - Verify final details with:
    - Florist
    - Bakery
    - Priest or Pastor
- **Two weeks before:**

- Pick up dress
- Perform hair/makeup test-runs
- Avoid too many fatty foods, chocolates or other items that might keep your skin from looking its best
- **One week before:**
  - Get plenty of rest and relaxation so you will look radiant on the day of your quinceanera
  - Check your planning list
- **The day of:**
  - Have a good breakfast
  - Decorate ceremony and reception sites
  - Get nails done
- **The day after:**
  - Send out thank-you notes

Smart Back-to-School Shopping

For kids, shopping for new clothes, electronics, sporting goods, and school supplies may be the only good thing about going back to school. However, you don't have to spend a fortune each year!

What's the best strategy for back-to-school shopping? Make a plan! Get organized, get your kids on board, know what you (and they) need, stock up on basics, and look everywhere for sales and promotions.

Back-to-school is the second-biggest shopping season of the year. Retailers and manufacturers know this, and do their best to encourage add-on purchases. Guess how much you *could* spend on those back-to-school notebooks, computers, clothes, and backpacks, and supplies: They can easily add up to $500 to $1,000 per child if you're not careful. The cost to go "back to school" keeps increasing: The National Retail Federation estimated that the average American family spends more than $600 on back to school supplies. That's only for an average student; college-age students often require many more—and more expensive—supplies, especially if they're moving into a dorm.

Even if your child's school or teacher hasn't provided a list of school supplies, you can't go wrong by sticking with the basics and taking advantage of back-to-school sales. Some retailers are a step ahead and have copies of supply lists from the schools in their area (Wal-Mart does, and sometimes Staples). Check with the school, too, in case they have the supply lists available at the front desk. You can also check on http://www.GreatSchools.org for recommended basics for elementary, middle school, and high school.

Start your back-to-school shopping with a strategic game plan.

- To start your list, first check to **see what you already have**:
    - Check the required supply list from your children's teachers.
    - Search your house for school supplies from last year, or extra office supplies.
    - Examine your kid's clothes: What still fits, what is worn out, what is out of fashion?
    - Donate what doesn't work anymore, so it's gone and not cluttering the closet or the house.
- **What sports or activities** will your children be participating in this year? See what equipment, clothes, and shoes you already have, what needs to be replaced, and what needs to be purchased.
- **Check the calendar** for upcoming events throughout the school year. Fairs, costumes, dances, and trips—all may have accompanying additional expenses.
- **Next, get your kids involved:**
    - Sit down and go over your list together. You'll be teaching them how to get organized (a skill that applies to more than shopping), how to budget, and that there's a limited amount of money to spend on things they want.
    - When they are drawn to this year's trendy items, go over the budget and list with them, and let them help set the priorities.

- Also suggest they start saving their allowance, or income from jobs, so they can buy the items that won't fit in the budget
- **Create your shopping list:**
  - Group like items together (office supplies, clothes, etc.).
  - Make a note of stores to go to, and where to shop online for each item.
  - Also note if there's a coupon, or discount code, for that item.
  - Keep a list of what you already have
  - Keep your list with you so you don't purchase an item twice, or miss out on a great deal.
- **Shop strategically**:
  - Don't shop when you're tired.
  - Don't bring your children with you unless it's for items they need to help make a decision on (clothes, etc.).
  - If you have big-ticket items on your list, think about getting the best deal on those first. You'll have plenty of opportunities to buy paper and pencils just about everywhere you go.
  - Plan out which items need to be higher quality. If that cheap backpack breaks after a month, it's not a bargain anymore. Items likely to stain (pens, markers, paints) should be able to be closed firmly. Some name brands are better for a reason: crayons, colored pencils, markers and water color paints simply have better packaging, brighter colors, and last longer.
  - Help out a teacher: Your child's teacher will thank you if you stick to supplies without gimmicks. Pencil sharpeners that light up, items that are in invitation to be thrown, and things that make noise are distractions in class. Keep supplies to the useful versus fun.
  - Hold off on trendy supplies until your child sees what everyone else in his or her class has.
- **Figure out where the deals are:**
  - For basic supplies, best-bet retail stores include dollar stores, office supply stores, Wal-Mart, Target, Costco, and supermarkets. For specialty items try Michaels, Joann's, or Craft Warehouse, art supply stores, HomeGoods or Marshalls, even Tuesday Morning. For higher ticket items, check online stores like Amazon, Best Buy, eBay, and even Craigslist and garage sales for some items.
- **Get a better deal:**
  - Shop end-of-summer sales. It will still be summer while you are shopping, and your kids will probably wear t-shirts well into the fall.
  - Start watching the weekly sales ads from the big retailers and your local supermarkets.
  - Collect coupons and discount codes: Look for coupons in the weekly ads, join your store's club for extra discounts, check your store's website for coupons and discounts offered only online (many can still be used in the actual store). Also search for online discount codes on http://www.RetailMeNot.com. Don't forget the Sunday newspaper, too.
  - Some retailers offer a 10% to 15% discount online (or in physical stores) if you sign up for their newsletter—which could also offer more discounts.
  - Local health departments in some areas offer free basic school supplies to parents who bring their children in for immunizations.
  - Keep all your ads and flyers with you—other stores may price match.
  - Does your local supermarket offer an extra 10% off for seniors one day a month? Go shopping with Grandma or Grandpa.
  - If you see an item you bought in the past 14 days on sale later, you can get the difference refunded at certain stores. You might not even need the item, just the receipt. Check at your store for details.
  - Many states have sales tax holidays, when shoppers can buy items without paying sales tax. Perfect time to stock up!
  - Retailers will often offer a discount on gift cards if you buy more than one. Why not buy a set to either that store or another where you'll be shopping? You'll be spending the money anyway, but now you effectively get a discount. Also look for discounted gift cards to stores in which you'll be shopping on sites like www.giftcards.com or http://www.plasticjungle.com. You'll save as much as 25% on cards whose original recipients don't want or can't use.

- Use social media: Follow your favorite and targeted stores on Facebook and Twitter, and watch for sales and special offers. If you can, use your coupons on those sales days for additional price savings.
- Online cash-back shopping venue http://www.Ebates.com acts like a shopping gateway. The website allows you to shop major stores and brands like Barnes & Noble, Dell, Kohl's, DWW, Macy's, and Wal-Mart online, all while giving you 6% or more cash back on your purchases.
- Buy basics in bulk. You know you'll need paper, notebooks, report folders, pens, pencils, glue sticks and erasers. Dollar stores, and warehouse stores are good sources for buying these and other basics like healthy single-serve snacks in bulk. If the quantities are too much for your own use, see if you can combine a shopping trip with a friend. Set up a supply shelf or storage container in your home for these basic supplies. They'll be easy for you and your child to find.
- Think about lunch supplies and gear while you're shopping for classroom supplies. Need a new lunch bag? Containers for lunch items? Think reusable. Bento boxes, high-quality plastic or metal containers, and real (inexpensive!) spoons require an initial investment, but will save money on plastic bags and utensils in the long run.
- Texting: Take advantage of mobile technology! See if any of your preferred stores offer coupons via text. Also look for scannable QR (Quick Response) codes in stores and ads.
- If you can, wait for the back-to-school sales. If you avoid the beginning of the season and buy *after* the rush, when items often go on sale for 50%-75% off retail prices, you can save a lot of money. It all depends on what you need and when your child's school starts.
- Other, non-traditional, places to shop: Find a list of children's clothing consignment stores at http://kidsconsignmentsales.com/seasonalsales.htm. Also try better-quality thrift shops, garage sales, Craigslist, and eBay.
- A word about dollar stores: Yes, they are cheap, but compare prices before you buy. You can sometimes get a better quality *and* quantity at a similar price at a "regular" store. That said, there are great deals to be had: from stickers to kid's scissors to some craft supplies (best pricing for poster board and foam core for class projects).

- **Sticking to your budget**
  - With all that merchandise out there, and clamoring kids, it's very hard to keep to your budget.
  - Always have your list with you, and stick to it!
  - Make sure you've checked for discounts.
  - Use cash instead of credit cards: Paying for supplies with cash allows you to keep an eye on your funds and to stay within your budget.
  - Start your shopping list with absolutely essential items. If you run out of money in your budget, some things—especially clothes—can still be purchased later.

Summer flies by quickly and before you know it, it's time for back-to-school. If you can, start planning early, as early even as the end of the prior school year. You'll want to be able to use every deal and coupon that comes your way!

Save on College Supplies

If you have a child heading to college, or are going to college yourself, then you will experience some serious sticker shock. From furnishings for a dorm room or apartment to textbooks, attending college is an exercise in new ways to spend money.

However, there are many ways to save!

In the process of applying to a college and for scholarships, make a list of other expenses you will have: outfitting a dorm room or apartment, textbooks, electronics, transportation. Assign a budget to that list, and stick to it!

Dorm or apartment essentials:

- Shop for rugs, sheets, furniture, and light cooking equipment at garage sales and thrift stores.
- Ask friends and family members if they have any appropriate items.
- If you are sending your child off to college, shop your own house first: extra towels and sheets? Chair you were about to take to Goodwill? A small set of dishes?
- Shop the back-to-college promotions at stores like Target and IKEA for mattress pads, lamps, shower caddies, and other helpful items.
- Don't forget Craigslist and http://www.Freecycle.org.

Study and class supplies:

- In general, what was good for high school will be good for college: No. 2 pencils, notebooks, yellow sticky notes, highlighters, pens, index cards, etc.
- Check the course lists for any specialty supplies, such as a specific calculator or art materials.
- Don't purchase these at the campus bookstore! Buy in bulk at Costco, and shop the back-to-school sales at stores like Target or Staples.

Electronics:

- A computer, after textbooks, might be the second-most costly item for which you will pay. A basic laptop will be fine.
- A small inexpensive black-and-white printer
- An e-reader for downloading textbooks

Textbooks:

- Don't buy at the campus bookstore. Their markup on textbooks is higher than at other retailers. The only exception: Custom-printed packets assigned by particular professors. These are printed and bound ahead of time, and you won't be able to get them anywhere *but* the campus bookstore.
- Other places to buy textbooks:
    - Online retailers Amazon, eBay, http://www.Half.com, http://www.CheapestTextbooks.com, or http://www.Textbookx.com.
    - Digital: http://www.CourseSmart.com or http://www.Cafescribe.com. You can save 50% or more on textbooks by purchasing a digital copy and downloading it to your e-reader.
    - Buy used: The market for used college textbooks is huge, since many students only use them for a single semester. Try used bookstores near your college campus, and online.
- Rent: Textbook rentals are popular, and even rental e-book versions of textbooks. Remember that physical textbooks will have to be in excellent condition when you return them, or you'll pay extra fees.
- Borrow: The college or public libraries are both good options for finding copies of more-common books. Libraries may not have a copy of a $175 quantum physics textbook, but they *are* likely to have copies of many texts used in liberal arts courses. Also check the public library used bookstore for popular classics.

For more ways to save, read the chapter on back-to-school shopping!

Negotiating: Not a Dirty Word

Negotiating: We've all done it at one time or another. Perhaps you negotiated your salary, benefits, or vacation at a new job. If you've purchased or sold a house, you most likely negotiated the sales price and other aspects of the sale. But did you realize that you could negotiate expenses in other aspects of your life?

Now, I'm not saying that you should go into the grocery store and haggle over the cost of your items at the checkout. But there are plenty of other ways you can save yourself money just by asking and by being diligent.

BIG TICKET ITEMS

Auto purchases: You already know this one! Be sure to arm yourself with information in advance: Know your desired car's worth. Kelly Blue Book, Edmund's, and True Car are all good information sources. Be polite but firm. Turn down all those extra add-ons the dealership will try to sell you. Just keep saying "no." Try shopping (with your desired car and price firmly in mind) on the dealer's off days or hours: Last day of the month, Saturday or Sunday an hour before closing, really bad weather days.

Medical bills: Now, this you might not be that familiar with. First off, thoroughly check over your medical bills, especially Medicare bills. Make sure the services listed are ones you actually received. At a minimum, you should be able to negotiate a payment plan with your provider. If you've received a very large bill from a hospital or other large service provider, be frank with them about your financial situation, and ask them to reduce your bill. Also: Ask before your visit for any special cash payment or uninsured discounts!

Rent: This works especially well if you are a good tenant. Before your lease is up, do a survey of comparable rentals in your area. If you find that other properties are priced a bit lower, or include other features (paid utilities, etc.), present that information to your landlord when it comes time to renew your lease. Be polite and friendly. Perhaps the landlord can pay one or more of your utilities, arrange to paint or do other not-urgent maintenance, provide landscaping, or simply reduce your rent. If you have been a good tenant, it will be cheaper and easier for them in the long run to keep you, rather than have the property vacant and risk someone new.

OTHER OPPORTUNITIES

Insurance: Check that you are getting the best price for your auto, home, or renter's insurance. First, know what you are currently paying, and then shop around for comparable rates. This is relatively easy to do online, or just by calling. Sometimes an insurance broker can help (make sure you select one that represents a lot of companies, not just one). Contact your current insurance company and ask them to meet their competitor's prices, and also ask if there are any discounts you are eligible for (clean driving record, bundled plans, safe driving and parking).

Cable and internet: Again, shop around, and see what other companies are charging, including their new subscriber deals. Then, call your company and ask them to match those, or their own new subscriber deal. If you've been with the company for a long time, they will consider this seriously. If not, go to another service and take them up on their lower price!

Credit card fees: If you haven't abused your credit card and have made payments on time, but recently made one late payment, call them to ask about waiving the fee.

Cell phone fees or plans: Again, express dissatisfaction about your plan or question the fees involved, and ask them to take a look at it—what can they offer you?

Damaged items: If the product you are purchasing is slightly damaged (and it's damage you don't care about, such as packaging), ask for a discount at the register. Checkout clerks at chain stores are frequently authorized to grant a 10% discount with no hassle.

KEY PHRASES TO USE

- I've been a good customer for a long time.
- X Company is offering a better deal.
- I'd hate to have to change companies.
- Can you work with me? Or, what can you do for me?
- I need to cut expenses.

Always be polite and friendly, but patient and determined. Good luck!

Personal Finance *for* Real People

About the Author

Sandra Winters is a financial blogger and consultant. Experienced in hospitality and foodservice, bookselling, marketing, and social media, she's also helped create small-business associations, and has served on the boards of local non-profits. She lives in Southern Oregon amongst the trees, and tries to pursue her dreams of being an artist one day. Her dog, Nigel, convinces her she needs to give him treats instead.

www.ingramcontent.com/pod-product-compliance
Lightning Source LLC
Chambersburg PA
CBHW080955170526
45158CB00010B/2806